On Fish

Nathan Outlaw
On Fish

A SEAFOOD HANDBOOK

SPECIES • TECHNIQUES • RECIPES

K
KYLE BOOKS

First published in Great Britain in 2026 by Kyle Books,
an imprint of Octopus Publishing Group Ltd
Carmelite House
50 Victoria Embankment
London EC4Y 0DZ
www.octopusbooks.co.uk

An Hachette UK Company
www.hachette.co.uk

The authorized representative in the EEA is Hachette Ireland,
8 Castlecourt Centre, Dublin 15, D15 XTP3, Ireland
(email: info@hbgi.ie)

Text copyright © Nathan Outlaw 2026
Photography copyright © Kate Whitaker 2026
Design & layout copyright © Octopus Publishing Group Ltd

Distributed in the US by Hachette Book Group,
1290 Avenue of the Americas, 4th and 5th Floors,
New York, NY 10104

Distributed in Canada by Canadian Manda Group,
664 Annette St., Toronto, Ontario, Canada M6S 2C8

All rights reserved. No part of this work may be reproduced or utilized in any form or by any means, electronic or mechanical, including photocopying, recording or by any information storage and retrieval system, without the prior written permission of the publisher.

Nathan Outlaw asserts the moral right to be identified as the author of this work.

ISBN: 978 1 80419 321 1
eISBN: 978 1 80419 322 8

A CIP catalogue record for this book is available from the British Library.

Printed and bound in China.

10 9 8 7 6 5 4 3 2 1

Publisher: Joanna Copestick
Senior Managing Editor: Sybella Stephens
Copy Editor: Emily Preece-Morrison
Creative Director: Jonathan Christie
Designer & Illustrator: Paul Palmer-Edwards
Photography & Props: Kate Whitaker
Food Stylist: Nathan Outlaw
Senior Production Manager: Katherine Hockley

Contents

Introduction 6

1 **Fish basics** 8
Fishing methods, Shopping & storing,
Fish preparation tools & equipment, Finishing & cooking techniques

2 **Flat fish** 22
Brill, Dover Sole, Lemon Sole, Megrim, Plaice, Turbot
Preparation techniques 30
Recipes 32

3 **Round fish** 58
Bass, Black Bream, Gilt Head Bream, Cod, Gurnard, Haddock,
Hake, John Dory, Ling, Monkfish, Ray & Skate, Red Mullet,
Grey Mullet, Trout
Preparation techniques 74
Recipes 80

4 **Oily fish** 144
Anchovies, Blue-fin Tuna, Herring, Mackerel, Pilchards/Sardines,
Smoked Fish
Recipes 152

5 **Shellfish & cephalopods** 178
Cockles, Clams, Mussels, Scallops, Crab, Lobster, Langoustine,
Squid, Cuttlefish, Octopus, Oysters
Preparation techniques 192
Recipes 200

Index 252

Acknowledgements & Glossary 256

Introduction

This very personal seafood handbook has been compiled from the notes I've kept daily over the last three decades. It contains what I consider to be the most important and most useful information about my favourite subject, and I've written it for everyone who wants to know more about seafood.

Over time, my thoughts on fish have altered due to changes in sustainability, tastes, better information or just what my tastebuds and my belly tell me. If you already have one of my previous books or you've heard me speak in the past, then you'll maybe find some contradictions here, but that is what's exciting about the life of a true seafood chef – every day is different. As nature moves forward and evolves, I have too.

My 30 years' of knowledge is hard to fit into these limited pages, so I've tried to cover only the most useful, helpful, important and tasty parts, to help you improve your knowledge and skill with seafood cookery. It's a handbook; treat it like one – add your own notes to the pages. I do that to all my books, jotting stuff down for future use when adapting or revisiting, as I cook each dish.

In the following chapters, I've written about my favourite seafood and created recipes for how I consider them best served right now – this is why it's a handbook personal to me and not a general encyclopedia on the subject.

Apart from the fact that very fresh seafood tastes wonderful, there are many health benefits to eating it. Current UK health guidelines suggest we should eat at least two portions of fish a week – not enough, if you ask me! Fish is an excellent source of protein, vitamins and minerals. Oily fish has the significant added bonus of being rich in omega-3 fatty acids, which help keep our heart, joints, skin and eyes healthy. And some of the smaller oily fish can be eaten whole, so they provide a particularly rich source of calcium and phosphorus.

For those who need to follow a low-fat diet, the obvious choice is white fish, although not deep-fried. Shellfish is also low in fat and a good source of zinc, iodine, copper and selenium. Mussels, oysters and crab provide a fair amount of omega-3 fatty acids, too.

Over the last 30 years, I've prepared, cooked and eaten all the seafood species available to me where I live and work. Of course, I have experience of cooking species from other parts of the world, but in this handbook I've covered what I know best: seafood from the North Atlantic Ocean.

Availability of seafood species can vary according to both the time of year and your location, so I've given alternatives for some of the dishes, but feel free to swap in your own choices too. And for each species, I've tried to cover all I think it is worth knowing.

What do people want to know about seafood? What puts people off cooking fish at home? How can I explain about the convenience of seafood as a product? These are some of the questions I've tried to ask myself while writing. I want this to be a book you can grab to quickly find what you need to know and how to do it; straight to the point and with the information you need. On the way, I have added tips, a few memories and some general knowledge about this fascinating subject.

I hope this book inspires you, answers some questions, gives you some useful tips, persuades you to try something different and becomes a well-used and favourite cook's handbook in your kitchen.

Best fishes, as always,
Nathan

1

Fish basics

Fishing methods, Shopping & storing,
Fish preparation tools & equipment,
Finishing & cooking techniques

Fishing methods

The different methods used to catch fish and seafood are chosen according to species and where in the sea they swim.

Research is constantly ongoing to ensure that fishing methods become more effective and less damaging for the environment, yet it is naïve to think that enough seafood to satisfy the human appetite can be caught by using only entirely sustainable methods. What we do need to do is check that the fish we buy is as sustainably caught as possible.

The most sustainable method is using **rod and reel**, the traditional way of fishing, which only catches fish that are actively feeding. It's selective, but time consuming. The chance of unwanted bycatch is rare; if some is caught alive, it can be put back for another day. Also, the likelihood of the fish being damaged is low, so it will always fetch the best price at market due to quality.

Shellfish such as mussels, cockles, clams, prawns, shore crabs, limpets, oysters and winkles, and also seaweeds, can be **hand-collected**, which is low impact. However, you need to know the area well, due to the chance of sewage outlets and other nasty stuff.

Diver-caught seafood is low risk regarding any damage to the seabed. However, large groups of divers picking a certain species from a small area can have a detrimental impact, especially when juvenile species are taken.

Lobsters and crabs are caught by **potting**, and there are specific pots for cuttlefish, velvet crabs, prawns and crawfish. 'Disco' scallop pots, so-called because the pot is fitted with a light that flashes and attracts the scallops, are starting to be used. This is an exciting development that could see a big move away from scallop dredging and all the negatives that come with it. However, greed has affected even pot fishing and some large vessels are shooting miles and miles of pots into the sea in certain areas. In my area, this has dramatically affected the edible brown crab population. It's certainly something that needs addressing.

In protected areas where motorized boats are not permitted, **sail and oar fishing** is used to catch oysters. This type of fishing is seasonal and can only be done in good weather, making it very sustainable with little impact on the oyster stocks.

Net fishing

Gill nets are set on the seabed. They can't be used during strong tidal flows or around spring tides, because the movement of the water is too strong and the nets' anchors can't handle the power of the tide. This is problematic, as they can become unattached and float around in the sea, entangling fish and mammals on their way. Other types of net fishing include: **tangle nets** which target turbot, crawfish, spider crabs and monkfish; **wreck nets** that are set over wrecks and reefs to catch cod, ling and pollack; **deep-water hake nets** and **red mullet nets**, which are species specific; and **trammel nets**, which are set in layers along the seabed. Most nets have mesh specific to the size of fish they are targeting. However, unintended loss of the nets is a big problem.

The large gill and trammel nets now incorporate what are known as 'pingers', little contraptions that give off a sonic noise to warn cetaceans and scare them off. They have been proven to work, but smaller, inshore gill netting fishermen are not yet required to use them. Netting, in general, is a selective way of catching certain species and, when done with care, is an okay fishing method, but like everything, there is bad practice too.

A very old, traditional method is **beach seine netting** which was used to catch salmon and trout in estuaries in the old days before they were overfished. This entails a long wall of mesh netting with a foot rope and buoyed head rope being taken out to sea in a semi-circle, with one end tethered on shore and the other brought back in when the net is full. The nets are large and are used to catch species like grey mullet and bass. When a shoal is seen offshore, one end of the net is taken out around the shoal, then brought back to shore and hauled in by hand. The problem is that if the catch is large (it could be several tonnes), manpower isn't strong enough to haul the net in and deal with the fish, so they have to be let go. For this reason, and because of the precise conditions needed, beach seine fishing isn't popular, but it is a method that doesn't impact upon the environment and there is little chance of unwanted catch like dolphins or seals being caught up.

Ring netting targets sardines, herrings, anchovies and sprats. In Cornwall, where I live, this method is well managed and usually happens within a six-mile limit from the shore. Due to the nature and importance of the oily fish caught, ring netting is a real skill and the skippers catching the best fish are extremely gifted at it. It is illegal to catch certain species this way and if there is evidence of other species in the net, the whole catch must be released.

Trawling

Demersal trawls are large nets that are dragged through the water with the bottom of the net touching the seabed. The mesh is spaced to a large size to let juvenile fish swim through, catching only the targeted size of the species. It does impact the seabed. However, many of the sandy areas have already been fished and scientists have shown that habitats regenerate faster than the fishermen can fish those environments again in certain cases.

On the other hand, **beam trawl nets** are dragged along the seabed, scooping up different species and leaving very little behind, including juvenile species, which are disturbed or destroyed. The flat fish species are generally caught this way; to use any other method would simply not keep up with demand. Technology is being developed and scientific research is being undertaken to find ways of improving this method, but there is no getting away from the destructive nature of it.

Shopping & storing

It goes without saying that you should buy the freshest fish available to you.

You may be lucky enough to have a good fishmonger on your doorstep, or even access to the fishermen themselves if you live near the coast. If not, some of the better supermarkets now employ trained staff on their fish counters, but I recommend online fishmongers like Rockfish and The Cornish Fishmonger which are both great for landlocked fish lovers.

Remember to take a cool bag with you to bring the fish home in, it will stay much fresher. And always check the cleanliness of wherever you're buying from. Is the fish displayed well? Check out the staff behind the counter; are they confident and do they handle their seafood cleanly and carefully? Ask questions. Staff should be able to answer any questions you have. If they can't, give the place a wide berth.

No fish or seafood should smell 'fishy' – if it smells at all unpleasant, don't buy it! Make sure the whole fish looks good. It should be intact with no visible damage to any part. Eyes should be bright and clear, gills should be vivid red, and any scales that you'd expect should be in place. Flat fish should be firm with some sea slime on their surface. Always check the underside of flat fish, as this is where they will show any signs of red bruising. Oily fish should have retained their natural, vibrant colours and be firm to the touch.

Lobster & crabs
When buying lobsters and crabs, again, they should be alive. Check for bubbles coming from their mouths – this is a sign that they have become stressed and will affect the quality of their meat. Lobsters should have long antennae; short ones suggest the lobster has been stored for a long while and has either begun to eat itself or been eaten by others!

Molluscs
Molluscs need to be alive when you buy them, so check their status. If clams, cockles, mussels or oysters have open shells, tap them firmly; if they don't close readily, don't buy them, as this indicates the shellfish have died.

One exception to the 'live' rule is scallops, which often come to the market ready prepared and cut from the shell. However, they should still smell sweet, and not 'fishy'. Also, make sure they feel firm and haven't been left to soak. If any of these criteria aren't met, leave them in the shop.

Cephalopods
Finally, the cephalopods – squid, octopus and cuttlefish – really need to be eaten within a couple of days of being caught. Eyes should be bright and skin should be intact with no signs of the colour changing to pink, as this suggests they've seen better days.

Storage
If you've found a fresh bargain or someone has brought you lots of freshly caught fish, don't turn it away – most fish freezes well. Store on a tray on a dry cloth, uncovered, in the coldest area of the refrigerator. Don't let it sit in water or ice, as sea fish don't live in fresh water and contact with ice or water increases the speed of decomposition of their flesh. The refrigerator needs to be between 0–2°C (32–36°F). Stored carefully, dry and on the bone, most fish will be fine for several days. The same applies to filleted fish.

If you won't be eating the fish within a few days, take it off the bone, make sure it's completely dry, then wrap tightly in clingfilm and put it in the freezer as soon as you can. It will keep quite happily for up to two months. In the case of lobster and crab, cook before freezing, pick or crack the meat from the shells, cool, then wrap securely before putting into the freezer. Freeze the shells too (for use in sauces and stocks). Always allow fish and seafood to defrost slowly in the refrigerator on a tray lined with kitchen paper or – even better – a perforated tray with another tray underneath to catch the water.

I can't stress enough the importance of keeping your fish dry while storing. It will last longer and cook better.

Fish preparation tools & equipment

Buying equipment for cooking can be daunting, as there's so much out there to choose from. I've put together below a list of items I would recommend if you're going to get seriously into fish cookery. Always buy the best-quality products you can afford. Trust me, skimp and you'll be buying again soon, so it will end up costing you more in the long run.

Knives

I strongly recommend investing in a selection of good knives for your kitchen. They may seem expensive at the outset, but most will last you a lifetime and serve you well. I currently use TOG knives and I've also used Robert Welch and Victorinox which are my preferred brands. I also have some unique knives made by Fingal Ferguson, an Irish knifemaker, too. Whatever you choose, handle them before buying to make sure the balance is right for you.

Filleting knife – There are many types of filleting knife on the market, with various uses. I use a thin, 17.5cm (7-inch) long, semi-flexible bladed one, which I designed with TOG, called 'Sakana'. You can get some filleting knives that are very flexible, but they are not easy to sharpen.

Carving or slicing knife – I use a 26cm (10½-inch) long TOG 'Sujihiki' carving knife, which is very sharp, for all my raw preparation and for slicing cured fish.

Cook's knife – I have two in constant use: a 21cm (8¼-inch) long TOG 'Gyuto' which is a multi-purpose cook's knife for most jobs, and a heavier 25cm (10-inch) Victorinox knife which I use for bashing lobsters and crabs and for steaking fish. It's much safer to use a heavy knife for jobs like this, so it doesn't bounce off and injure you.

Paring knife – An essential. Don't be tempted to buy one that's too big, as it will be clumsy when peeling small items. Keep it nice and sharp.

Serrated knife – A strong serrated knife is useful for cutting off fish heads. When I'm dealing with bigger fish, I always cut the head off first, as I find it allows more control when filleting.

Oyster knife – It took me years to find an oyster knife that I like to use. The one I own, and love, has a wooden handle and a firm but short blade. I always keep it sharpened so it slices through the muscle cleanly, leaving a presentable oyster.

Boning knife – I use a firm-bladed boning knife for opening scallops. This is not technically the correct use of this knife, but I find it is the best knife for this job. If you're planning to open lots of scallops, I'd suggest investing in one.

Knife sharpener

I've always been terrible at keeping my knives sharp, it's just not an interesting job. However, the discovery of a sharpener with a guided sharpening wheel on it has been a revelation. A great investment!

Kitchen scissors

I use the shape of scissor that is traditionally used for cutting fabric! I find the flat-bottomed blade easier to handle when, for example, cutting off the fins of a Dover sole. I can also sharpen them if they get blunt.

Microplane grater

For zesting citrus fruit and grating cheese, garlic and chocolate, the Microplane grater is one of the most frequently used pieces of kit in my kitchen and worth every penny. One word of warning: they are very sharp, so mind your fingers!

Mandoline
A mandoline is a real time-saver for finely slicing vegetables, such as fennel, for salads and pickles, and I use a Japanese-made one. Note: fingers and mandolines don't mix – take care and always use the safety guard provided.

Pin-boning tweezers
An essential item for your fish prepping kit. Make sure you buy a pair that have no flex to them; flexible ones seem to struggle to grab smaller bones. I use the same type of tweezers that fishermen use to get hooks out when they catch a fish.

Chopping boards
It's worth investing in a good-quality, blue plastic chopping board if you plan to do lots of fish prep, as it is easy to clean when you've finished using it. My tip is to always wash it with cold water first rather than hot, as hot water will 'cook' any fish debris and make the board smell. For all other food prep, I love using a large, wooden chopping board.

Digital scales
Try to get scales that have a decent-sized platform and weigh in metric and imperial for both dry goods and liquids. Take care, though, they are delicate and easy to break.

Sieves
A fine-mesh sieve is best for straining stocks, purées and sauces.

Pans
For a good investment, choose saucepans and frying pans with heavy bases and tight-fitting lids. If they're ovenproof, even better. A thicker-based pan helps cook food more evenly and gives you lots of residual heat when you take it off the heat source. They are also good to braise in, hence the need for a tight-fitting lid. For pan-frying fish, a good-quality nonstick frying pan is essential. Look after it and don't leave it on the heat if you're not cooking with it – if you do, the coating will eventually burn off and leave bits of nonstick coating in your food.

Baking trays & grill trays
Whether you are grilling or baking, you need to invest in good-quality trays. Too thin and they will buckle under the heat and the food won't cook evenly. Buy a range of sizes, from trays big enough to hold a couple of fish fillets up to one big enough to take a whole fish. A little tip: to avoid rusty trays, put the cleaned tray in a warm oven to thoroughly dry out before storing.

Steamer
Steaming fish shows off its freshness and the purity of its flavour. I prefer to use a simple Chinese bamboo steamer – you can't go wrong with them.

Finishing & cooking techniques

Having sourced the best seafood available, now you need to decide what to do with it. It's important to consider the finishing and cooking techniques – these form the basis to my cooking and how I devise dishes and my menus. Here are the techniques I use at my restaurants and at home.

Raw

Although nearly all seafood is edible, not all is edible raw. For me, the best species for raw preparation are scallops, tuna, bass and bream. However, they need to be super-fresh when purchased, with the quality of the fish of utmost importance. Good hygiene is also paramount. I always buy fish that has been line-caught and killed swiftly, or in the case of scallops, diver-caught and looked after carefully afterwards.

Bleeding the fish is important, otherwise the bitterness from the blood will transfer to the flesh and remove the actual character of any given species. I believe that raw seafood dishes, more than any other preparation with fish, need to be kept simple. A powerful sauce or dressing will overpower that subtle flavour and beauty of raw fish. Seasoning with salt is also important – and fascinates me, because fish live in saltwater, so you would think that salt wouldn't be an issue. In fact, given a few grains of sea salt, raw slices of fish will sing.

Cured

The term 'cured' is generally applied to fish that has been fermented, pickled or smoked to preserve it. In my kitchen, it describes fish that has been cured in a wet or dry salt-cure mixture. (We think of fermenting, pickling and smoking as processes that we can apply to our cured fish.) Our aim isn't for an extended shelf life, although that is an advantage. For me, it's the magical change in texture that makes our cured dishes unique.

An effective way of preserving food, salting draws out moisture and inhibits the action of bacteria and other potentially harmful micro-organisms which are unable to function in a salty environment. Table salt is commonly employed for curing, but I use Cornish sea salt, as I think you can taste the anti-caking agents in table salt in the finished cured product.

Curing allows us to make some of the less flavoursome species taste special. Currently, my favourite fish to cure are bream, mackerel and brill, but we are constantly developing new cured dishes so this could change tomorrow! That's why I love curing; the adventure is endless.

There are a few traditionally cured fish that I buy already prepared, notably salt cod, salt herring and canned anchovies, which are convenient standby ingredients.

Pickled & soused

Fish is well suited to pickling and sousing, and for centuries these methods have been used for preserving fish. Probably the oldest and most common preparation is found in classic soused herring, which dates back to the Middle Ages, specifically in Dutch, German, Swedish and British culinary traditions.

So, how do pickling and sousing differ? In pickling, the fish is immersed in a cold, acidic liquid (usually wine vinegar), with spices and/or other aromatics added. Sousing is similar, but vegetables are included in the pickling liquor, then it's added hot to the fish. The acidity works well with fish, and shellfish, particularly scallops, oysters and lobster, can also be enhanced beautifully with a light pickling liquor. It goes without saying, but I will say it: always use the freshest fish and shellfish for these techniques. What I like most about pickling and sousing is the scope they offer for experimentation. By using different vinegars (or other acidic liquids) and varying the herbs, spices and vegetables, you can create your own unique take on pickled fish.

My favourite fish to pickle are sardines, pilchards (large sardines) and mackerel; favourites to souse are Dover sole and ray.

Smoking

Smoking is a traditional and ancient method of preservation applied to many foods, but throughout history it has been particularly useful for fish, which goes off relatively quickly. In times past, most fishermen had a smokehouse attached to their cottage. Typically, they would salt the fish for storage, then dry it and smoke it with heat for eating. With refrigeration and freezers, smoking is no longer necessary for preserving, but the technique is still used for the wonderful flavours it lends to the fish.

Over time, the smoking process has been adapted and refined. Nowadays there are basically two types of smoking: cold and hot. Cold smoking takes place between 20–24°C (68–75°F), which isn't hot enough to cook the fish or eliminate pathogens, so it is essential to refrigerate it. Smoked salmon is the most popular cold-smoked fish. Hot smoking, which is carried out between 70–80°C (158–176°F), cooks the fish and changes the texture. The best example of hot-smoked fish is smoked mackerel, which is a particular favourite of mine.

There are two methods of smoking: traditional and mechanical. For the former, the fish is suspended in smokehouses over smouldering wood, usually overnight, slowly taking on smokiness. With mechanical smoking, smoke is distilled and used in liquid or solid form, so the process is akin to painting on the flavour. It's a quick, cheap way to produce smoked fish for supermarkets, but it's not great in my opinion.

Traditionally smoked seafood is far superior to its commercial counterpart, so buy this, unless, of course, you are going to smoke the fish yourself, which I would definitely recommend trying. Smoking fish is an adventure. You will, of course, need something to smoke it in. That can be an actual smoker (either a Bradley smoker – my choice, or if you know a good carpenter, he could make you one, like a shed). If you don't want to go to that expense, you can simply use a large bucket or metal box with holes drilled into it. You will also need untreated wood shavings.

For hot smoking, you can get good-quality, inexpensive stovetop smokers and I recommend buying one of these. You put wood shavings in the bottom and get these smoking over a flame, then place your fish on the rack, put it inside the smoker and slide on the lid – it's as simple as that. If you're indoors, make sure you have your extractor on full – you'll need it! Hot smoking can also be done on your barbecue.

My favourite fish for cold smoking are bream and bass; favourites for hot smoking are grey mullet, bass and mackerel.

Steamed

In recent years, I've come to appreciate how a fish that has been steamed has the purest flavour of all. If you want to know what a particular fish or shellfish really tastes like, the answer is to steam it. You'll have a wonderful clean flavour and succulent flesh, as long as it's been cooked correctly. I would go so far as to say my favourite way of cooking fish now is steaming. The purity it gives you when the dish is perfect is sublime.

It is imperative to use super-fresh fish for steaming. Techniques like roasting and pan-frying can hide slightly older fish, as the caramelized flavours produced can mask the pure taste of the fish. Steaming, however, is one technique that will tell you if your fish is old – not only in taste, but also in appearance. If, once steamed, your fish is off-white, even slightly yellow, rather than pearly white, it is not spanking fresh.

Such a gentle heat works like magic, especially with delicately textured fish, like brill and plaice. It's also the healthiest way to cook fish and shellfish, as it locks in the nutrients as well as the flavour – and you can avoid adding any oil or butter, if you wish.

You will need a steamer of some sort to cook your fish. I've found that a Chinese bamboo steamer works a treat. You can steam small to medium whole fish, such as bream or bass, but I usually steam fillets, as they cook more evenly.

Steaming is also the technique for opening bivalves, mainly mussels, cockles and clams. Typically, a little wine or cider is heated in a large pan, then the shellfish is added and the lid fitted tightly. The shells open in the steam created by the liquor in minutes, ready to be picked or eaten straight from the shell.

My favourite fish to steam are turbot or brill, and for shellfish, it's cockles and mussels.

Poached

Poaching can be one of the most flexible and adventurous of cooking techniques for fish and shellfish, which can be poached in a variety of different liquids, from a classic court bouillon, fish or shellfish stock to salted butter, various oils, milk or cream. Poaching is like cooking and marinating at the same time. It's also a technique that gives you a little leeway when you are cooking. Fish can overcook and become dry quickly under a grill or in a hot frying pan, but poaching is a little more forgiving because the seafood is immersed in liquid.

You can poach seafood either on the hob or in the oven. Poaching on the hob calls for a large, deep pan that can hold all the liquid and the fish comfortably. The heat that you poach at is slightly under a simmer (90–95°C/194–203°F). At this temperature, the liquor should not be bubbling but you should see steam rising from the surface.

For oven-poaching, preheat the oven to about 140°C Fan (325°F), Gas Mark 3 and put the fish into a suitable oven dish. Warm the poaching liquor in a pan until hot but not scalding, then pour it over the fish to two-thirds cover it. Put the lid on or cover the dish with greaseproof paper and foil. At this temperature, you will get perfectly cooked, succulent fish and a lovely, tasty stock to use as a base for a sauce or dressing.

I prefer to use either a salted butter or a highly flavoured court bouillon for poaching – both bring something special to the fish. My favourite seafood for poaching are turbot, bass, scallops and brill.

Boiled & braised

Boiling and braising both involve cooking in liquid. Boiling entails immersing the seafood in a pan of fast-boiling water and is only used to cook crustaceans, such as lobster, crab and langoustines, in my kitchen – to boil a piece of fish in liquid would be to ruin it! Braising is a gentler method of cooking by partially or totally immersing the fish in liquid and can be done in the oven or on the hob in a covered dish.

Boiling is straightforward. The water needs to be bubbling away rapidly before you add the shellfish and you need to add plenty of salt (around 30g/1oz salt per 1 litre/1¾ pints of water).

If there is not enough salt in the boiling water, the crustacean(s) will become waterlogged and their flavour will leach out and become lost. Also, you need to time the cooking carefully. The great thing about this technique is that it is consistent. Once you've boiled a crab or a lobster correctly, you've cracked it. You really cannot beat a freshly boiled crab served with a homemade mayonnaise and some good bread.

Braising is an excellent technique for cooking cuttlefish and big squid. Immersed in their braising liquor, these cephalopods tenderize as they cook slowly and gently for around an hour. Chunky fish steaks also respond well to braising, but they cook much more quickly. Braised with a few shallots softened in butter and a glug of wine in a suitable pan covered with a tight-fitting lid, a thick piece of fish should emerge beautifully succulent and flavoursome. There's also the added advantage of a lovely braising liquor to use as the base of a sauce. Just add a splash of cream and some freshly chopped herbs or some olive oil and fresh tomato and you have a delicious sauce to accompany your fish. With your ingredients prepared, that should take you around about 8 minutes to cook. That's convenience food for you!

My favourite fish to braise are chunky turbot, brill, plaice or sea bass; all shellfish boiled is utterly delicious.

Grilled

Other than pan-frying, grilling is probably the most popular way to cook fish. It takes little effort, after all, to pop a fish under the grill and there's nothing wrong with an easy option. Some of the best seafood I've eaten and cooked has been grilled.

Before you start, it's important to heat the grill to the correct temperature for cooking. If you don't, the skin won't colour and lightly crisp before the fish is cooked through and you'll be disappointed with the result. Generally, a medium to medium-high heat is used, depending on the thickness and density of the fish you're cooking. Mackerel, for example, can handle a fairly high heat, whereas bass needs a medium heat to ensure that it cooks through to the middle before overcooking on the outside.

Size is an important consideration when you're grilling fish. A large fish will dry out on the outside before it's cooked through, so I rarely grill a whole fish that weighs more than 1kg (2lb 4oz). Filleted portions can be grilled successfully provided they are of a reasonably even thickness. For me, it's essential to grill fish with the skin on. It protects the delicate flesh from the intense heat and is delicious to eat, as it acquires a delicate crispness and slightly caramelized favour under the grill.

Use a really strong grill tray that won't buckle under the heat and oil it lightly before you add the fish. I always oil and season the fish too before putting it under the grill – this helps to prevent it sticking to the tray. Always remember that the tray remains very hot when you remove it from the heat and the residual heat will continue to cook the fish.

My favourite fish to grill are bream, sea bass and mackerel.

Barbecued

Before you start barbecuing, you need to make sure your barbecue is hot enough, especially if you're cooking fish or shellfish. Personally, I don't think gas barbecues cut the mustard for seafood – they just don't get hot enough and the fish sticks.

For me, barbecuing is all about cooking over coals. And the coals need to be white hot, so hot that you can't hold your hand anywhere near the rack. It's this intense heat that stops the seafood from sticking and ensures it cooks quickly and remains succulent. The coals also give seafood an incomparable flavour.

Generally, I only ever barbecue whole fish on the bone; without the protection of the skin, the flesh can dry out very quickly over the intense heat. Butterflied fish can work well, too, but I'd never cook fillets on a barbecue. Similarly, crustaceans need to be in their shells; the flesh effectively steams within the shells and takes on the flavour from the coals without drying out.

My golden rules are: Get the coals white hot and be patient, it takes at least 45 minutes to 1 hour to get to that stage. Cook fish on the bone and with the skin on. Cook crustaceans, scallops and oysters in their shells. Only ever barbecue fish and shellfish that is spanking fresh. Stick to these golden rules, and you will be cooking some of the tastiest seafood ever!

My favourite seafood to cook over coals are mackerel, turbot, lobsters and gilt-head bream.

Baked

From simply baking whole fish on the bone dotted with butter and herbs, to cooking it in a tart or pie, baking fish in the oven is incredibly versatile. It's important to protect the fish from the dry heat of the oven and there are several ways of doing this. If you're baking a whole fish, leave it on the bone with the skin on and baste it with melted butter or oil a few times during cooking, to keep it moist. In a pie, the fish is kept succulent within a sauce under the pastry or mashed potato crust.

Baking in a salt crust is a great way to cook whole bass or bream. Simply enclose the fish in a thick layer of wet salt before it goes into the oven. This forms a crust, which seals in the fish, keeping in its flavour and moisture; the crust is broken and removed before serving. Cooking fish such as bass and sea trout *en croute* (in pastry) also works well.

One of the simplest ways to protect fish in the oven – whole or fillets – is to wrap them in foil with a little liquid, such as wine, some herbs and a few aromatics, like onion and garlic. Effectively, the fish steams in the sealed package and stays deliciously moist.

Similarly, fish fillets can be cooked *en papillote* (in sealed baking parchment or greaseproof paper parcels). This is a really nice way to bake fish, using different herbs, liquids and vegetables in the bag with the fish. When I cook fish this way, I open the parcels at the table so guests can savour all the delicious aromas as they are released.

My favourite way to bake fish is a nice chunky portion of hake fillet in foil, or a simple fish pie.

Pan-fried

This is probably the most common of all seafood cooking techniques. What I like most about pan-frying is the speed and convenience. It takes no time to pan-fry a fillet of fish, so make sure you have everything else for your dish prepared before you begin and don't start cooking until your guests are ready to eat. Another potential pitfall is to fry your fish in a pan that is too hot – you need a medium rather than a high heat.

For me, a good-quality nonstick pan is the way to go. Buy the best you can afford – a good-quality nonstick pan is a pleasure to use and will last a lot longer.

Fish fillets with skin lend themselves well to pan-frying. Always do most of the cooking on the skin side, as this acts as a protective layer, keeping the flesh moist and succulent. If you're pan-frying skinless fillets, you'll need to be very careful. Thin fillets, particularly, will dry out very quickly in a hot pan and are better steamed or briefly grilled.

The most important stage of pan-frying, for me, is when you turn the fish over. I fry the fish fillets skin-side down until the flesh is still slightly opaque in the middle, then turn off the heat and turn the fish over so the skin-side is uppermost. There's no need to turn the heat back on, as the fish will finish cooking in the residual heat of the pan. This slow finish to the cooking will give you time to plate up your garnish, sauce and any other accompaniments.

The other great thing about pan-frying is all the lovely juices and oils released by the fish as it cooks. Once you've removed the seafood, add a splash of wine to the pan to deglaze it, stirring to lift all that flavour in the sediment. Add a few softened shallots and a touch of cream, simmer for a minute, then add some herbs, and there you have it – a simple pan sauce.

My favourite seafood to pan-fry are scallops, mackerel, squid, grey mullet and red mullet.

Deep-fried
This may not be the healthiest of cooking methods, but there really is nothing quite like a piece of fresh, battered fish deep-fried to perfection. Deep-frying is, in fact, a good technique for protecting the fish and sealing in its moisture and flavour. Generally, the fish is coated in batter or breadcrumbs before frying or simply dusted with flour and dropped straight into the hot oil.

A thermostatically controlled deep-fat fryer is convenient and easy to use, but only worth buying if you deep-fry often. A deep, heavy saucepan on the hob will suffice, but do use a cooking thermometer to check the temperature, and don't fill it more than halfway with oil.

Be careful when you are deep-frying thick pieces of fish, as a crisp, golden coating may suggest they are cooked but the heat may not have penetrated all the way through to the centre. If you think this is a possibility, pop the fish into a hot oven for a few minutes after frying and it will be good to go.

When fish is deep-fried correctly, it doesn't become greasy. You'll only have this problem if the oil isn't hot enough.

Obviously, you need to get the oil in your deep-fryer up to the correct temperature before you add any food; the optimum temperature range for deep-frying fish is 175–190°C (347–375°F). Don't put too much into the pan in one go, or you will bring the temperature of the oil down; cook in batches to avoid this.

For me, the best way to deep-fry fish is in batter. I love the contrast of a crisp, golden, well-seasoned batter against the seafood.

I adore fish and chips as long as they're crispy – and I'm not alone. Whenever I put anything deep-fried on the menu, it always flies out of the kitchen!

My favourite fish to deep-fry are haddock, gurnard and squid.

2

Flat fish

Brill, Dover Sole, Lemon Sole,
Megrim, Plaice, Turbot

Brill

A lovely fish that is good served in several different ways; brill is always welcome on the menu.

Smaller fish hang about in estuaries feeding on plankton, but larger ones head out to sea, living on the seabed in the Atlantic Ocean and Mediterranean and Baltic Seas on a diet of crustaceans and small fish, which gives them a lovely, sweet flavour. Brill are fished by beam or demersal trawling, so always check the traceabililty with your fishmonger.

(Side note: I'd been told by fishermen that turbot and brill interbreed, but never believed them, until a few weeks ago when one of these fish arrived in my kitchen. Even after 30 years prepping fish, there's more to learn!)

Notes

In late spring and summer, the females carry huge amounts of roe, which – unless you plan to use it – is an expensive waste.

Growing to 75cm (30 inches) in length and 3kg (6lb 8oz) in weight, fishmongers usually sell them at around 1–2kg (2lb 4oz–4lb 8oz). For me, 2kg (4lb 8oz) is the ideal size.

Before buying, check the white underside of the fish for bruising; this indicates poor handling and will render parts of the flesh inedible, which is a very costly discovery if you don't check before buying! Also, check how fresh the fish is (see page 12); realistically it will have been out of the sea for at least 2 days.

Best time to eat

October–April.

Cooking & serving

- For me, curing fillets cut from a 2kg (4lb 8oz) fish is the ideal thing to do (see page 16).

- Brill has tiny scales that become translucent when cooked and are not nice to eat. Wipe them away with kitchen paper, but avoid washing the fish if you can. Fresh water speeds up the aging process and the fish will spoil more quickly.

- Steam fillets from a big fish (see pages 17–18) or breadcrumb and fry those from a smaller fish.

- Brill can handle big, bold flavours. I've served it at different times with red wine sauce, mustard dressing and jalapeño mayonnaise.

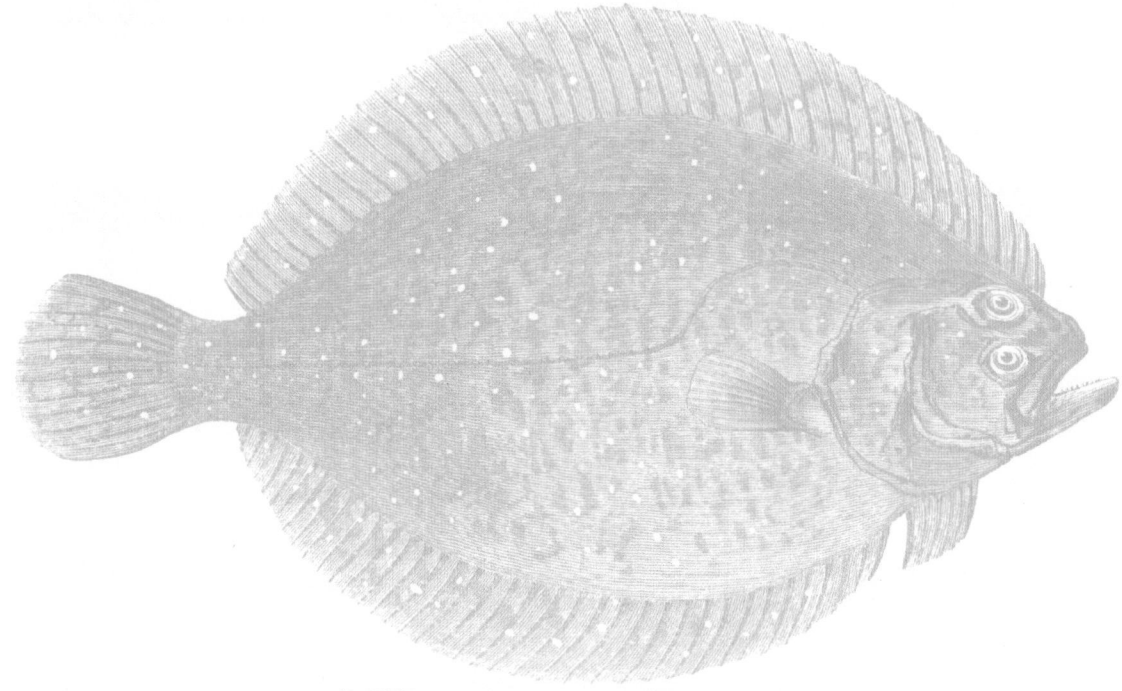

Dover Sole

Despite its name, Dover sole doesn't come from Dover! It was named after the Kent port because in times past, this was the most reliable land route to the London fish market. In the early to mid-nineteenth century, the bigger the Dover sole on your table, the richer you were thought to be. Sadly, cooks tended to serve them with lavish sauces, completely masking the wonderful flavour of the fish.

They are caught across the Atlantic, but those from around the UK coast are deemed the best in the world. In Cornwall, the fishing industry has taken part in a successful EU Dover sole recovery plan, which means part of the Cornish north coast is closed off for fishing and becomes a breeding ground. This has seen Dover sole populations increase. At the time of writing, Dover sole is a good sustainable choice. Modern fishermen are very experienced and, due to the value of Dover sole as a quota species, are very cautious when fishing for them.

The young feed on planktonic larvae, usually in tidal inlets, estuaries and bays, until big enough to move to the nursery areas of the seabed. At about 2 years old, they move to deeper waters where they feed at night, hiding half buried in the sand, waiting for small crustaceans and fish to cross their path.

They spawn at roughly 3 years old when they are about 30cm (12 inches) in length, the minimum landing size in Cornwall. I think this should be increased to give the species a few cycles of breeding, especially as the females produce millions of eggs when spawning. This simple act would give more juvenile fish a better chance to reach maturity.

They're fished using various trawled methods, some more detrimental to the seabed than others. Trawling also risks catching other species accidentally. Improving fishing methods and new technology are helping to rectify this.

Notes
Living up to 40 years, we tend to see them at around 5–6 years old; you'll rarely see one over 15 years old these days. The 500–600g (1lb 2oz –1lb 5oz) fish are the most popular size, but I like the larger fish, or 'doormats' as the fishermen call them. Small Dover soles, called slip soles, are a great option as they are less expensive. A brace of these makes an excellent main course or use one as a starter.

When it comes to Dover sole, I invariably think 'cook whole'. This is probably because of its structure and texture. The fillets have dense, tightly packed, juicy flakes making it the perfect fish for cooking whole.

Best time to eat
May–January.

Cooking & serving

- I think the best way of cooking Dover sole is a technique I call 'soused on the bone' (see pages 16 and 39), but a simpler, classic way would be to pan-fry on both sides (always on the bone!) and finish with a lovely flavoured butter.

- Dover sole can handle big flavours, but I tend to be gentler with it, because the natural taste of the fish is so fine it would be a shame to lose it with an overpowering accompaniment. Dover sole fetches a very high price; it's not a fish you want to ruin!

- If you attempt to cook a very fresh, stiff Dover sole you will find it tough and tasteless, and it will probably curl up during cooking and might also split across the fillet, leaving you with an unattractive result. It benefits from a few days in the refrigerator or dry-ager.

- Ask your fishmonger or online fish supplier how long their Dover soles have been out of the sea; don't be shocked if they say over 3 days! This is normal due to the nature of the fishing methods the fishermen use when targeting flat fish. Anything under 4 to 5 days with Dover sole is too fresh, in my opinion.

Lemon Sole

Lemon sole deserves more respect as a species. In my opinion, when cooked gently and simply, it has such a lovely, unique flavour that there's nothing else like it. It also has a melt-in-the-mouth texture, so it's an ideal fish to introduce to children or first-time fish eaters. Once under-used, it's more popular now that its eating qualities are more widely appreciated; it's also a bit cheaper than most other flat fish.

Quite where the name 'lemon sole' comes from is a bit of a mystery. Its flavour isn't lemony, and it isn't even a sole, belonging instead to the same family as plaice and halibut! Living on the gravelly seabed, they can live up to 20 years, swimming at depths of 20–200m (65–650ft). They feed at night on small crustaceans and barnacles, which gives their flesh shellfish overtones.

Caught by beam and demersal trawling, Cornwall's and the EU's own sustainability standards say that only fish over 25cm (10 inches) in length should be targeted. They're mostly sold at around 4 years of age.

Notes
Avoid during the spawning season – spring and early summer; they have large roes and the flesh becomes spongy and not good to eat.

Best time to eat
Autumn and winter.

Cooking & serving
- When serving whole, scale the fish first, unless you want scales in your sauce!

- My favourite way to serve is to simply fillet and skin the fish, then steam (see pages 17–18). Alternatively, bake gently.

- Do not pan-fry. Lemon sole is far too delicate, the fillets are too thin and the skin gives little protection to the flesh.

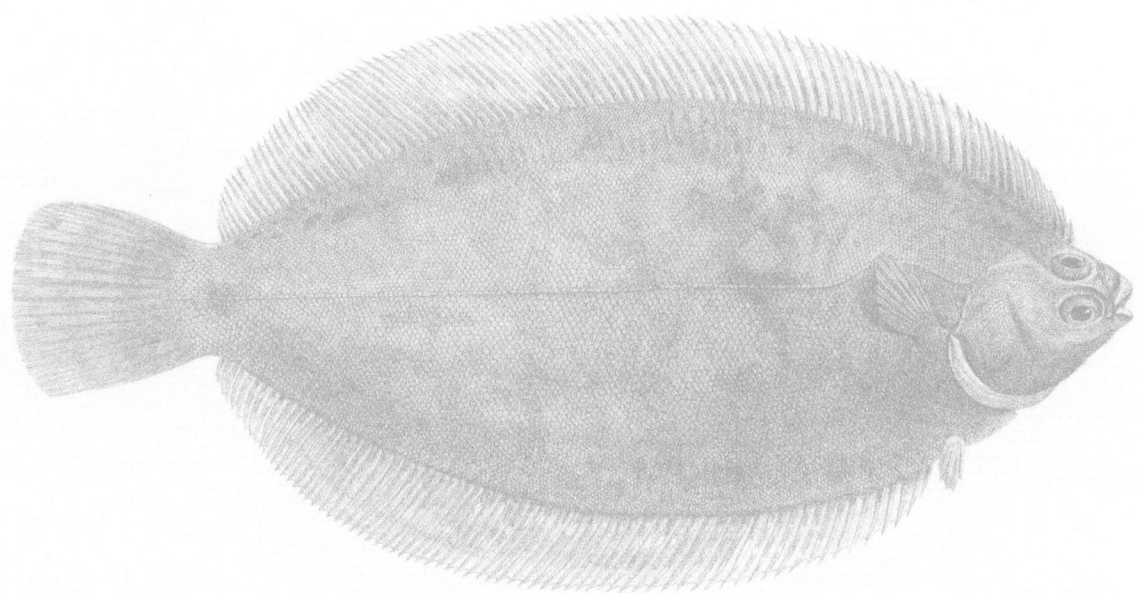

Megrim (or Cornish Sole)

Megrim sole is classed as a common flat fish. In the past, it wasn't eaten much in the UK and the catch would go to France or Spain, but Brexit has made that difficult. Coupled with a demand for something different and cheaper, and an increased awareness of sustainability, megrim has started to become more popular with UK consumers. Commonly caught off the Cornish coast, it's often sold as 'Cornish sole'. This sounds quite cool and certainly helps them fly out of the kitchen when they're on the restaurant menu!

The EU minimum landing size is 20cm (8 inches), but Cornwall operates an inshore fisheries and conservation scheme, which has set a minimum landing size of 25cm (10 inches) to give the species a chance of spawning and increasing stocks. Most trawlers in southwest England are using square mesh panels that allow juvenile fish to escape, some even using CCTV to monitor the release of the little ones. At the present time, megrim is a sustainable choice.

Generally found on the continental shelf of the north-east Atlantic, they tend to be caught at various depths between 50–800m (165–2,600ft), but mostly at about 200m (650ft). Megrim sole can live for up to 15 years and grow to around 60cm (24 inches) in length, but the fish we usually eat tend to be 3–5 years old and 35–40cm (14–16 inches) long. Like all flat fish, they live happily at the bottom of the ocean and are partial to a few little fish. They have huge mouths for a flat fish, so they are not shy about hanging around the seabed buffet table, feeding mostly through the summer on small fish and crustaceans.

Notes
I like to buy and cook bigger 1kg (2lb 4oz) fish, which a good fishmonger should be able to get for you, as I find the texture to be more appealing. Smaller fish can be a bit soft and nothing special – leave them in the sea to get bigger and tastier!

Best time to eat
May–December.

Cooking & serving
- Megrim is good for serving to children, as they make lovely posh fish fingers.

- My favourite way to cook and eat megrim is trimmed and baked whole in the oven (see page 47). I think you get the true flavour and texture cooking the fish this way.

Plaice

A great alternative to its expensive cousins, brill and turbot, plaice is one of Europe's most important commercial species, but this popularity means sustainability has become an issue.

Masters of hunting, they can change colour to match their surroundings, hiding in the sand or shingle and waiting for anything edible to come past for their dinner. They spend most of the day inactive, coming out at night to feed, especially on mussels. At certain times of the year they can be found loitering around areas where mussels are young and relatively easy picking; they also enjoy small crabs. They much prefer mussels and small, broken-up crab to the line fishermen's bait and are not easy to catch.

Plaice are usually caught on the bottom of the ocean mainly with beam and demersal trawlers, and occasionally gill nets. The minimum landing size in the UK is 27cm (10¾ inches) and the main fishing for plaice happens about 20 miles offshore, usually off the south coast. Unfished, they are a long-lived species, some up to 30 years old, but generally we see them at 5–6 years old.

Notes
Growing up to 42cm (16½ inches) in length, at this size they're fantastic cut into steaks and grilled on the bone. Most of the time though, plaice are sold at around 30cm (12 inches), when they are great as fillets or served whole.

Best time to eat
Late April–end December.

Cooking & serving

- You can always pick plaice out on the fishmonger's counter, as it's distinguished by the orange spots on its green-brown back and eyes directed to the right.

- I much prefer to cook the less fashionable, larger plaice, as they have the qualities of brill and can stand up to some big flavours.

- Be warned! This isn't a fish that needs much cooking. If you do overcook it, it will become very dry and tasteless.

- Cook with care using a method such as braising and you will have beautiful, moist white fillets of fish.

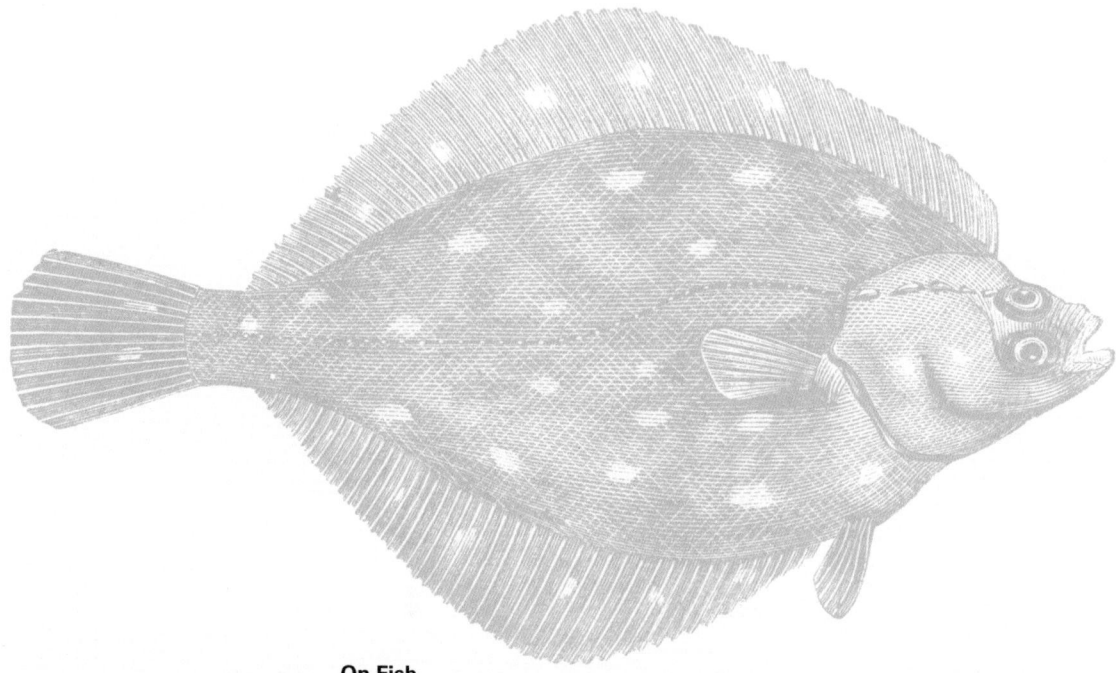

On Fish

Turbot

Turbot is considered the king of the sea in UK waters. Great tasting and very expensive, it's welcome on any menu, albeit with a staggering price tag!

A large, flat fish, turbot is related to brill, flounder and plaice. Fascinatingly, it starts life as a round fish, feeding off plankton and after the first 6 months it gradually transforms itself into a flat fish, living around the seabed in mostly sandy areas, becoming a 'bottom feeder' that loves to eat small fish and crustaceans. Like other flat fish, turbot is adept at camouflage, blending in with its environment. A sedentary species, it hunts successfully by remaining still on the seabed and waiting for dinner to arrive.

Turbot spawn from roughly 3 years old when they are about 30cm (12 inches) long; the minimum landing size in Cornwall. Maybe this should be increased to give the species a few cycles of breeding, especially as the females produce millions of eggs. This simple act would give more juvenile fish a better chance to get to a mature age.

A fast-growing, powerful flat fish, turbot can grow up to 1m (3¼ feet) in length and up to 25kg (55lb) in weight. I've never seen a fish this big, and can only imagine it would be a pointless catch and best left in the sea to breed. The quality would be awful eating-wise, due to the size.

Turbot are generally caught at depths between 15–60m (50–195ft), nearly all landed by gill netters using tangle or trammel nets set on the seabed, and rarely off the shore with rod and line – you'd have to be a very good angler to do this.

Amazingly, the management of turbot stocks is poor and I find it unbelievable there is no set quota at the time of writing. However, the efforts made with closed fishing areas off the south-west coast for cod and sole may, in turn, help turbot stocks recover. Also, the sad fact that there are fewer fisherman fishing nowadays due to costs could be of benefit to the species. Neither of these things are being scientifically monitored at present, so let's hope there is some study soon so we can eat turbot without worry in the future.

Notes
Avoid from March–June, its spawning season. The roes are very big and, unless you have use for them, it would be a very expensive, wasteful buy. The fillet quality will be poor, too.

Best time to eat
In season between July–February, but at its peak when the water and weather is coldest.

Cooking & serving
- The perfect size for cooking is 2–3kg (4lb 8oz–6lb 8oz); this will feed 4–6 people easily.

- The biggest I've ever prepped is about 10kg (22lb), too big in my opinion. When it is this size, the big fillets are very hard to cook perfectly, tending to overcook and dry out.

- The best way to cook turbot is to steam it, if the fish is filleted, or cut into steaks across the bone if you buy a whole one (see pages 52–7).

- This is not a species I would say is good raw or cured, due to the firm and tough texture.

- Turbot can handle bold flavours, but due to the cost and superior quality I always keep the flavours simple to let the fish shine through.

Flat fish

Preparation techniques

Filleting & pinboning flat fish

1. Make sure your chopping board is secure by placing a cloth underneath. Begin by scraping any slime present from the fish. Place the fish on the board dark side up and head facing away from you. Look for the line that runs down the centre and, using a sharp knife, make an incision around the neck and down the centre. Cut around the neck, keeping as close to the bone as possible, then cut down the centre to the tail.

2. Using a sharp knife at a slight angle, cut along the fillet as close to the bone as possible. Continue until you reach the tail.

3. Continue to run the knife as close as possible to the bone, releasing the fillet.

4. Turn the fish around, head towards you. Starting at the tail, repeat steps 2 and 3.

5. Release the fillet by keeping your knife as close as possible to the bone.

6. Turn the fish over and repeat steps 2–4

7. Remember to keep close to the bone to release the fillet.

8. Turn the fish around and release the final fillet, repeating steps 4–5.

9. The filleted turbot.

Flat fish

Serves 4

500g (1lb 2oz) thick brill fillet (from a 2kg/4lb 8oz fish), skinned
100g (3½oz) sea salt
100g (3½oz) caster sugar
100ml (3½fl oz) dry white wine

For the basil oil
60g (2¼oz) basil leaves, washed
150ml (5fl oz) light olive oil
sea salt

For the pumpkin seeds
4 tablespoons pumpkin seeds
a drizzle of light olive oil
sea salt and freshly ground white pepper, to taste

To serve
juice of 1 lime
12 crisp red grapes, sliced

Brill Cured in White Wine
with Grapes, Pumpkin Seeds & Basil Oil

Brill is my favourite species to cure; the texture is perfect for this technique. It is firm but not sinewy and that's what I want when eating cured fish. I have cured brill in many ways, but the simplicity of this white wine cure, with just enough acidity coming from the wine, is perfect. Cured fish is a great 'get out of jail free' dish, because it freezes very well and once thawed is ready to go. That may seem strange because freezing fish isn't traditionally deemed the 'done thing', but I truly believe in this case the texture is better for it.

1. To cure the brill, place the fillet into a snug tray and sprinkle over the salt and sugar. Pour over the wine and turn the fish in it a few times. Place in the refrigerator for 3 hours, turning the fish every hour.

2. To make the basil oil, bring a small pan of salted water to a simmer and have ready a bowl of cold water with a few ice cubes in it. When the water is simmering, add the basil leaves and blanch for 30 seconds. Remove the basil and plunge it straight into the iced water to cool. When the basil is cold, drain and squeeze out all the excess water. Place the basil into a small food processor and add the oil. Blend for 1 minute, then transfer the oil to a container to settle for a couple of hours before straining through muslin into a clean container. Store in the refrigerator for up to 1 week (it can be frozen, too).

3. For the pumpkin seeds, preheat the oven to 160°C Fan (350°F), Gas Mark 4. Lay the seeds on a baking tray in a single layer, then drizzle with oil and season with salt and white pepper. Roast in the oven for 10 minutes, then give them a stir and spread them out again. Return to the oven for 5 minutes. Remove from the oven and leave to cool.

4. Wash the curing mixture off the fish under cold running water, then pat dry with a tea towel or kitchen paper. For best results, wrap the fish tightly in good-quality greaseproof paper and freeze it until firm – this will enable you to cut neat slices.

5. When you are ready to serve, place the frozen fish on a chopping board for 10 minutes to thaw slightly. Using a sharp, serrated knife, slice the fish as thinly as you like. Lay the slightly frozen slices on to serving plates – the fish will defrost after 20 minutes and will then be ready to eat.

6. Just before serving, add a squeeze of lime juice to each slice of fish and drizzle around the basil oil. Arrange the slices of grape on top of the fish slices, with a pumpkin seed on each slice, then serve.

Serves 4

2 teaspoons fennel seeds
2 teaspoons sea salt
8 slices of smoked streaky bacon or pancetta
2kg (4lb 8oz) brill, filleted and portioned into 4 x 120g (4¼oz) portions
2 tablespoons olive oil
a drizzle of extra virgin rapeseed oil, to finish

For the pea, shallot & cider stew
50g (1¾oz) unsalted butter
2 tablespoons rapeseed oil
12 shallots, peeled and left whole
200ml (7fl oz) dry cider
1 sprig of rosemary, finely chopped
300ml (10fl oz) fish stock
200g (7oz) fresh peas, podded
100g (3½oz) clotted cream (ideally Cornish, of course!)
1 tablespoon chopped mint leaves
1 tablespoon chopped flat-leaf parsley leaves
sea salt and freshly ground black pepper, to taste

Steamed Brill
with Pea, Shallot & Cider Stew

A filleted portion of brill from a good-sized fish, lightly steamed, is a comforting and pleasurable delight. Brill is such a delicate species that harsher techniques of cooking tend to dry out the edges of the fish. In this recipe, I've paired the fish with a subtle fennel salt that brings out its character. Beneath the fish pools a fresh, but rich, stew of peas, bolstered with cider and clotted cream. A wonderful, delicate plate of food, I hope you'll agree!

1. To make the stew, heat the butter and oil in a medium saucepan over a medium heat. When the butter is bubbling, add the shallots and gently let them colour all over, stirring occasionally, for 15–20 minutes. Don't cook them too quickly – if they start to colour fast, reduce the heat. Once the shallots are well coloured, add the cider and rosemary and increase the heat to allow the cider to reduce quickly. When the cider has reduced by three-quarters, pour in the fish stock and simmer until reduced by half. Add the peas and simmer for a further 20 minutes.

2. Meanwhile, set up a large bamboo steamer or switch on your steamer oven. Crush the fennel seeds and sea salt together in a mortar and pestle and set aside. Cook the bacon until crispy under a hot grill or in a frying pan and set aside.

3. Season the brill with 2 teaspoons of the fennel seed salt and drizzle with the olive oil. Place the fish on a sheet of baking parchment and steam for 4–5 minutes.

4. While the fish is cooking, add the clotted cream to the stew. Bring to a simmer and whisk it in, then add the chopped herbs. Taste and add salt and pepper as you like.

5. To finish, ladle the stew into bowls. Peel the skin away from the brill and sprinkle the flesh with 1 teaspoon of the fennel seed salt. Place the fish on top of each portion of stew and add 2 slices of crispy bacon to each bowl. Drizzle a little extra virgin rapeseed oil over the fish and serve. I would serve this with either new or mashed potatoes.

Whole Baked Dover Sole
with Blistered Olives & Tomatoes

Serves 4

4 x 500g (1lb 2oz) Dover sole, skinned and trimmed

For the spice rub
4 teaspoons fennel seeds
1 teaspoon dried chilli
2 teaspoons coriander seeds
2 teaspoons sea salt

For the dressing
60g (2¼oz) black olives, pitted
60g (2¼oz) green olives, pitted
20 cherry tomatoes, halved
olive oil, for drizzling and cooking
4 tablespoons extra virgin olive oil
zest and juice of 1 lemon
2 teaspoons fennel seeds
1 teaspoon chilli flakes
2 garlic cloves, finely chopped
2 sprigs of rosemary, picked and chopped
1 red onion, finely chopped
12 new potatoes, washed and cooked
1 x 50g (1¾oz) can of anchovies in olive oil, sliced lengthways (reserve the oil)
a handful of flat-leaf parsley leaves, chopped
sea salt and freshly ground black pepper

Cooking Dover sole on the bone is the only way to cook the species, in my opinion. This recipe is a really lovely way to keep it simple, but with a little touch of difference by using a spice rub. Colouring the fish first in a pan may seem a bit of a faff, but that touch of direct heat gives the fish a slight caramelized edge that really brings out the wonderful, sticky, lip-smacking character of Dover sole. Baking the fish in essentially a dressing of all the ingredients creates a lovely delicious marriage of flavours. By all means play around with your own spice rub and mixture of ingredients with this technique. The end results are just right for this type of fish.

1. First, make the spice rub for the fish. In a frying pan over a medium heat, lightly toast the spices with the salt for 5 minutes. Take care, as you don't want them to burn! Transfer them to a spice grinder and blitz until fine. Transfer to a bowl and leave to cool.

2. Preheat the oven to 180°C Fan (400°F), Gas Mark 6.

3. Place the olives and cherry tomatoes on a baking tray and sprinkle with salt and a drizzle of olive oil. Roast in the oven for 15 minutes until blistered. Remove from the oven and leave to cool. Keep the oven on for the fish.

4. In a small saucepan, combine the extra virgin olive oil, lemon zest, fennel seeds, chilli flakes, garlic and rosemary. Gently heat over a low heat for 10 minutes, then set aside to infuse further.

5. To cook the fish, heat a large frying pan over a medium heat (depending on the size of your pan, you may need to cook in two batches). Drizzle some oil into the pan. When it's hot, add the red onion and cook for 5 minutes until it softens and starts to colour. Transfer the onion to the tray with the blistered olives and keep warm.

6. Season each fish with 2 teaspoons of the rub. Wipe out the frying pan and drizzle in some more oil, then carefully lay the fish into the pan and cook for 2 minutes. Turn them over and cook for another 2 minutes.

7. Lift and transfer the fish to a roasting tray large enough to hold them all. Scatter the new potatoes, olives, tomatoes, red onion and anchovies with their oil over the fish, then pour over the infused oil. Bake in the oven for 8–10 minutes until cooked through. Remove from the oven and squeeze over the lemon juice, then sprinkle with 1 teaspoon of the rub and the chopped parsley.

8. Transfer the fish to serving plates and spoon the cooking juices and vegetables equally among each plate. Serve simply with a green or tomato salad.

Soused Dover Sole
with Sweet & Sour Beetroot & Shallots

Serves 4

olive oil
1 onion, sliced
2 garlic cloves, finely chopped
50g (1¾oz) fresh root ginger, peeled and sliced
2 sprigs of thyme
175ml (6fl oz) white wine vinegar
200ml (7fl oz) dry white wine
2 Dover sole, about 600g (1lb 5oz) each, skinned and heads removed
sea salt and freshly ground black pepper
extra virgin olive oil, to finish

For the beetroot & shallots
400g (14oz) raw beetroot, cleaned
2 teaspoons sea salt
75ml (2½fl oz) white wine vinegar
a drizzle of olive oil
2 banana shallots, finely sliced (a mandoline is useful here, but mind your fingers!)
1 garlic clove, finely chopped
50g (1¾oz) fresh root ginger, finely chopped
100ml (3½fl oz) sherry vinegar
25g (1oz) caster sugar
2 sprigs of thyme, leaves picked
fennel herb or dill, to serve (optional) and chopped

For the dill & lemon yogurt
100g (3½oz) full-fat Greek yogurt
4 teaspoons chopped dill
zest of 1 lemon
a pinch of sea salt

This is a different way of cooking Dover sole compared to the usual method of serving a whole fish. I developed this technique to allow us to serve Dover sole fillets that had been rested on the bone, which allows the fish to stay firm and juicy without the fillet shrinking. It also allows you to pre-cook in advance to take the pressure off trying to get it right at the last minute. In fact, this whole dish can be made in advance and sit in your refrigerator waiting to be served. Just remember to take it out an hour before serving to allow it to come to room temperature.

1. Start with the beetroot. Place the raw beetroot into a pan and cover with water. Add the 2 teaspoons of salt and the white wine vinegar. Bring to a simmer and cook the beetroot for 20–30 minutes until tender. To test, prick the beetroot with a small knife or skewer. Once cooked, leave the beetroot to cool in the water until it can be handled without burning your hands.

2. Preheat the oven to 180°C Fan (400°F), Gas Mark 6.

3. Meanwhile, cook the fish. Heat a large frying pan over a medium heat and add a drizzle of oil. When hot, add the onion, garlic and ginger and cook for 3–4 minutes until the onion starts to soften. Add the thyme sprigs, vinegar and white wine and bring to a simmer. Pour the mixture into a roasting tray large enough to hold the fish.

4. Wipe out the frying pan, add a fresh drizzle of olive oil and heat over medium heat. Season the fish all over with salt and pepper. When the oil is hot, add the fish and fry for 2 minutes, then turn over and cook for a further 2 minutes. Transfer the fish to the roasting tray, spooning some of the onion mixture on top. Bake in the oven for 8–10 minutes until cooked through, then leave to rest until it is cool enough to handle.

5. Carefully remove the cooled fish fillets from the bone and place in a separate deep tray. Strain the liquid remaining in the roasting tray through a sieve and pour it over the cooked fillets.

6. To finish the beetroot, peel off the skin using a knife or your hands (with gloves!), then slice and place in a bowl. Heat a frying pan over a medium heat and add a drizzle of oil. When hot, add the shallots, garlic and ginger and cook until the shallots start to soften. Add the sherry vinegar, sugar and thyme and season with salt and pepper. Pour the contents of the pan onto the beetroot and mix together carefully.

7. Lay the beetroot onto 4 plates (you will have some extra to serve on the side) and lay the fish fillets on top. Mix the yogurt with the chopped dill, lemon zest and a pinch of salt and spoon some onto each plate.

8. Finally, mix equal quantities of the sousing liquid, beetroot liquid and extra virgin olive oil and taste. Add some seasoning if you feel it is needed. Spoon the dressing equally over the 4 plates. Scatter over the fennel herb or dill, if using, then serve.

Lemon Sole in Sherry Sauce
with Braised Lettuce & Green Peppers

Serves 4

2 lemon sole, about 800g (1lb 12oz) each, filleted and skinned
4 tablespoons extra virgin olive oil, to finish

For the spice rub
1 tablespoon cumin seeds
1 tablespoon coriander seeds
1 tablespoon picked thyme leaves
sea salt and freshly ground black pepper

For the sauce
1 tablespoon olive oil
1 banana shallot, finely chopped
50g (1¾oz) unsalted butter
1 garlic clove, finely sliced
250ml (9fl oz) dry sherry
500ml (18fl oz) fish stock
150ml (5fl oz) double cream
1 tablespoon lemon juice
a handful of chopped flat-leaf parsley leaves

For the braised lettuce
olive oil
50g (1¾oz) unsalted butter
4 baby gem lettuces, halved and washed
100ml (3½fl oz) dry sherry
100ml (3½fl oz) fish stock

For the green peppers
2 green peppers, halved lengthways, seeds removed
2 tablespoons sherry vinegar
a drizzle of olive oil

This dish is well worth the effort to impress someone or as a treat for yourself. I can't stress enough how important it is to get everything ready before you start cooking, as lemon sole is very thin and cooks quickly. Sit everyone down, pour the drinks, then cook the fish. I serve this with couscous or rice.

1. First, make the spice rub. Toast the cumin, coriander seeds and thyme in a dry frying pan until aromatic. Transfer to a mortar and pestle or small food processor, add some salt and black pepper, and grind to a fine powder. Set aside 5 teaspoons of the spice rub for the peppers and sauce. Lightly season the fish fillets with the remaining rub, then set aside.

2. To make the sauce, place a large saucepan over a medium heat. When hot, add the olive oil and sweat the shallot, stirring occasionally, until it softens and starts to colour slightly. Add the butter, garlic and 3 teaspoons of the spice rub and cook for a further 2 minutes, then add the sherry. Simmer until the sauce reduces and becomes syrupy, then add the fish stock and continue to simmer until reduced by half. Pour in the cream and simmer for 5 minutes, then season the sauce to taste with the lemon juice, salt and pepper. Keep warm, or, if making in advance, allow it to cool, then cover and store in the refrigerator for up to 3 days.

3. For the braised lettuce, heat a large nonstick frying pan over a medium heat. Add a drizzle of olive oil and the butter. Once bubbling, add the lettuces, cut-sides down, and season with salt and pepper. Cook for 2 minutes until the cut surfaces are starting to brown, then flip the lettuces over and colour for 2 minutes on the other side. Add the sherry and fish stock and bring to a simmer, then cover and cook for 5 minutes.

4. Transfer the lettuces to a plate. Simmer the cooking liquid until reduced by half, then return the lettuces to the pan. Remove from the heat, spoon the reduced liquor over the lettuces and keep warm.

5. For the green peppers, preheat the oven to 180°C Fan (400°F), Gas Mark 6. Place the peppers in a baking dish, cut-sides up. Season with salt, pepper and the remaining 2 teaspoons of the spice rub. Drizzle over the sherry vinegar and some olive oil, then bake for 30 minutes until the peppers start to collapse but still have some structure. Divide the braised lettuce among the pepper halves and keep warm while cooking the fish.

6. Set up a large bamboo steamer (or steamer of choice). When your steamer, sauce and peppers are ready, cook the fish. Lay the seasoned fish on a piece of greaseproof or baking paper and steam for 3 minutes. Make sure the fish fits into the steamer comfortably, but don't overfill it. If you need to, steam in two batches.

7. Add the chopped parsley to the warm sauce, then spoon it onto warmed plates. Carefully transfer the fish fillets to the plates and place a pepper half alongside. Drizzle with extra virgin olive oil, then serve.

Serves 4

Crispy Breaded Lemon Sole
with Cucumber & Ginger Mayonnaise & Herb Oil

100g (3½oz) plain flour
2 eggs, beaten
100g (3½oz) panko breadcrumbs
4 lemon sole, 400–500g (14oz–1lb 2oz) each, filleted and skinned
sunflower oil, for deep-frying
sea salt and freshly ground black pepper

For the mint & coriander oil
30g (1oz) mint leaves
30g (1oz) coriander leaves
200ml (7fl oz) light olive oil

For the cucumber & ginger mayonnaise
50g (1¾oz) fresh root ginger, peeled
50ml (2 fl oz) lime juice, plus the juice of 1 extra lime
1 tablespoon white wine vinegar
1 cucumber, peeled, deseeded and chopped
2 egg yolks
2 teaspoons Dijon mustard
300ml (10fl oz) sunflower oil

To serve
1 cucumber, peeled, deseeded and sliced
a small handful of mint leaves, washed and picked
a small handful of coriander leaves, washed and picked

There are many ways to cook lemon sole, it's such a versatile fish, but I don't think you can beat it breaded, fried until crisp and perfectly steamed inside crunchy breadcrumbs. I suppose, for me, there is a nostalgia element attached to this as well. My first seafood experience wasn't *fruits de mer* in the south of France – it was fish fingers, from the Captain, of course! I think this dish is a level up from those orange fish rectangles. The mayonnaise sauce is delicious and will work in several ways if you want to change the juice element for another citrus.

1. First, make the mint and coriander oil. Bring a small pan of salted water to a simmer and have ready a bowl of cold water with a few ice cubes in it. When the water is simmering, add the herbs and blanch for 30 seconds. Remove the herbs and plunge them straight into the iced water to cool. When the herbs are cold, drain, and squeeze out all the excess water. Put the blanched herbs into a blender with the olive oil and blitz for 2 minutes. Strain through a fine sieve or muslin and transfer to a container. Chill until needed. Leftover oil will last for 1 week in the refrigerator.

2. For the cucumber and ginger mayonnaise, put the ginger, 50ml (2fl oz) lime juice, white wine vinegar and a pinch of salt into a blender or food processor, add the cucumber and blitz for 3 minutes. Strain through a sieve lined with muslin into a bowl, twisting and squeezing the cloth until you cannot extract any more juice. Set the juice aside and discard the contents of the sieve.

3. Place the egg yolks and mustard into a food processor and blend for 30 seconds. With the motor running, slowly add the sunflower oil until incorporated and you have a thick mayonnaise. Place in a small saucepan over a low heat, add the strained cucumber and ginger juice and whisk together; do not let it boil or it will curdle. Add lime juice to taste. When you see steam rising from the sauce, it's ready. Remove from the heat.

4. For the crispy lemon sole, have the flour, beaten egg and panko ready in three separate bowls. Pass each fish fillet first through the flour, then the egg and finally the breadcrumbs to coat.

5. Heat a deep-fat fryer to 180°C (350°F) or heat some sunflower oil in a deep, heavy-based pan (not filling more than two-thirds full). Deep-fry the breaded lemon sole in the hot oil for 2 minutes until golden. Using a slotted spoon, remove to drain on kitchen paper and season with salt and pepper.

6. Mix the cucumber slices and herbs together and season with salt.

7. Share the mayonnaise sauce among warmed plates, arrange the cucumber and herbs in the middle and place two lemon sole fillets on top of each portion. Finish with the cucumber and herb oil.

Deep-Fried Megrim Sole
with a Chilli & Seed Dressing

Serves 4

sunflower oil, for deep-frying
100g (3½oz) Farina potato starch
4 megrim sole, 300–400g (10½–14oz) each, filleted, skinned and trimmed

For the dressing
2 tablespoons pumpkin seeds
1 tablespoon sesame seeds
1 teaspoon cumin seeds
3 ripe plum tomatoes, deseeded and chopped
a handful of coriander leaves, washed and chopped
juice of 2 limes
1 red chilli, deseeded and chopped
1 teaspoon fresh oregano leaves
1 garlic clove, finely chopped or grated
200ml (7fl oz) olive oil
sea salt and freshly ground black pepper

This is a very simple, quick recipe that makes the best use of megrim sole. The fillets are coated in potato starch before frying and that's enough to keep the fish moist and prevent it overcooking. The dressing is an interesting collection of flavours that go so well with fried fish, plus a good kick of chilli! If chilli isn't for you, just leave it out. This technique will work well with all flat fish. Rice or chips work well as a side.

1. To make the dressing, toast the seeds in a dry frying pan over a medium heat for 5 minutes. Using a mortar and pestle or a small blender, blitz three-quarters of the toasted seeds, reserving the rest for later.

2. Place the tomatoes, coriander, lime juice, chilli, oregano, garlic and olive oil together in a bowl and season with salt and pepper. Mix well, then add the toasted and blitzed seeds. Leave for the flavours to mingle while you cook the fish.

3. To cook the fish, heat a deep-fat fryer to 180°C (350°F) or heat some sunflower oil in a deep, heavy-based pan (not filling more than two-thirds full). Meanwhile, season the potato starch with salt. When the oil is hot, pass the fish, fillet by fillet, through the potato starch. Tap off the excess and place them on a tray. Deep-fry the fish for 2 minutes. Unless you have a big fryer/pan, do this in two batches. Remove with a slotted spoon to drain on kitchen paper.

4. Plate the fish fillets and share the dressing among them. Finish with a sprinkling of the reserved seeds.

Baked Megrim Sole on Fennel
with Orange & Gochujang Butter

Serves 4

1 teaspoon fennel seeds
1 teaspoon coriander seeds
½ teaspoon woody herbs
  (such as rosemary and thyme)
1 orange, zested, then peeled
  and segmented
3 teaspoons sea salt
4 megrim sole, 350–400g
  (12–14oz) each, scaled,
  trimmed and heads removed

For the butter
3 tablespoons gochujang
  chilli paste
2 tablespoons chopped chives
1 tablespoon chopped rosemary
  leaves
zest of 1 orange
250g (9oz) unsalted butter,
  softened

For the fennel
2 tablespoons olive oil
2 banana shallots, halved
  lengthways and sliced
  lengthways
2 fennel bulbs, sliced as finely as
  you can, fronds reserved
3 garlic cloves, finely chopped
juice of 1 orange
200ml (7fl oz) white wine
sea salt and freshly ground
  black pepper

Megrim sole, a.k.a. Cornish sole, is perfect to bake whole in the oven. The gentle heat allows the fish to cook evenly, avoiding any chance of overcooking. Try to get the bigger size of megrim sole if you can, as they tend to be better eating due to the thickness of the fillets. Fermented gochujang chilli paste is available in most supermarkets and online now. It's a great product from Korea that works well with fish species that may lack in the flavour department. The butter can be frozen if you don't use it all, but I think you will! I like to serve this with boiled rice and a salad of fresh leaves.

1. First, make the butter. Put the gochujang, chives, rosemary and orange zest in a bowl and add the softened butter. Mix with a spatula until evenly blended. Season with salt to taste. Spoon the butter onto a sheet of clingfilm and wrap it up, rolling it into a long sausage and tying the ends to secure. Chill for 2 hours before using.

2. Preheat the oven to 180°C Fan (400°F), Gas Mark 6.

3. To prepare the fennel, heat the oil in a large sauté pan over a medium heat. Add the shallot and cook for 1 minute, then add the fennel and cook for a further 3 minutes. Add the garlic, then when it starts to colour, add the orange juice and white wine, and season with salt and pepper. Bring to the boil, then transfer the mixture to one or two roasting trays, depending on the size of your fish and oven. Leave to cool slightly.

4. In a food processor, blitz together the fennel seeds, coriander seeds, woody herbs, orange zest and the sea salt. Season the fish with the mixture, then place them on top of the fennel in the roasting tray/s. Slice the chilli butter into thick slices and place on top of each fish – be generous. Bake in the oven for 8–10 minutes.

5. Scatter a few orange segments and fennel fronds over the fish and serve straight away, spooning over the melted butter and roasting juices from the tray.

Serves 4

2 x 1kg (2lb 4oz) plaice, fins trimmed, heads removed, cut down the centre into 4 steaks, skin scored
olive oil

For the rub
4 star anise
2 teaspoons white peppercorns
zest of 2 lemons
2 tablespoons sea salt

For the onion & chicory
a drizzle of olive oil
75g (2½oz) unsalted butter
1 large onion, finely sliced
2 garlic cloves, halved
4 white chicory, halved
2 sprigs of thyme
2 sprigs of tarragon
50ml (2fl oz) white wine vinegar
200ml (7fl oz) white wine
200ml (7fl oz) fish stock
50g (1¾oz) honey

To serve
2 tablespoons chopped tarragon
1 lemon, zested, then peeled and segmented

Grilled Plaice on the Bone
in a Star Anise & Lemon Rub with Braised Onion & Chicory

Grilling plaice on the bone when the fish are bigger in size is a delight. I think when the fish gets over 1kg (2lb 4oz) in size, the character and texture rises to a whole new level and cooks excellently. Plaice can sometimes be seen as boring, but it shouldn't be. Using a rub like the one in this recipe adds an element of class and complements the fish so well. The bitterness of the chicory with the earthiness and sweetness of the plaice works wonderfully. My favourite accompaniment is mashed potatoes.

1. To make the rub, blitz the star anise, peppercorns, lemon zest and salt in a small food processor until fine. Set aside.

2. Preheat the oven to 160°C Fan (350°F), Gas Mark 4.

3. To braise the onion and chicory, heat the oil and butter in a large ovenproof pan with a tight-fitting lid over a medium heat. When the butter starts to bubble, add the onion and cook for 5 minutes, stirring occasionally. Next, add the garlic and chicory and cook for 3 minutes, stirring occasionally. Add the thyme and tarragon sprigs, vinegar, white wine, fish stock and honey, then season with 2 teaspoons of the rub. Cover with the lid (or kitchen foil) and transfer to the oven. Cook for 45 minutes.

4. Meanwhile, season the fish all over with the remaining rub and allow it to come to room temperature. This will help with even cooking.

5. Remove the pan from the oven and, using a slotted spoon, lift the chicory onto a plate, leaving the liquid in the pan. Reduce the liquid until it is syrupy in consistency, then return the chicory to the pan. Keep warm.

6. Preheat the grill to medium-high.

7. Place the fish onto a sturdy baking tray that won't buckle under the grill. Oil the fish well and place on the middle rack of the grill, orange-dotted-side up. Cook for 10–12 minutes. Insert a small knife or skewer into the thickest part of the fish, leave for 5 seconds and then remove and touch it to the back of your hand – if it feels warm to hot, the fish is ready. Remove from the grill and leave to rest for 2 minutes, then transfer to 4 plates.

8. Add the chopped tarragon to the chicory and mix in carefully. Spoon on to serving plates, scatter over the lemon zest and a few lemon segments, then serve.

Plaice, Aubergine & Mushroom Curry
with a Lime Oil

Serves 4

4 x 130g (4½oz) plaice fillets
olive oil
sea salt and freshly ground black pepper

For the curry powder
6 whole smoked chillies
1 tablespoon raw basmati rice
1 tablespoon coriander seeds
1 tablespoon cumin seeds
2 teaspoons mustard seeds
2 teaspoons black peppercorns
1 teaspoon Szechuan peppercorns
1 teaspoon ground turmeric
2 teaspoons sea salt
10 makrut lime leaves
zest of 1 orange

For the lime oil
zest and juice of 3 limes
400ml (14fl oz) light olive oil

For the curry
1 large aubergine, peeled and chopped into cubes
200g (7oz) chestnut mushrooms, halved
2 teaspoons ground turmeric
2 teaspoons ground coriander
4 teaspoons sea salt
2 tablespoons coconut oil
1 red onion, finely sliced
1 cinnamon stick
4 curry leaves
½ teaspoon fenugreek seeds
½ teaspoon nigella seeds
1 fresh red chilli, deseeded and chopped
400ml (14fl oz) can coconut milk
2 tablespoons chopped coriander leaves, plus extra to serve
1 tablespoon chopped mint leaves, plus extra to serve

Gently baking plaice fillets is a good way to cook a fast dinner and to use the smaller fish. This curry is delicious – I've used aubergine and mushrooms, but you can use pretty much anything. I've also cooked this dish with mussels and clams steamed into the sauce, so feel free to do that too. It's more of a guide than a 'you must' recipe. The lime oil is best left for 24 hours to infuse, but it wouldn't be the end of the world if you used it straight away, just make sure you strain out the bits!

1. To make the curry powder, gently toast everything in a large dry pan over a medium heat for 10 minutes. Leave to cool slightly, then blitz in a spice grinder. Sift the powder onto a large tray and leave to dry slightly. When dry, store in an airtight container.

2. To make the lime oil, put both the ingredients into a blender and blitz for 2 minutes. Pour the mixture into a container and leave to infuse for 24 hours. Strain the infused liquid through a fine sieve or muslin cloth into a clean container or bottle, store in the refrigerator and use within a month.

3. Preheat the oven to 180°C Fan (400°F), Gas Mark 6.

4. To make the curry, put the aubergine and mushrooms in a large bowl, add the turmeric, ground coriander, sea salt and 6 teaspoons of the curry powder and toss to coat. Leave for 10 minutes.

5. Heat a large pan over a medium heat and add the coconut oil. When the oil is hot, add the red onion and fry for 3 minutes, stirring occasionally, then add the aubergine and mushroom mixture and cook for another 3 minutes. Add the cinnamon stick, curry leaves, fenugreek, nigella seeds and the red chilli, season with salt and cook for 3 more minutes. Pour in the coconut milk and cook gently for 10 minutes. After this time, add the chopped coriander and mint and check the seasoning. Keep warm.

6. Season the plaice fillets well with salt, pepper and 2 teaspoons of the curry powder. Place in a roasting tray and oil the fish well. Cook in the oven for 5 minutes, then remove.

7. Share the curry among 4 bowls, then top with the plaice. Finish with the lime oil and a sprinkle of chopped herbs.

Steamed Turbot Fillet & Parsley Sauce
with Roast Garlic Potato Dumplings

Serves 4

4 x 140g (5oz) skin-on turbot portions, filleted from a 2kg (4lb 8oz) fish
a drizzle of olive oil
sea salt, to taste

For the roast garlic potato dumplings
300g (10½oz) potato, baked until tender
1 Roasted Garlic bulb, puréed (see page 250)
1½ tablespoons grated Parmesan
1 egg yolk
65g (2¼oz) '00' flour (pasta flour), plus extra for dusting
2 teaspoons olive oil, plus extra for cooking
2 tablespoons fine capers in vinegar, finely chopped
3 tablespoons chopped flat-leaf parsley leaves
sea salt and freshly ground black pepper

For the parsley sauce
2 tablespoons olive oil, for cooking
50g (1¾oz) unsalted butter
1 small onion, chopped
1 garlic clove, chopped
1 floury potato (Maris Piper), peeled and thinly sliced
200ml (7fl oz) Roasted Fish Stock (see page 250)
30g (1oz) flat-leaf parsley, picked and washed
30g (1oz) curly parsley, picked and washed
60g (2¼oz) spinach, picked and washed
sea salt and freshly ground white pepper, to taste

To serve
1 lemon, peeled and segmented
a handful of flat-leaf parsley leaves, finely sliced
Lemon Oil (see page 251 or shop-bought)

Steaming is, for sure, the cooking method that showcases the beauty of turbot. Steaming is subtle and delicate and that's exactly what you want with a filleted piece of fish like turbot. This parsley sauce is very different from the flour-and-milk-based traditional parsley sauce served with fish, with a much cleaner taste and a vivid colour. A sauce made this way can also be turned into a soup, if you want, just add more stock. The potato dumplings are exactly like gnocchi, that delicious Italian classic, but here I've shaped them into little squares and given them a touch of colour in the pan.

1. To make the potato dumplings, scoop the flesh out of the baked potato and pass through a ricer or drum sieve into a bowl. Add the garlic, Parmesan and egg yolk and lightly fold together; avoid overworking as this will make your dumplings tough and heavy. Lightly fold in the flour, oil, capers and parsley. Season with salt and pepper. Turn the dough out onto a floured surface and roll into a long sausage, then cut into bite-sized pieces the size of large marbles. Shape them into squares or balls, if you wish.

2. Bring a large pan of water to the boil, salt well and add a little oil. Have ready a bowl of iced water. Blanch the potato dumplings in the boiling water, in batches if necessary, until they float to the surface, about 2 minutes. Transfer to the iced water to cool quickly. Once cold, dry on a tea towel. Unless serving straight away, gently toss the dumplings in a little oil in a container to stop them sticking together. They will keep in the refrigerator for a few days.

3. To make the parsley sauce, heat a large pan over a medium heat and add the oil and butter. When the butter is bubbling, add the onion and garlic and cook for 5 minutes until the onion is soft. Add the sliced potato and season with salt and white pepper. Cook for 1 minute, then add the stock and cook until the potato is soft and falling apart, about 5 minutes.

4. Meanwhile, in a separate pan, heat a little more oil until hot and fry off the parsley and spinach for 30 seconds until wilted. Transfer the parsley and spinach together with the potato and stock to a blender and blitz for 2 minutes. If you are making this in advance, you will need to chill the sauce over an ice bath to cool it down quickly, so that it retains its vivid green colour.

Recipe continued overleaf

Recipe continued

5. To cook the dumplings, heat a non-stick frying pan and add a drizzle of oil. Fry the dumplings in the hot oil for about 3 minutes, turning often, until they are lightly golden brown all over. Drain on kitchen paper and keep warm.

6. Set up a bamboo steamer or switch on your oven steamer. Cut 4 pieces of greaseproof paper slightly bigger than the turbot portions. Oil and salt the fish portions and lay them on the paper, skin-side up. Place the turbot into the steamer and cook for 4 minutes.

7. While the fish is cooking, warm the sauce gently, stirring all the time.

8. To serve, warm 4 bowls and place a few potato dumplings in each one. Peel the skin off the turbot and lift the fish from the steamer to the plates. Season with salt, scatter with lemon segments and sliced parsley, then pour in the sauce. Finish with lemon oil and serve.

Roast Turbot Steak
with Mustard Sauce & Butter Beans

Serves 4

4 turbot steaks
olive oil
1 small butternut squash, peeled and diced
½ Savoy cabbage, shredded
sea salt and freshly ground white pepper
extra virgin olive oil, to finish

For the butter beans
200g (7oz) dried butter beans, soaked in cold water overnight
2 garlic cloves, peeled
1 carrot, peeled,
1 celery stick
2 bay leaves
1 rosemary sprig
sea salt

For the sauce
2 small shallots, chopped
1 garlic clove, chopped
1 sprig of thyme
1 bay leaf
1 star anise
100ml (3½fl oz) white wine
50ml (2fl oz) double cream
250g (9oz) unsalted butter
1 tablespoon wholegrain mustard
1 tablespoon chopped chives

Cooking turbot as a steak is very good and if I wanted to impress someone, this would probably be my go-to. If you get the cooking right, you end up with a lovely, almost crispy, white skin that has been protecting the precious flesh that sits beneath. Cooking on the bone this way, as opposed to as a fillet, allows you to rest the fish before serving and stops it overcooking so quickly, therefore it's great for home cooking. The sauce technique is based on the classic beurre blanc but with the addition of a few ingredients. The acidity and richness of the sauce is perfect with the turbot. The butter bean recipe works for all dried beans. In fact, dressed with a touch of vinegar, some herbs and extra virgin olive oil they would make a lovely simple starter or side dish for another time.

1. Drain the soaked beans and rinse under cold running water. Take a large pan and add the garlic cloves, carrot, celery, bay leaves and rosemary sprig along with the beans. Add enough water to cover generously and salt lightly. Bring to a simmer and skim off any foam that comes to the surface. Cover and simmer gently for 25 minutes.

2. Now top up the water and taste a bean. Is it still chalky? Then it needs more cooking. Cooking beans always seems to vary, so I suggest you now taste one every 5 minutes until they are creamy and don't forget to top up with water if need be. When the beans are cooked, take the pan off the heat and leave them to cool in the cooking water. You can now store them like this or drain them ready for serving.

3. To make the sauce, put the shallots, garlic, thyme, bay leaf, star anise and wine in a pan and cook until the wine has almost totally reduced. Add the cream and turn the heat down low. Now add the butter, piece by piece, whisking all the time; do not allow the sauce to boil or it will split. Once all the butter is incorporated, season with salt and white pepper to taste. Strain the sauce through a sieve into another pan and whisk in the mustard. Cover the surface with clingfilm or baking parchment to prevent a skin forming. Keep warm.

4. Preheat the oven to 180°C Fan (400°F), Gas Mark 6.

Recipe continued overleaf

Recipe continued

5. Bring a pan of salted water to the boil and add the diced squash. Cook for 5 minutes, then add the cabbage. Cook for a further 3 minutes. Drain and keep warm.

6. Place a large, ideally ovenproof, nonstick pan over a medium-high heat and drizzle in some olive oil. When the oil is hot, season the turbot all over with salt and white pepper. Place the steaks gently into the pan, white-skin-side down, and cook for 3 minutes until the edges start to become golden. Transfer the pan to the oven. If your pan isn't suitable for the oven, transfer the fish to a baking tray lined with baking parchment. Cook the fish for 8 minutes, then remove from the oven and leave to rest for a few minutes.

7. While waiting, drain the butter beans and discard the carrot and other vegetables. Gently heat up the butter beans and season with salt and white pepper. Add the cooked butternut squash and cabbage to the beans and mix gently.

8. Warm the sauce gently and add the chopped chives. Warm 4 plates. Peel the dark skin off the turbot steaks and sprinkle each one with a touch more salt.

9. To serve, place the fish in the centre of the plate with the white skin up, share the beans, squash and cabbage equally between the plates and spoon the sauce around. Serve immediately.

3

Round fish

Bass, Black Bream, Gilt-Head Bream,
Cod, Gurnard, Haddock, Hake,
John Dory, Ling, Monkfish, Ray & Skate,
Red Mullet, Grey Mullet, Trout

Bass

With a beautiful flavour and succulent, part-oily, part-creamy, flaky flesh, bass is as good as it gets. It's excellent cooked whole or as fillets and served very simply, but is also robust enough to take a strong shellfish sauce or even one made with red wine. Raw and cured preparations are perfect too, due to the firm, but tender bite.

As the demand for this amazing fish has increased over the last 30 years, the price has escalated. It's certainly not the cheap alternative to cod that it once was.

Bass is the ultimate hunting and fighting machine, and it's a bully. Whether small and moving around in a group, or a large adult hunting alone, it's a deadly predator. Reaching maturity at about 6–7 years, bass can live to a ripe old age of 25. I like to get them in the 2–3kg (4lb 8oz–6lb 8oz) size range and never buy one measuring less than 42cm (16½ inches) – under this size, they are banned across Europe and are illegal to land.

Trawling for bass has taken its toll, but much of the bass landed in southwest UK is now line caught and targeted as such – a much more sustainable option.

Notes
I've bought some bass that has been caught and dispatched the Japanese ikijime way (a method of killing fish that quickly and directly kills the fish's brain dead and stops movement in the spinal cord). The process allows the fish to die before it suffocates and, when done correctly, the fish relaxes and stops all motion, which stops lactic acid and ammonia building up and getting into the flesh, making the raw fish less sour and the texture firm. This technique is better for raw and cured preparations, and you can tell the difference when you eat it. If cooking the fish, I'm not sure it makes any difference.

Best time to eat
Towards the end of the summer.

Cooking & serving
- When you prepare a bass from scratch you will, at some point, inevitably stab yourself with one of its many sharp spines. Beware!

- An all-rounder, bass can be served whole, filleted, raw, cured, simply grilled with a wedge of lemon or with robust shellfish or red wine sauces.

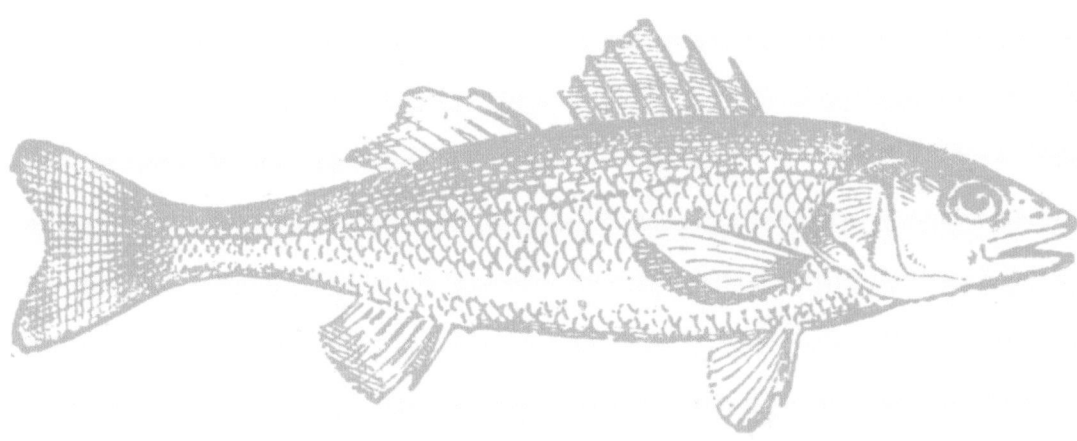

Black Bream (or Porgy)

The first time I used black bream, I was asked to use it in a curry recipe. As a young chef I did as I was told, but I thought it was a bit strange considering the delicate texture of the fish. Later in my career, after tasting it simply grilled, I realized I should have questioned it back then. The delicate texture and flavour would have been totally lost in that curry! Black bream has a similar texture to bass and is not massively popular. It is cheaper and worth buying if you see it, and it's great for cooking whole, too.

Black bream is found in the Mediterranean and the eastern Atlantic around the south and southwest of England. A shoal fish, they live in areas where there is seaweed that they can forage and are caught by a variety of targeted and mixed catch nets.

Notes
A species that can change sex, they start out as female and at about 20cm (8 inches) some change to male. Female fish remain smaller, while the males grow up to 40cm (16 inches).

Unusually, during spawning, it's the males that create nests for the eggs and protect them. Unfortunately, black bream can be a victim of bottom trawling, with the spawning process interrupted and nests destroyed, so try to buy line-caught or fixed-net-caught fish if you can.

Best time to eat
Any time outside of spawning which is between April–May, optimum between October–February.

Cooking & serving
- I always cook black bream gently pan-fried, skin on (see page 86). The skin crisps up beautifully and protects the flesh from the harshness of direct heat.

- It's not good cooked in sauces or curries, as the flesh breaks up.

Other bream species I've cooked and you may be lucky enough to find

Red sea bream (or black spot sea bream)
Mainly found throughout the eastern Atlantic and Mediterranean, but have been caught as far up as Norway. Black bream and red bream are similar in appearance apart from the obvious colour differences. Both have the ability to change sex. Adults have a distinctive black spot on their shoulder that gives them their alternative name of black spot bream. The French call them *gros yeux*, which means 'big eye'. In Japan, they are known as *tai* and are regarded as a lucky fish. Sometimes people mix them up with Couch's bream (see below) due to the red colour, but they are different. The larger fish are the best to eat. Cooking them whole, perhaps baked in salt (see page 90), is a brilliant way to appreciate the flavour and texture.

Couch's bream (or red porgy or common sea bream)
Found in shallow waters on either side of the Atlantic Ocean and the Mediterranean, it feeds on the seabed and can grow to 75cm (30 inches), but most we see are half that size. The few times I've used them, I've prepared them lightly cured and cut like sashimi; I've also grilled the fillets. I recently had a Couch's bream and found the flesh incredible for raw preparation – it was late February and the sea is very cold at this time – I do think the cold water and weather make a big difference to the quality.

Gilt-Head Bream

There are hundreds of different bream species around the world, but gilt-head is the best one in our waters. They are a southern species, common in the Mediterranean, but going further north each year. They now swim the Atlantic mainly from the UK down to the Canary Islands.

Living in estuary and bay areas, they can grow as big as 70cm (28 inches) and live for up to 11 years. They're predatory, living either solitary lives or in small shoals, feeding on worms, crustaceans and small fish, with rather impressive teeth to rip mussels off rocks!

Gilt-head bream is highly prized by anglers and fishermen, but little is known about the stock numbers; crazy considering the superiority of the fish and the high price that fishermen can get for it! No minimum landing size, no restrictions, no quota; it's simply stupid. This needs to change to protect this amazing species. If you do buy wild gilt-head bream, for peace of mind, buy hook-and-line-caught rather than netted if you can. This method is, and will always be, sustainable due to the tiny number of fishermen doing it.

Farmed gilt-heads are a very common, cheaper alternative in fishmongers and at fish counters, but like all things farmed, they really aren't the same.

Notes
A beautifully defined fish, you can always tell if it's a wild gilt-head bream by the striking gold band across its nose between the eyes.

All gilt-head bream start life as males, but at around 3 years old some change sex to become female.

Best time to eat
April–October.

Cooking & serving

- If you do get a super-fresh wild gilt-head bream, try it raw (see page 89). The flavour and texture is excellent.

- If you cook it, I'd suggest pan-frying, skin-on (see page 86); the skin will crisp up and taste almost like pork crackling.

- If you are lucky enough to get a large gilt-head bream that is 1.5kg (3lb 5oz) or more, try salt-baking it (see page 90). It makes a great showpiece when entertaining.

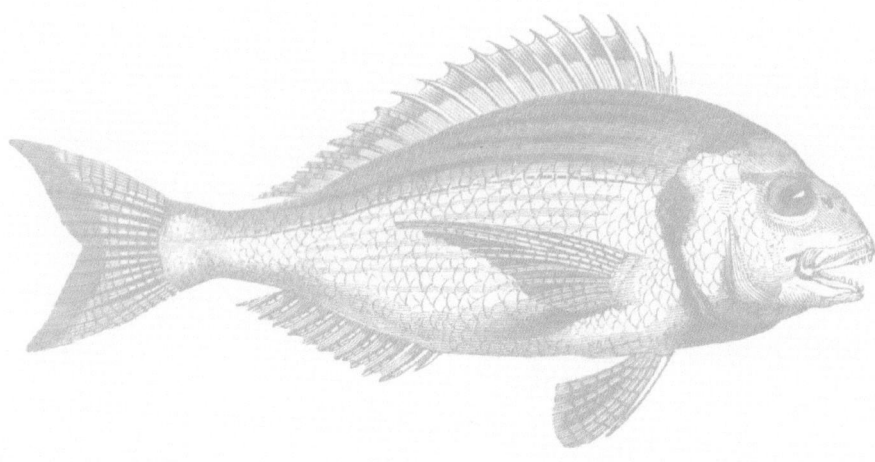

On Fish

Cod

The nation's favourite fish has undoubtedly suffered for its popularity, its biggest enemy being overfishing. For decades, the species has been decimated and we need to use discretion when buying it, otherwise cod could disappear altogether. As I write this, I recommend you just try another species, unless you know an angler or fisherman who has by chance caught a fish on a line, the only sustainable method as far as I know. Please just don't buy it, try something else.

A cold-water species, cod don't like the warming climate. They're pretty lazy, hanging around waiting for their lunch to come along rather than hunting, but they're incredibly strong and greedy so not much gets past.

Usually caught when they are 3–5 years old, they can reach 50 years old or more if they manage to avoid predators, especially humans. When you're line fishing, you can usually tell when you've caught cod because it puts up the briefest of fights, then gives up, so reeling one in is a piece of cake.

Notes

Cod has delicately flavoured, flaky white flesh. Because the majority of its oil is stored in its liver, the flesh itself has virtually no fat and is very high in protein.

Due to concerns for this species, I've not included any cooking or serving advice, or specific recipes, in this book.

Round fish

Gurnard (or Sea Robin or Croaker)

Gurnard is a real treat to eat, but perhaps owing to its weird appearance, it has taken a while to become properly appreciated in the kitchen. Fisherman have certainly taken a while to appreciate them – until only recently, they would use them as bait for lobster pots or just throw them back.

There are three main types of this amazing and strange-looking, small, predatory, demersal fish that we use – the red, the grey and the tub – but there are hundreds of species around the world. The red is the most common and smaller than the tub, which is the biggest and has blue marking on the fins. The grey is smallest. Although they usually swim in warmer waters, you may occasionally find the long-finned and piper gurnard, and also the streaked gurnard, which is of great quality.

Gurnard has an interesting feeding pattern, eating whatever it fancies from wherever it finds it. It uses its almost hand-like fins to feel around on the seabed looking for small prawns, crabs and lobsters, but also likes to have a go at chasing small fish.

Most gurnard are caught by demersal or beam trawling, but they can be line-caught too.

Due to the funny croaking noise made when landed, gurnard are also known as sea robins or croakers. It's thought that this croaking sound is how they communicate below the waves. They're called feeler fish, too, due to the sensory organs that they 'walk' on.

Notes
When I've caught gurnard, it's always been on fishing trips for mackerel. It's a joy and surprise to all on the boat when you pull one in.

Their firm, creamy-white flesh has an excellent texture and subtle flavour. If you get a chance to buy gurnard, do so.

Best time to eat
Late summer–end of winter.

Cooking & serving
- They're an all-rounder and cook well in many ways. My favourite methods are curing the fillets or using their meaty texture in a curry (see page 95). It's great for battered fish too.

- Gurnard is also very tasty barbecued when spanking fresh (along with the mackerel you may have caught on that fishing trip!).

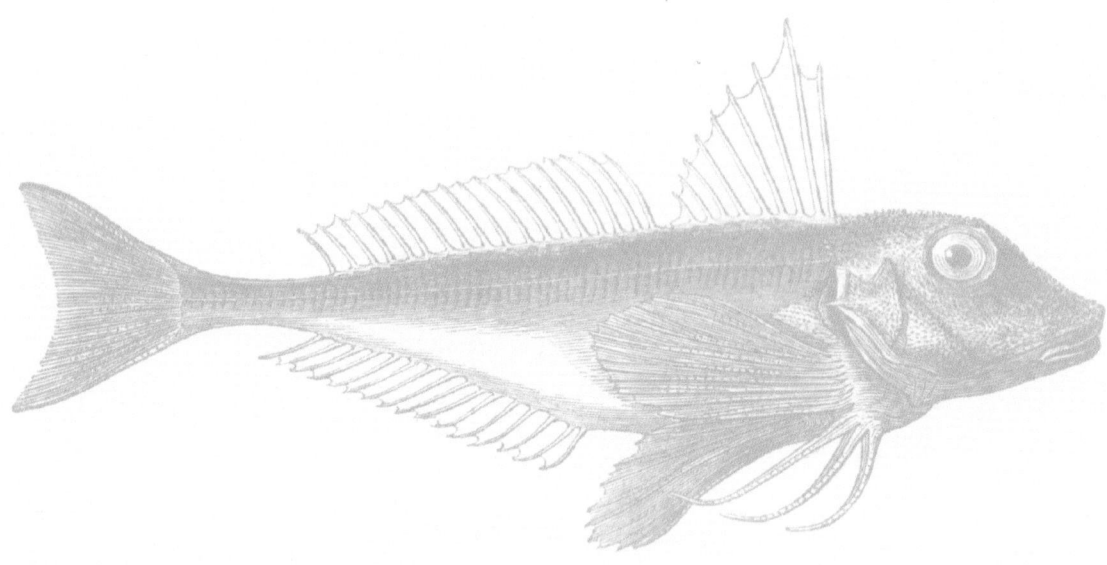

Haddock

Haddock is a member of the cod family and, like cod, is one of those unfortunate fish in such high demand that it's been overfished for decades.

Living for up to 10 years, haddock feed on crustaceans and small fish, feeling around the ocean bed with their barbule, which hangs from the lower jaw and looks like a goatie beard. In winter they move to deeper waters and colder temperatures to spawn.

Haddock can be line-caught and there have been schemes to increase that, but they're mainly caught with beam trawling and gill nets. There have been issues with discards of juvenile fish due to these fishing methods, when fishermen are aiming to catch a mixture of species, but modern fishing gear and improved nets with larger mesh are addressing this.

I've caught them off Cornwall a few times in the past on my mackerel feathers, along with cod and whiting. They're not the hardest of fish to catch, unless you are looking to target a big one.

Notes
The haddock fisheries in the Nordic regions are very well managed and so fish from there is a good option. It grows quickly, so we could see an increase of this important fish in future if quotas are obeyed and the fishing industry works hard on the way it's fished.

Best time to eat
Summer and autumn.

Cooking & serving

- The best size to buy is 1kg (2lb 4oz) plus.

- At the fishmonger, look for haddock that has most of its scales intact – this means it's been well handled by the fisherman.

- Simply grilling haddock is a fantastic way to cook this fish – the skin protects the flesh and becomes golden brown, tasting really good.

- Poaching haddock gently in milk or fish stock is a classic cooking method, which retains the succulent qualities of this fish.

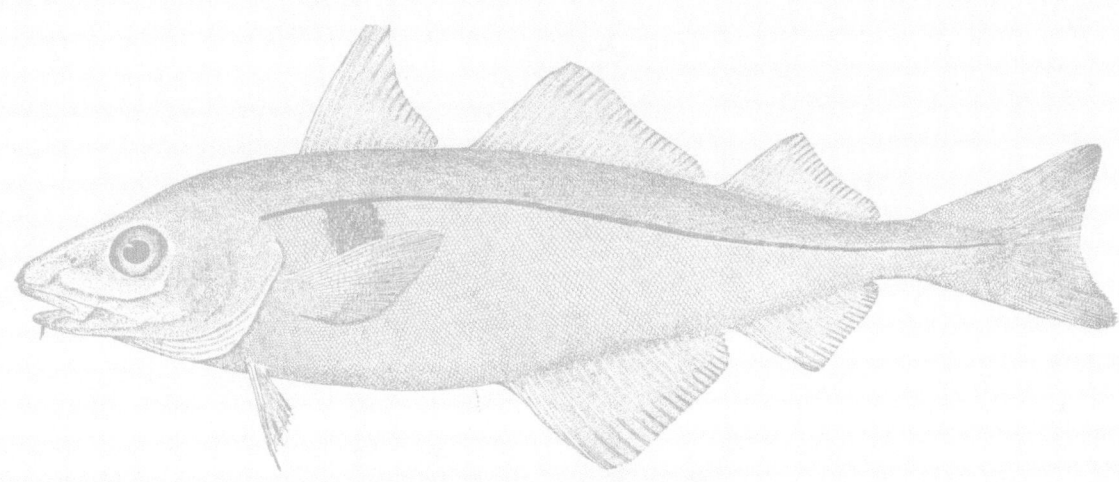

Hake

One of the most fearsome and ugly-looking fish in the sea, but don't judge a book by its cover... Hake is a delicious fish and in prime condition has a unique eating quality. Chunky and soft, with a very moist mouthfeel, it's great simply roasted or grilled and enjoyed on its own. Hake is from the same family as cod but is very different in physique and temperament.

Swimming at around 70–300m (230–985ft), it stays close to the seabed during the day, rising at night to feed. With a mouth full of sharp, pointed teeth and a long, slender body, it really is a hunting machine. Hake mainly like to feed on squid (who doesn't?) and sometimes juvenile hake.

In the late 1990s, a hake recovery plan was introduced to stop overfishing, mainly due to the demand in Spain where it's a delicacy and a way of life. The recovery effort was strictly controlled and now stocks are far larger than they have been for years. The Cornish hake gill net fishery was certified as sustainable by the Marine Stewardship Council in 2015.

Most hake landed to Cornish ports is caught using gill nets and it's a requirement that Cornish vessels over 12m (40ft) long and fishing outside the 12-mile zone use electronic 'pingers' that scare dolphins and other cetaceans away from the nets.

Notes
Hake doesn't live well in captivity, so you'll never see one in an aquarium.

They can reach a weight of 15kg (33lb), which is huge, but I find 3–4kg (6lb 8oz–8lb 13oz) fish to be best.

Best time to eat
Late autumn and early winter.

Cooking & serving
- Cornish hake is a great choice for cooking at home and choosing in a restaurant.

- It's a versatile fish and can be cooked in various ways, my favourites being grilled or breaded and fried.

- It's definitely not a species for raw or cured preparation, in my opinion.

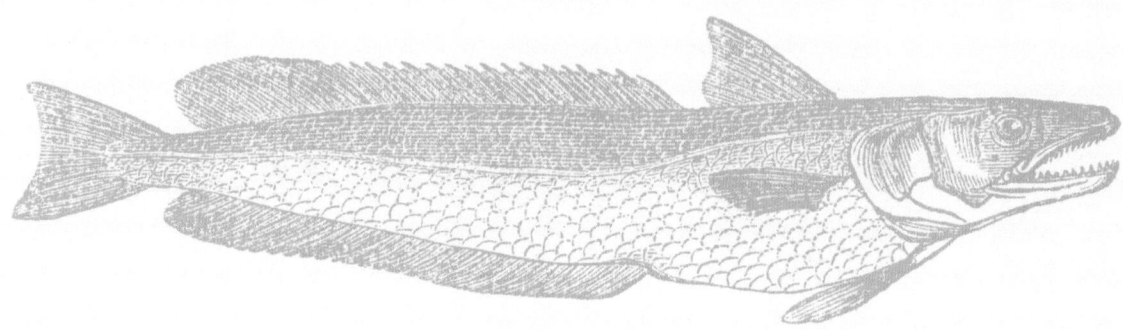

John Dory

Some say ugly, I say unusual. John Dory is one of my favourite fish to cook. It's a treat, because it isn't always available; you may not see it for ages. In the UK, as far as I'm aware, there aren't any fishermen who target John Dory; it's seen as by-catch rather than the gem it is. It can be pretty expensive but don't let this put you off. If you get a chance to buy or eat John Dory, do so; its texture and appearance are different to any other fish. In my view, it's fantastic!

John Dory can be found around most of Britain's coastline and because of its almost invisible head-on appearance, it is an amazing hunter. It swims up, opens its huge mouth and swallows its prey whole, in a flash. It also has some pretty good defence mechanisms in the form of barbed thorns on its body, and sharp fins. The large, dark mark on its side looks like a giant eye to other fish – some say it was a thumbprint bestowed by Saint Peter as he was pulling the fish from the sea of Galilee at Christ's request, hence its nickname 'Saint Peter's fish'.

Little is known about the stocks of John Dory, it's not a well-researched species and that leaves it a bit vulnerable, which is crazy considering the quality and value it has. I recommend you resist smaller fish, under 35cm (14 inches), as they haven't yet reached the stage where they have been able to breed.

In southwest UK, the majority is caught near wrecks with trawl nets. However, they are caught with beam and demersal trawls, and gill nets, too.

Notes
It's so cool that the Latin name for the European species is Zeus faber, possibly after the king of the Greek gods!

Best time to eat
Late spring–late summer.

Cooking & serving

- John Dory is unique in that it yields six fillets – three on each side – which are not the easiest to fillet from the bone, but are worth the effort.

- Beware of the very sharp, almost barbed, thorns on its body and sharp fins too.

- My favourite way to eat John Dory is to braise the fillets gently in a flavourful sauce or stock (see page 110), or trim it up and bake (see page 113).

- On a sunny day, they're great trimmed and cooked whole on the barbecue.

Round fish

Ling

A relatively inexpensive fish to buy, ling is one of the biggest fish I've ever prepared. They can grow to 2m (6½ft) in length, although they're quite awkward to prepare at this size. The largest member of the cod family, in structure ling has the head of a cod and the body of a conger eel, so it looks like a cross between the two. Their texture is firm and meaty, more like monkfish than any of the cod family, and they taste great.

A migrating species found all over the northeast Atlantic, ling swim at depths between 100–400m (330–1,300ft). It's very slow-growing, usually not breeding until around 5 years old, and can live up to 25 years old.

The majority are caught using beam trawlers, netters and demersal trawlers; some are line-caught, but this is rarely available. There have been fewer landed over recent years, possibly due to a reduced effort of fishing for them and not using the longlining fishing method.

Notes

Ling has been heavily fished, so ask your fishmonger how it has been caught and avoid fish less than 80cm (31 inches) in length, as they won't have had a chance to breed.

Ling feed lazily off the bottom and will eat almost anything. I've come across all sorts when preparing them, even a coin!

Best time to eat

During the winter months when the water is cold.

Cooking & serving

- The best size to use is about 3kg (6lb 8oz).

- Deep-fry (see page 114) or pan-fry with the skin on (see page 117).

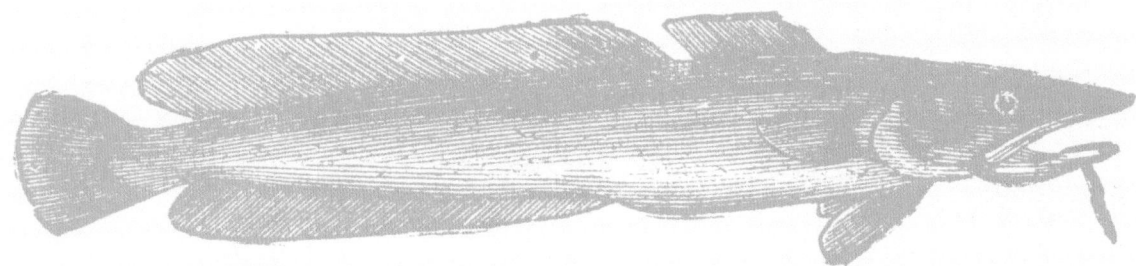

Monkfish

With a huge head in comparison to its body, a strange, evil-looking face and wide mouth full of razor-sharp teeth, monkfish is an ugly beast to say the least! There are two species of monkfish that we get in the UK: the white and the black-bellied. They look very similar and until they are prepared you won't see much difference. The black-bellied species has a black lining on the belly side of the fish. I use both and don't really find much difference in the taste or texture.

Perhaps because of its unfortunate appearance, it took a while for people to warm to this fish. Fifty years ago, it would most likely have ended up in a tin of cat food or as bait for lobster pots, but over the years chefs and home cooks have come to appreciate its attributes. Monkfish tastes great, has a lovely meaty texture and is extremely versatile, not least because it can handle lots of different flavours.

Extending from the top of its head are flexible spines with nodules on the ends, hence their nickname 'anglerfish'. To other fish, these look like tasty little fish swimming about in the water. Glowing in the dark, they attract prey even in murky, stormy conditions. The unfortunate fish swim up, undeterred by the monkfish's gigantic head, which resembles a giant rock and blends perfectly with the environment. All the monkfish needs to do is lie in wait for dinner... hunting doesn't get much easier!

Notes
Monkfish are quite slow-growing and can live for a long time. The best choice to buy is net-caught, or fish caught with demersal trawlers; both day-caught for the best quality and freshness. Ask your fishmonger to be sure.

Best time to eat
Late autumn–early spring.

Cooking & serving
- Monkfish has only one central bone to contend with, making it a pretty easy fish to prepare.

- I'd say the best fish to buy is a 2kg (4lb 8oz) tail, with no head (you're unlikely to see one with the head on anyway).

- My favouite way to cook is on the bone (see page 121), on a charcoal barbecue, under the grill, or cured (see page 118).

- It is not good raw.

- Monkfish livers are amazing. If you get a chance, buy them and use to make a tasty pâté, or pan-fry and eat on toast.

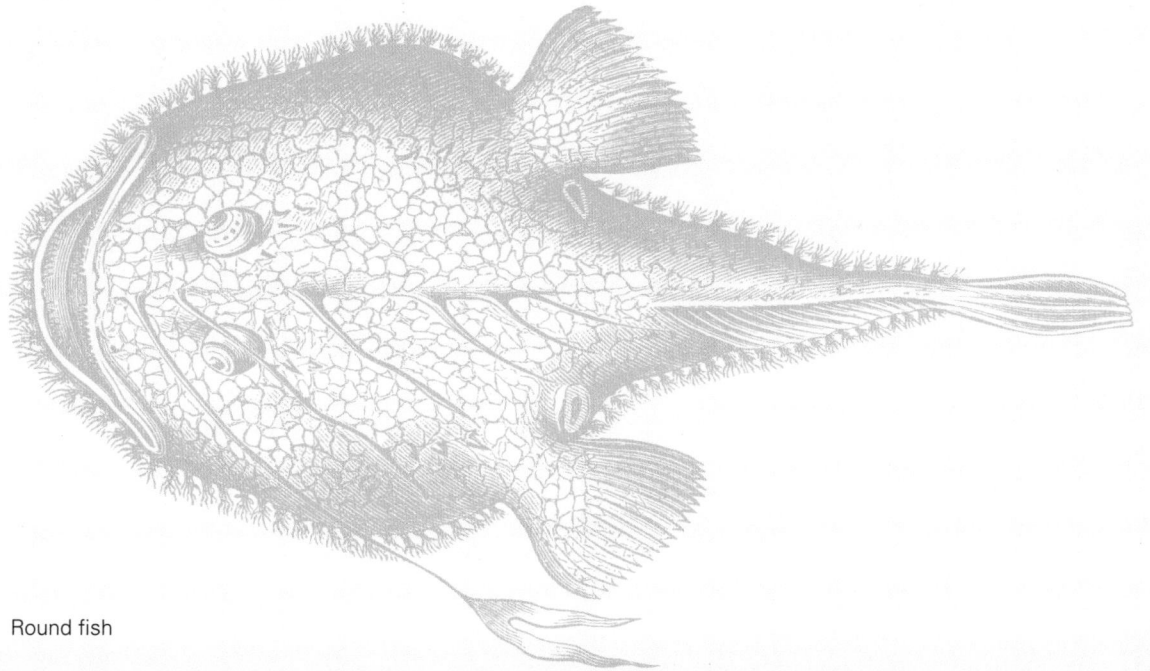

Ray & Skate

You will come across 'skate' on most UK fish restaurant menus at some point, but I very much doubt it will actually be skate, which has become scarce. It is more likely to be ray of some sort. Members of the same family, they're both flat and cartilaginous and it's difficult to differentiate between them.

Ray and skate are effortless to eat because, once cooked, the flesh slides easily from their cartilaginous framework. That has made them extremely popular, but has also caused sustainability issues.

We see a variety of ray species in this country so you could be offered any of these: blonde, cuckoo, shagreen, small-eyed, spotted, undulate or thornback. However, at the time of writing, the only ray we should be eating are cuckoo, small-eyed, thornback and undulate; all skate should be avoided.

Mainly bottom-dwellers, they are the camouflage kings of the seabed, laying buried in the sand, waiting to feed on small fish and crustaceans that come by. Most are landed on boats targeting flat fish and, once caught, are generally prepared onboard – where they are skinned and the 'wings' cut from their body, hence the difficulty identifying which species you are buying.

Notes

Ray give birth to live young whereas skate lay egg cases, known as mermaid's purses, which take 6 months to hatch into little skates.

Before 3 days of aging, the flesh is tough, a bit tasteless and has a slight whiff of urine owing to the presence of urea, which protects the fish from the salt in the sea and prevents them from dehydrating. The urea is purged from the flesh naturally during those first 3 days after landing, leaving the flesh sweet and tender to eat. Kept for more than 5 days after landing, they develop a smell of ammonia, which obviously isn't nice either. A good fishmonger will sell them to you at the right stage for eating.

Best time to eat

Various, according to species: October to February.

Cooking & serving

- For ray, the best size is a 1kg (2lb 4oz) wing – this gives 3 portions.

- If you plan to fry ray, make sure you use good-quality kitchen paper to dry the fish before cooking – this will remove the maximum amount of moisture, meaning less steam when cooking and ensuring a delicious golden crust to the cooked flesh.

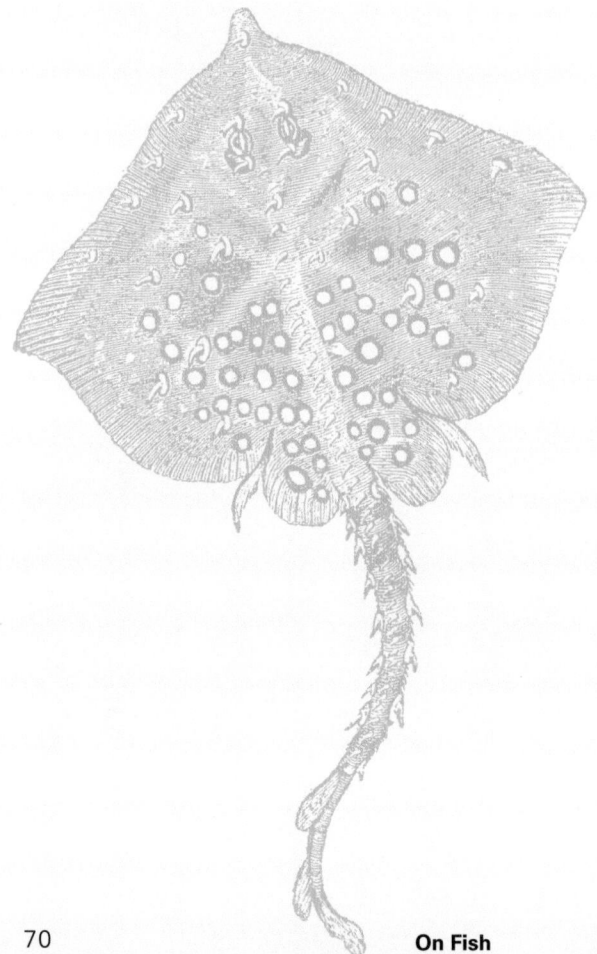

Red Mullet

Strictly speaking, this striking fish isn't really a mullet at all. A far relative of grey mullet, it's more a member of the tropical goatfish family. With the seas around Britain warming, red mullet has taken up residence. In the past, they would just visit for the summer, but now commercial fisherman can usually rely on catching them right through the year.

A very sociable fish, red mullet swims with others in groups of 10 to 20, pecking at the mud and silt to find small crustaceans and worms. They grow quickly, reaching maturity at around 2 years old, which should be great from a sustainability angle, but unfortunately red mullet stocks have decreased over the last few years.

It's highly likely that you'll never see red mullet fresh in a supermarket due to the delicate nature of the species. Once caught, quick deterioration is an issue. I suggest buying from a fishmonger or direct from a fisherman if you are lucky enough to live by the sea. This way, you can ensure the fish have been looked after properly. Buy red mullet caught using species-specific nets from inshore day boats and you can eat them happily without concern for sustainability.

Notes
Also known as goatfish or striped mullet, red mullet was so highly valued in Ancient Rome that they were sold for their weight in silver.

Best time to eat
Traditionally between August–October; more recently I've found the quality of red mullet to be good between January–March.

Cooking & serving

- Size does make a difference when cooking red mullet. I prefer to cook the bigger ones that weigh 500–800g (1lb 2oz–1lb 12oz) as they seem to have a better, meatier texture, cook more evenly and are much more forgiving. The smaller fish lack the meaty texture and overcook very quickly – they are best for soup.

- Red mullet has a few slight variations with the change in size. The larger, almost orange/red fish have a lighter flavour and less of the shellfish flavours you find in the smaller ones, which have redder skin and a golden stripe along the entire length.

- In my view, the finest way to experience red mullet is butterflied and grilled until the skin crisps up and becomes almost like fish crackling, while the flesh within stays moist and juicy (see page 133).

- When red mullet is super-fresh you can eat the livers, which are amazing chopped, pan-fried and spread on a piece of toast.

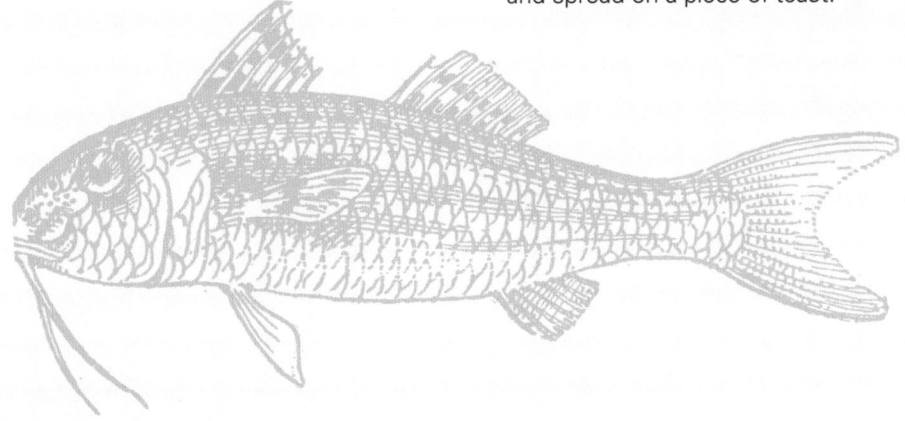

Grey Mullet

There are three main species of grey mullet: thick-lipped, thin-lipped and golden grey. If you see a golden grey mullet, which is easy to identify by the golden dot on the side of the fish, buy it!

This is the species you see in harbours around the UK and most places in Europe; they tend to inhabit estuaries and keep close to the coastline, but that doesn't mean they're easy to catch. They're very clever and can spot an angler fishing on an estuary bank or harbour wall easily. They tend to only eat small morsels of food and have small, soft mouths, making hooking them rather more difficult than you'd expect.

Grey mullet is a slow-growing fish and doesn't reach maturity until between 9–10 years old. All three species spawn at slightly different times and they don't always breed every year. Due to the long-lived, late-maturing nature of the species and their erratic spawning patterns, they are vulnerable to overfishing. Stocks aren't managed and there is little evidence or knowledge of the species. My advice, as it is with nearly all species, is ask your fishmonger how the fish was caught and where. If they have no information, it's best to avoid it.

The best caught mullet will come by hook and line, by a spearfisherman, or commercially by beach seine nets and gill nets.

Notes
In my experience, some grey mullet is best avoided due to the nature of their habitation. Estuary and harbour locations are not always the cleanest of places and this is something to consider when purchasing. I would recommend the usual quality points for buying fish (see page 12), but get the fishmonger to scale and gut it for you. If there are any quality issues at that stage, the fishmonger will notice. If they want to keep a good reputation and the quality isn't good enough, they'll advise you to choose something else!

Best time to eat
Autumn/winter.

Cooking & serving

- The best size to use is 2kg (4lb 8oz) or more.

- Raw, cured and pan-fried (see pages 137) are three excellent preparations and cooking methods for this species; you won't be disappointed. If you want crispy skin, mullet is a great species to cook. The natural oil that renders out of the fish as it cooks is delicious, but don't get your pan too hot or you will burn the natural fat.

- It is also a good fish to home smoke (see page 17). You never see it pre-smoked in shops, but if you fancy a kitchen adventure, have a go at smoking it.

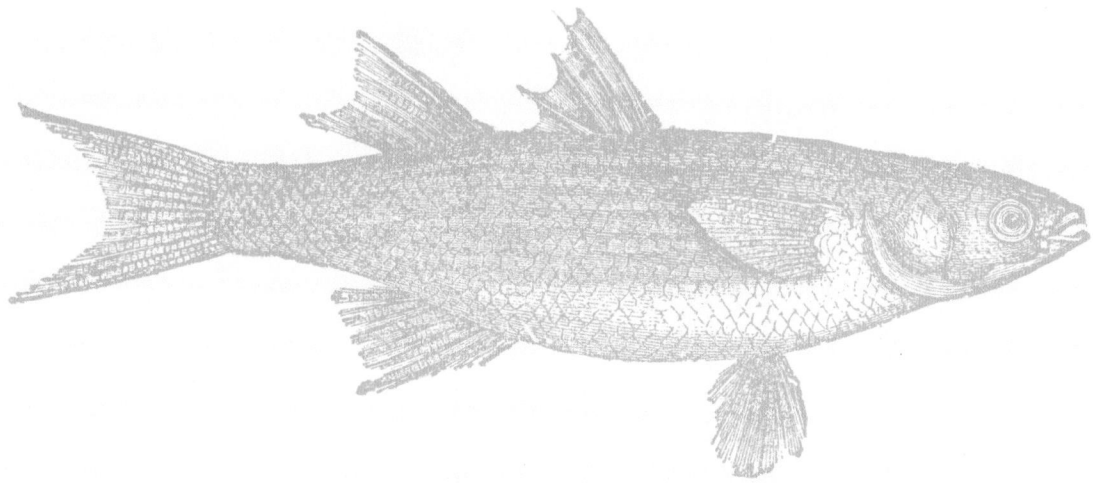

Trout

I buy farmed trout from an extremely small, family-run farm in Boscastle, Cornwall, just 15 miles from my restaurants in Port Isaac. Issues with farmed fish are well documented, so before I began buying farmed trout I scrutinized the whole operation – it's everything you would want to see: 3 large pools holding the fish at 3 stages of life over 2½ years until they reach 3kg (6lb 8oz). The fish are not over-crowded and the owners produce only 5,000 fish per year. Fresh water enters and drains through granite contours from the moors of Bodmin, travelling through the farm and down to the ocean in Boscastle. Their feed is fishmeal made from the waste from processing fish, fish bones, fish oil and non-GM soy, all certified by the Marine Trust and the Marine Conservation Society. I've never tasted or cooked such lovely trout. Zero earthiness and such a beautiful texture.

Notes
There are a few farmed trout producers popping up, and something I'm seeing a lot of is chalk stream trout – I've eaten it and it was delicious! It's a much better alternative to farmed salmon, which I tend to avoid.

Best time to eat
Farmed trout is available throughout the year, but I find it better during the colder months.

Cooking & serving
- The skin on trout is delicious and well worth the effort of scaling the fish well, so that you can eat it.

- Raw or a simple ceviche of trout is a great and quick way of serving it.

- The oiliness of trout against any type of citrus or a good vinegar works brilliantly.

Preparation techniques

Filleting round fish (shown with bass)

1. Scale the fish, then remove all the fins with kitchen scissors.

2. With the head towards you, cut from tail to head along the spine.

3. Cut around the neck and ribcage.

4. Run your knife along the bone to begin releasing the fillet.

5. Carefully release the tail end of the fillet, leaving the tail behind.

6. Release the bottom of the fillet where the guts would have been, towards the ribcage.

7. Turn the fish around and carefully work around the ribcage.

8. Release the fillet.

9. Pay special attention at the ribcage. With bass you can cut around it but with other species, such as mackerel, you will need to cut through it.

10. Now repeat the above steps on the other side of the fish.

11. Different species have different amounts of pin-bones but they always run down the centre of the fillet. Always remove pin-bones at the same angle as the bone grows or you will rip the flesh.

12. To skin the fillets, hold the tail end firmly then bring your knife above the skin but below the flesh and hold it at a slight angle.

13. Always flip the fillet over halfway through skinning to make sure you are not cutting into the flesh. The aim is to have no flesh left on the skin afterwards.

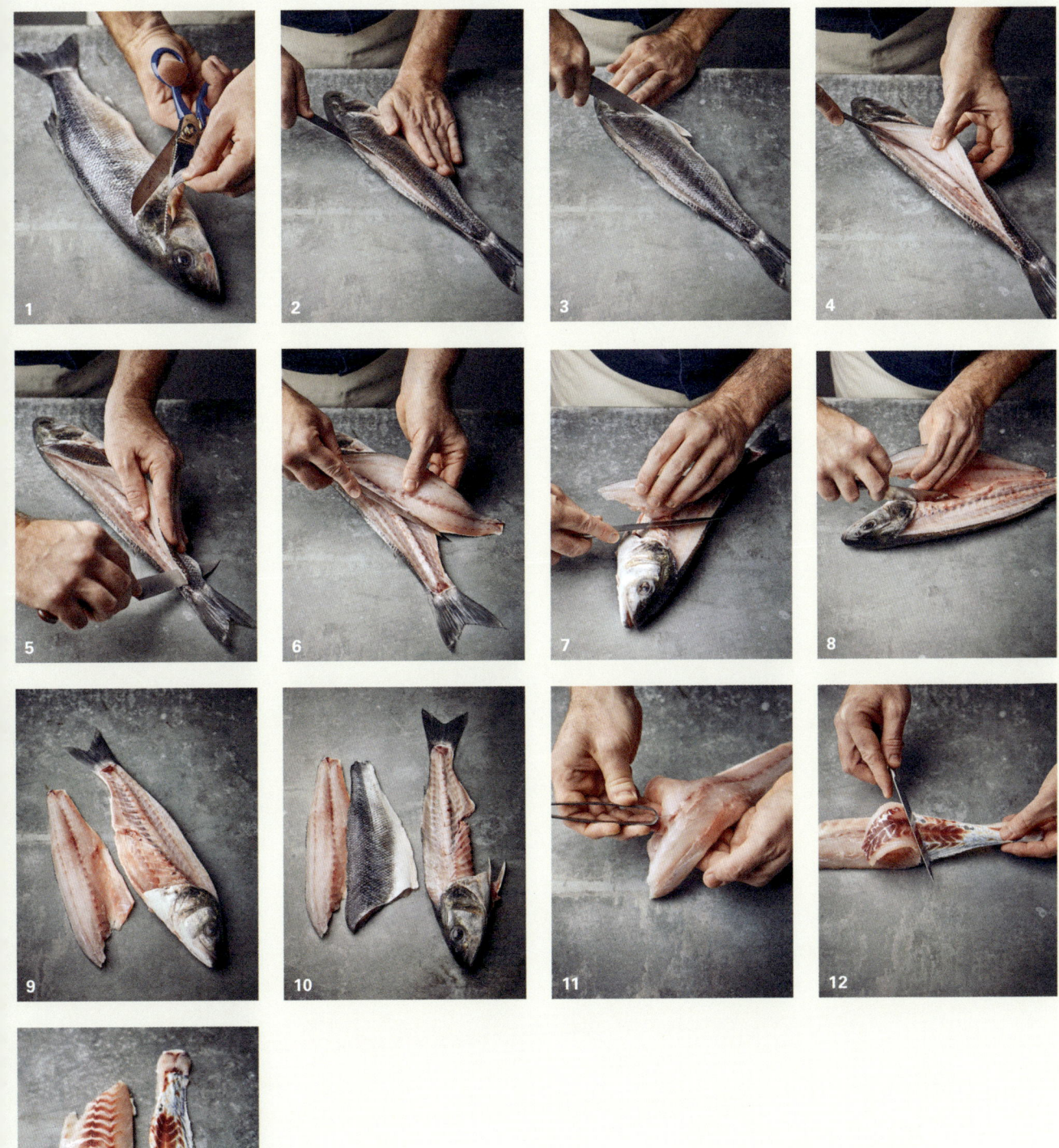

Round fish

Preparation techniques

Skinning round fish

1. Place the fillet on a secure chopping board, skin side down, and trim the outer edges to neaten.

2. Hold the skin at the tail end and, holding your knife at a slight angle, slide the blade between the skin and flesh to release the fillet. Avoid being too aggressive!

Cooking whole

1. Using scissors, cut off the fins, trim the tail and cut out the gills.

2. To gut the fish, hold it belly-side up with the head pointing away from you.

3. Insert your knife tip at the anal vent and make a shallow cut along the belly up to the throat. Pull out the guts, taking care in case there are hooks or small spiny fish inside.

4. Rinse the cavity well.

Tranching

1. Mark the fish so that portions are equal-sized or they won't cook evenly.

2. Slice straight though, using a mallet or rolling pin to force the knife though the bone.

Descaling

1. Hold the fish by the tail and using a knife or descaler, push firmly against the skin from tail to head. Don't push too hard or the skin and flesh will be damaged.

2. Turn the fish over and repeat.

3. Wash and dry the fish, checking for any stray scales as you do so.

Pin-boning

1. Lay the fillet on a chopping board, skin-side down.

2. Using your fingers, feel along the centre of the fillet for any bones.

3. Using a pair of strong tweezers, grab the bone and pull firmly towards the head end of the fish to remove.

Butterflying (shown with mackerel)

1. Gut and scale the fish and remove the head, gills and fins (see Cooking whole, opposite). Clean the fish then, holding it upside down with the tail away from you, cut down the fillet on one side as close as you can to the bone without piercing the skin at the top.

2. Repeat on the other side.

3. Open the fish up and gently push the fillets flat so that the spine is exposed.

4. Using scissors, cut out the spine, taking care not to cut through the skin.

5. Using a flexible filleting knife, cut around the ribcage then pin-bone the fillets, removing the pin-bones at an angle in the same direction as they grow.

6. The butterflied mackerel.

Round fish

Preparation techniques

Filleting monkfish

1. You'll rarely see monkfish with the head intact, it's too big. You'll usually only see monkfish tail. Begin by cutting through where the top fins are, this will release the skin.

2. Turn the tail away from you then, starting at the thickest part of the fish, firmly grip the skin and pull to remove it.

3. Continue by wrapping the skin around your hand and gradually pulling it off bit by bit. Once at the tip of the tail, discard the skin.

4. Turn the fish onto its back and, using a sharp knife, cut all the way down from the thickest part to the tail, keeping your knife against the bone.

5. Repeat on the other side of the spine.

6. Your fish should now look like this. There should be almost nothing left on the backbone.

7. Release the fillets from the tail by slicing through.

8. You should now have 2 fillets and the cartilage (spine).

9. Left, a trimmed fillet which is ready to be portioned. Right, a fillet prior to trimming.

10. To trim the fillets, with the tail end towards you, insert your knife at a slight angle and cut away from you to trim off any sinew.

11. Trim off the sinew on the sides of the fillets.

12. Once the sinew has been trimmed from the bottom of the fillet, continue around to remove sinew from the top too.

13. Flip the fish over and trim off any sinew you've missed.

14. You'll see along the centre of the fillet a pale pink line; this is stringy sinew.

15. Cut at either side of the stringy sinew in a 'V'-shaped angle, remove and discard.

16. Two fully trimmed monkfish fillets, ready to be portioned and cooked.

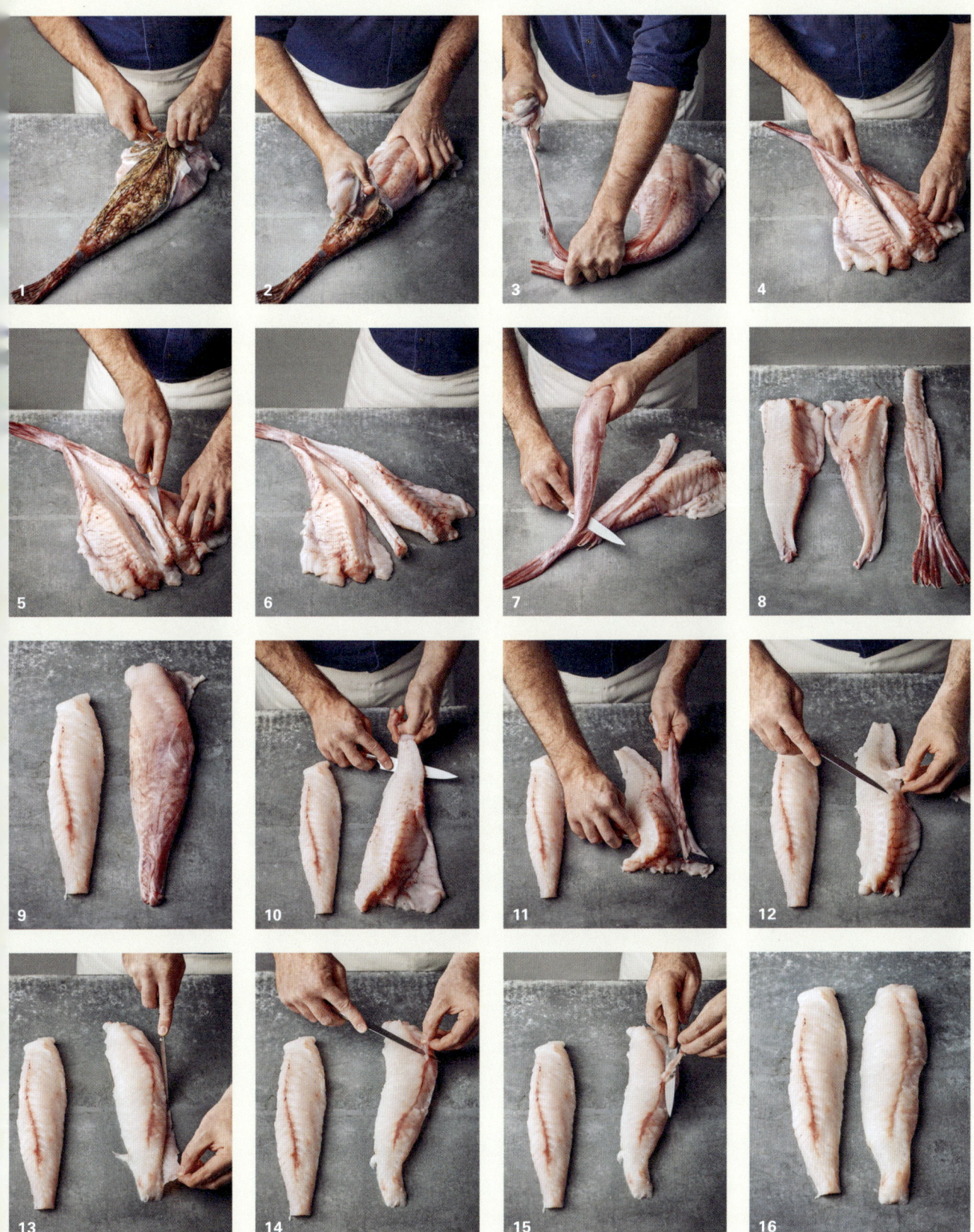

Round fish

Serves 4

400g (14oz) very fresh bass fillet, skinned and pin-boned
100g (3½oz) sea salt
50g (1¾oz) caster sugar
100ml (3½fl oz) dry white wine

For the tomato dressing

6 very ripe tomatoes, roughly chopped
50g (1¾oz) fresh horseradish, peeled and finely grated (use a Microplane)
1 garlic clove, sliced
a pinch of caster sugar
3 tablespoons extra virgin olive oil
sea salt and freshly ground black pepper

For the horseradish salad cream

2 egg yolks
4 teaspoons creamed horseradish
1 teaspoon caster sugar
zest and juice of 1 lemon
300ml (10fl oz) sunflower oil
50ml (2fl oz) double cream
1 tablespoon chopped flat-leaf parsley leaves

To serve

200g (7oz) selection of ripe tomatoes
very finely sliced flat-leaf parsley leaves

Cured Bass
with Tomato & Horseradish

We get some fantastic bass when it's in season. It's a fish that's plentiful where we are, due to the closed fishing season helping with sustainability. Thank goodness, I say, otherwise we wouldn't be able to do dishes like this one. The curing process is pretty much the same with all the species we prepare this way, timing is the main difference. The bigger the fillet, the longer it takes. Bass always takes between 2 and 3 hours the way we do it. The texture change you get from the cure makes the fish feel firmer and more flavourful. This dish works well with the tomatoes and horseradish; not the most usual combination, but with good judgement and balance it won't overpower. I could eat this all day, every day!

1. To cure the bass, put the salt, sugar and white wine into a food processor and blitz thoroughly. Lay the fish on a tray and pour the cure mixture over it. Turn the fish over a few times to ensure it is completely coated. Cover the tray securely and place in the refrigerator for 2 hours, turning the fish halfway through.

2. To prepare the fish for serving, wash off the cure mix and pat the fish dry with kitchen paper. Wrap tightly in clingfilm and place in the freezer to firm up for 2 hours.

3. Unwrap the fish and place it on a very clean chopping board. Using a sharp knife, slice the fish thinly and lay it onto a tray to defrost. The cured fish will be easier to slice because it is partially frozen; by the time you have sliced and plated it all, it will have defrosted fully. (If you have more fish than you need for the plates, freeze it, wrapped well, for another time.)

4. To make the tomato dressing, put the tomatoes, horseradish and garlic into a food processor with some salt, pepper and the sugar and pulse-blend 4 times. Transfer to a sieve lined with muslin set over a bowl. Squeeze out the juice and keep in the refrigerator (discard the contents of the muslin).

5. To make the salad cream, put the egg yolks, horseradish, sugar and lemon zest and juice into a bowl and whisk together for 1 minute. Gradually add the oil, drop by drop to begin with and then in a steady stream, whisking constantly until it is all incorporated. Finally, whisk in the cream and parsley. Season with salt and pepper to taste. Transfer to a lidded tub and refrigerate until needed.

6. To finish the dressing, take the tomato juice from the refrigerator and measure out 5 tablespoons into another bowl. Add the extra virgin olive oil and whisk to combine. Taste and season with a little sea salt if you wish.

7. Slice the tomatoes and arrange with the cured fish on 4 plates or a large platter. Finish with the dressing and sliced parsley and serve the salad cream on the side. Serve with bread to mop up the juices.

Bass Baked in Puff Pastry
with a Red Wine & Tomato Sauce

Serves 4

1 bass, weighing 1.5–2kg (3lb 5oz–4lb 8oz), scaled, gutted, filleted, pin-boned and skinned (reserve the bones and trimmings for the sauce)
800g (1lb 12oz) shop-bought puff pastry (or see below)
1 tablespoon chopped tarragon leaves
1 tablespoon chopped chervil leaves
1 egg plus 1 tablespoon milk, for egg wash
sea salt and freshly ground black pepper

For the rough puff pastry
400g (14oz) plain flour, plus extra for dusting
10g (¼oz) fine sea salt
400g (14oz) ice-cold butter, cut into 1cm (½ inch) dice
200ml (7fl oz) ice-cold water

For the red wine & tomato sauce
a drizzle of olive oil
bass head and fish bones (blood, gills and organs removed), chopped or cut up with scissors
2 onions, chopped
1 garlic bulb, halved
2 sprigs of thyme, picked
2 bay leaves
500ml (18fl oz) red wine
1 litre (1¾ pints) fish stock
6 very ripe tomatoes, chopped
2 firm tomatoes, deseeded and chopped
50ml (2fl oz) double cream
100g (3½oz) unsalted butter
2 tablespoons chopped chives
1 tablespoon lemon juice

A recipe like this is a lot of work and at home is certainly a challenge, but sometimes a good challenge is what we need. You will be so chuffed, and the results will speak for themselves if you give yourself time to cook this bass dish. Once all the work is done, serving is very simple. If you want to make the dish a bit simpler, you could buy the puff pastry. Resting the pastry is important and will result in a lovely flaky crust. I serve this with mashed potatoes and seasonal vegetables, asparagus being a favourite.

1. To make the pastry, put the flour, salt and butter into a bowl and rub in the butter using your fingertips until the pieces are roughly half the size. Add the cold water and mix to a dough. On a floured surface, roll the dough out to a neat rectangle, about 50 x 20cm (20 x 8 inches). Fold the top third down, then the bottom third up over the top. Wrap in clingfilm and rest in the refrigerator for 30 minutes.

2. After this time, give the dough a quarter-turn, then roll out and fold as before, twice more. Wrap the pastry and rest in the refrigerator for a further 30 minutes.

3. Dust your work surface with flour and roll out the pastry to the thickness of a £1 coin. Carefully slide onto a tray and rest again in the refrigerator for at least 30 minutes.

4. To make the sauce, drizzle some oil in a large frying pan over a medium heat. Once hot, add the bass head and bones and colour all over for 5 minutes, turning occasionally. Remove from the pan and set aside. To the same pan, add the onions and a drizzle more oil and cook for 10 minutes over a medium heat, stirring occasionally. Add the garlic, thyme and bay leaves and cook for 1 minute. Transfer to a large stock pot and add the bass head and bones.

5. Deglaze the frying pan with the red wine, cooking until reduced by half. Pour the wine into the stock pot and add the fish stock and ripe tomatoes. Simmer for 1 hour, then pass the liquid through a sieve (strainer) into another pan. Discard the bones. Bring to a simmer and reduce the liquid to 10 tablespoons, then add the tomatoes. Keep warm, or chill and refrigerate for up to 3 days.

6. For the onion confit, heat a large pan over a medium heat and add a drizzle of oil. Once hot, add the onions, thyme and bay leaves and cook for 25 minutes, stirring occasionally. When the onions are soft and caramel in colour, add the sugar, lemon zest and juice. Season with salt and pepper and cook for another 5 minutes. Transfer to a tray to cool.

7. For the pancake batter, whisk the milk and eggs together in a jug, then pour them into a large mixing bowl with the flour and whisk to form a smooth batter. Whisk in the melted butter, then season with salt and pepper and stir in the chives.

For the onion confit
a drizzle of olive oil
2 onions, finely sliced
3 sprigs of thyme
2 bay leaves
2 teaspoons sugar
zest and juice of 1 lemon

For the pancakes
300ml (10fl oz) full-fat milk
3 large eggs
140g (5oz) plain flour
50g (1¾oz) unsalted butter, melted
3 tablespoons chopped chives
sunflower oil

8. To cook the pancakes, heat a large nonstick frying pan over a medium heat. Add a drizzle of oil, then wipe out the excess with kitchen paper, leaving just a film on the pan. Pour in a ladleful of the batter and tilt the pan to spread it around in a thin layer. Cook for 1–2 minutes until golden at the edges, then flip the pancake and cook for a minute on the other side. Repeat so you have 2 large pancakes.

9. Take the puff pastry from the refrigerator and transfer it to a baking sheet lined with baking parchment. Lay 1 pancake on the pastry and place the first sea bass fillet on top. Add the herbs. Spread the onion confit on the fillet and then sandwich the other fillet on top and season. Place the other pancake on top and tuck in to seal the fish into a parcel. Brush the outer edges of the pastry with egg wash and carefully bring it over the fish to form a parcel, then crimp and trim. Brush the top and sides with the egg wash and chill for 30 minutes.

10. Preheat the oven to 170°C Fan (375°F), Gas Mark 5.

11. Bake the fish parcel for 30 minutes until the pastry is golden brown and evenly baked. While the fish is baking, finish the sauce by adding the double cream and whisking in the butter. Finish with chives and a squeeze of lemon juice.

12. Slice the baked parcel with a sharp knife and serve with sauce on the side.

Round fish

Rosemary & Garlic Pan-Fried Bass
with Baked Red Peppers

Serves 4

1 x 2kg (4lb 8oz) bass, gutted, scaled, filleted, pin-boned and cut into 4 equal portions (140g/5oz each) (reserve the bones and head for the sauce)
1 tablespoon chopped rosemary
1 garlic clove, finely chopped
olive oil
sea salt and freshly ground black pepper

For the sauce
a drizzle of olive oil
bones and the head from the fish (blood, gills and organs removed)
2 shallots, sliced
1 celery stick, sliced
1 fennel bulb, sliced
2 garlic cloves, crushed
1 red pepper, deseeded and sliced
zest and juice of 1 small orange
4 ripe tomatoes, chopped
2 star anise
2 teaspoons fennel seeds
½ teaspoon chilli flakes
1 teaspoon saffron
180ml (6fl oz) white wine
1 litre (1¾ pints) fish stock
1 teaspoon cornflour
2 teaspoons cold water

For the peppers
2 large red peppers, halved lengthways and deseeded
4 ripe plum tomatoes, cores removed
1 teaspoon finely chopped rosemary leaves
1 garlic clove, finely chopped
4 teaspoons capers, drained
4 tablespoons extra virgin olive oil

Bass is traditionally frowned upon when making stocks and sauces; I can't abide wasting the bones from any fish, so Pete Biggs, my right-hand man, set about creating a great bass sauce and here it is. I think it's delicious and worth all the effort. If you want to impress, this is the dish to do it. I would serve this with new potatoes, crushed with olive oil, olives and herbs.

1. For the sauce, heat a large frying pan over a medium heat and add a drizzle of oil. Season the fish head and bones with salt and gently fry for 4–5 minutes until golden brown all over. Transfer them to a large saucepan.

2. Heat the frying pan again and add another drizzle of oil. Once hot, add the shallots, celery, fennel, garlic and red pepper. Gently sweat the vegetables for 5 minutes, stirring occasionally. Season with a little salt and pepper. Add the orange zest and juice, tomatoes and spices and cook for a further 5 minutes until the tomatoes start to collapse. Now add the white wine and cook for 5 minutes, then pour in the fish stock.

3. Pour everything over the fish head and bones and bring to a simmer, skimming off any impurities occasionally. Cook for 30 minutes. Using a ladle and sieve, pass the stock into another pan, making sure you push out all the liquid you can. Discard the remains. Bring the stock to the boil and continue to skim and cook until reduced. Taste the stock as it reduces – when the flavour is full and starting to get salty, stop. You need about 250ml (9fl oz). Keep warm.

4. While reducing the sauce, bake your peppers. Preheat the oven to 180°C Fan (400°F), Gas Mark 6.

5. Season the peppers with salt and pepper. Halve the tomatoes lengthways and place inside the peppers. Share the rosemary, garlic and capers equally among the peppers halves, then drizzle over the oil. Place the stuffed peppers into a snug-fitting oven dish and bake in the oven for 30–40 minutes until collapsed. Remove and keep warm.

6. Season the bass fillets on the flesh side with salt, rosemary and garlic. Turn the oven up to 200°C Fan (425°F), Gas Mark 7.

7. Take a large nonstick ovenproof pan, or a seasoned cast-iron pan, and place over a medium–high heat. When the pan is hot, add some olive oil and lay the fish skin-side down (you may need to do this in batches, depending on the size of your pan). Gently fry the fish fillets for 3 minutes until the edges start to turn golden, then slide the pan into the oven, still skin-side down, and cook for 4 minutes. Carefully remove the pan from the oven and turn the fish over. The residual heat will finish the cooking.

8. To finish the sauce, bring it back to a simmer. Mix the cornflour and cold water until smooth, then whisk into the sauce. Cook for 2 minutes.

9. Warm 4 plates and spoon 3 tablespoons of sauce onto each plate. Top with a stuffed pepper and a portion of the fish, then serve.

Pan-Fried Black Bream
with Asparagus & Spiced Beurre Blanc

Serves 4

20 asparagus spears (about 2 bunches), peeled and trimmed of any woody parts
2 black bream, each 500–600g (1lb 2oz–1lb 5oz), scaled, filleted and pin-boned
2 tablespoons olive oil
sea salt

For the spiced beurre blanc
2 small shallots, finely sliced
1 garlic clove, chopped
zest and juice of 1 lemon
10 rasps of a whole nutmeg
a small pinch of cayenne pepper (be careful not to add too much)
150ml (5fl oz) white wine
50ml (2fl oz) double cream
250g (9oz) unsalted butter, cut into small pieces
1 tablespoon chopped flat-leaf parsley leaves
sea salt and freshly ground black pepper

To serve
1 tablespoon finely chopped flat-leaf parsley leaves
1 lemon, peeled and segmented

Pan-frying successfully relies on a few things: the pan must be nonstick; the fish skin must be as dry as you can get it, otherwise the contact between the fish skin and the hot pan surface will create steam instead of searing; and the heat must be controlled – too hot and the fish will scorch or burn, too cold and you won't get the desired crispness or golden colour. I always pan-fry at a medium level of heat. The spiced beurre blanc here is a take on one of my favourite flavour marriages, usually seen with potted shrimp or crab. The combination of lemon, nutmeg, cayenne and parsley is great with fish. I've taken a classic French sauce and added a bit of British tradition, and I think it works well!

1. To make the spiced beurre blanc, put the shallots, garlic, lemon zest and juice, nutmeg, cayenne pepper and wine into a pan and simmer over a medium-high heat until the wine has almost totally reduced. Add the cream and reduce the heat to low. Now add the butter, piece by piece, whisking all the time; do not allow the sauce to boil or it will split. Once all the butter is incorporated, season with salt and pepper to taste. Cover and keep warm.

2. Blanch the asparagus in a pan of salted boiling water for 3 minutes, then drain.

3. To cook the fish, heat a large nonstick pan over a medium heat. Season the fish all over with salt. Pour the oil into the pan and when hot, gently place the fillets into the pan, skin-side down. Make sure the oil isn't too hot; you want it to gently fry. Cook for 2–3 minutes on the skin side until the edges of the fish start to turn golden. Carefully flip the fish and turn off the heat, it will continue to cook in the residual heat.

4. Gently warm the sauce, add the parsley and stir in. Spoon the sauce equally between 4 warmed plates, top with the asparagus and then the bream. Sprinkle with parsley and place a few lemon segments around. Serve immediately.

Raw Gilt-Head Bream
with Pickled Fennel & Horseradish Crème Fraîche

Serves 4

1 gilt-head bream, 800g–1kg (1lb 12oz–2lb 4oz), scaled, gutted, filleted, skinned and pin-boned
4 tablespoons extra virgin olive oil
juice of 1 lime

For the pickled fennel
1 fennel bulb, finely sliced, reserve the fronds
1 small shallot, finely chopped
1 small green chilli, deseeded and finely sliced
50ml (2fl oz) white wine
50ml (2fl oz) white wine vinegar
50g (1¾oz) caster sugar
4 tablespoons water
sea salt

For the horseradish crème fraîche
4 tablespoons full-fat crème fraîche
2 tablespoons fresh horseradish, grated
zest of 1 lime

At the time of writing, gilt-head bream has become my favourite fish. It looks stunning and the quality of a line-caught, large fish is incredible. My 'go-to' is raw preparations, due to the quality and flavour – it's a pleasure to slice and serve with simple accompaniments. In this recipe, I've gone for a few little garnishes that complement the fish and don't overpower it. The fennel is a no-brainer for me, the anise works so well with raw fish, and the crème fraîche is light yet rich at the same time. If you're lucky enough to find wild gilt-heads, buy them – you won't be disappointed.

1. To make the pickled fennel, place the fennel, shallot and chilli into a heatproof mixing bowl. Pour the white wine, vinegar, sugar and water into a small pan and bring to the boil, then season with salt. Pour the pickle liquid over the fennel to submerge and leave to cool.

2. To make the horseradish crème fraîche, mix all the ingredients together and add salt to taste. Keep chilled.

3. Using a very sharp knife, slice the bream as thinly as possible and share equally between 4 cold plates.

4. Drain the fennel and discard the pickle liquid.

5. When you are ready to serve, drizzle the raw fish with olive oil and lime juice, then season with salt. Spoon the horseradish crème fraîche onto the plates and arrange some of the pickled fennel next to it. Finish with a few fennel fronds and serve immediately.

Salt-Baked Bream
with Cider & Brown Butter Dressing

Serves 4

1.5kg (3lb 5oz) sea salt
2 egg whites
4 tablespoons dry cider
2 gilt-head bream, each weighing 600–800g (1lb 5oz–1lb 12oz), scaled, gutted and fins removed
1 lemon, sliced
2 sprigs of rosemary

For the dressing
200g (7oz) salted butter
1 garlic clove, crushed
1 sprig of rosemary
200ml (7fl oz) dry cider
50ml (2fl oz) cider vinegar
50g (1¾oz) caster sugar
1 shallot, finely chopped
1 green apple, peeled and finely chopped (keep in lemon water to stop it going brown)
2 gherkins, finely chopped
4 teaspoons capers
2 tablespoons chopped chervil leaves
sea salt, to taste

Baking fish in salt is nothing new, but it always gets a great reaction when you do it. It's actually a very delicate way of cooking fish, which steams inside the hot salt. The salt also draws out excess moisture, condensing the flavour. You can cook fish of any size in salt, but it must have the skin on to protect the flesh from the harshness of direct contact with salt. You can wrap skinned fish in cabbage or large spinach leaves for protection, but don't eat the leaves – they would be too salty. I've cooked bass, turbot and grey mullet this way with success. It might seem daunting, however it really is quite straightforward and a great centrepiece to impress friends and family. I like to serve this with some new potatoes tossed in butter and mint, and a big green salad dressed with cider vinegar and olive oil.

1. Take the fish out of the refrigerator 1 hour before needed, to ensure it cooks evenly.

2. Preheat the oven to 200°C Fan (425°F), Gas Mark 7.

3. Mix the sea salt, egg whites and cider in a large bowl until well combined. Spread one-third of the salt mixture across a large roasting tray, shaping it into a rectangle that is slightly larger than both fish. Place the fish on top and tuck the lemon slices and rosemary sprigs into the gut cavities. Cover the fish with the remaining salt mixture and press into shape – the fish should be completely sealed within the salt crust. Bake for 20 minutes.

4. Meanwhile, melt the butter in a pan over a medium heat with the garlic and rosemary sprig until the butter turns golden. Remove from the heat.

5. In another pan, heat the cider and cider vinegar with the sugar and shallot until the sugar dissolves, then bring to a simmer and cook until the liquid becomes syrupy. Remove from the heat. Strain the butter through a sieve and add it to the cider reduction. Set aside and keep warm.

6. Remove the fish from the oven and let it rest for 10 minutes. A metal skewer inserted through the salt crust into the thickest part of the fish for 5 seconds should feel warm when touched to your wrist. Crack the crust with a spoon and gently remove the salt, using a pastry brush to sweep away any excess. Working from the head to the tail of the fish, use the tip of a knife to gently lift the skin from the flesh and discard. Following the body line in the centre of the fish, use a large spatula to lift the fillets from the bones and transfer to a serving platter or plate. Check for any remaining bones and remove them. Gently grab the tail end of the bone and pull it up toward the head to remove the fish's backbone and ribs. Gently remove the rest of the fish, leaving the skin behind. Place all the fish onto a platter or 4 serving plates.

7. Add the drained apple, gherkins, capers and chervil to the butter pan. Taste and add salt if required. Spoon the dressing over the fish and serve.

Gurnard Soup
with Gurnard Fritters & Green Olive Tapenade

Serves 4

2 gurnard, about 600g (1lb 5oz) each, scaled, gutted, filleted (heads and bones reserved)

For the fritters
1 tablespoon olive oil
150g (5½oz) unsalted butter
2 banana shallots, finely sliced
4 garlic cloves, chopped
1 red chilli, deseeded and finely chopped
zest of 1 orange
120g (4¼oz) plain flour, plus an extra 50g (1¾oz) for coating
450ml (16fl oz) Roasted Fish Stock (see page 250)
2 tablespoons chopped flat-leaf parsley
1 tablespoon chopped chives
2 eggs, beaten
100g (3½oz) breadcrumbs
sunflower oil, for deep-frying
sea salt and freshly ground black pepper

For the soup
olive oil
1 large onion, chopped
2 carrots, peeled and chopped
1 red chilli, deseeded and chopped
1 red pepper, deseeded and chopped
4 garlic cloves, crushed
1 tablespoon good-quality tomato purée
10 ripe tomatoes, chopped
1 bay leaf
1 sprig of rosemary
finely pared zest and juice of 1 orange, or as needed
1 litre (1¾ pints) Roasted Fish Stock (see page 250)

I like my fish soup recipe…a lot. Over the last decade, I've made it thousands of times and every time I tweak to improve it. I've recently added green olive tapenade, and kick myself as to why I didn't do it sooner – sometimes the best things are right under your nose! This soup is a great example of using everything up from the fish. The heads and bones make the incredible broth and all the fillet goes into making the fritters, which, incidentally, can be made with any fish. I suppose the same can be said for the soup, too, but today we make the soup with gurnard and it's a fine use of this fantastic fish. Both the soup and the fritters freeze well.

1. To make the fritters, heat a large pan over a medium heat and add the olive oil and butter. When the butter is bubbling, add the shallots, garlic, chilli and orange zest and sweat for 5 minutes, stirring occasionally. Stir in the 120g (4¼oz) flour and cook for a further 2 minutes. Heat the fish stock and add it to the vegetable mixture in roughly 4 pours, cooking for 1 minute after each addition. Season with salt and pepper, then leave to cool.

2. Slice and chop the gurnard fillets into roughly 1cm (½ inch) cubes and stir into the cooled sauce along with the parsley and chives. Place in the refrigerator for up to 1 hour to firm up.

3. Meanwhile, make the soup. Heat a large saucepan over a medium heat. When hot, add a drizzle of oil, then the onion, carrots, chilli, red pepper and garlic. Cook for 5 minutes to soften, stirring every minute to avoid the vegetables catching.

4. In a separate frying pan, fry off the heads, bones and trimmings from the fish in olive oil for 3–4 minutes until golden.

5. Add the fish bones and trimmings to the vegetable pan, along with the tomato purée, and cook for another 2 minutes, stirring again every minute. Add the tomatoes, bay leaf, rosemary sprig and orange zest and juice. Cook for a further 2 minutes, giving the mixture a good stir every 30 seconds. Pour in the fish stock and bring to a simmer, then reduce the heat and simmer gently for 20 minutes – do not allow it to boil!

6. Pass the soup through a mouli or a large potato ricer if you have one, into another saucepan. (If you don't have a mouli or potato ricer, you can blitz the soup in a blender, then pass it through a sieve, but you won't achieve quite the same clarity.) Taste the soup, correcting the seasoning with orange juice, salt and pepper as needed. Keep warm over a very low heat.

7. To make the tapenade, place all the ingredients into a small food processor and blitz until well blended but not super-fine. Taste and season with salt and pepper. Set aside.

Ingredients & recipe continued overleaf

Recipe continued

For the green olive tapenade
200g (7oz) green olives, pitted
1 tablespoons capers in brine or salt
1 small green chilli, deseeded
2 salted anchovy fillets
1 garlic clove, finely chopped
1 tablespoon olive oil

To serve
1 orange, segmented
a drizzle of good olive oil

8. When the gurnard fritter mix is firm, divide it into 12 portions, each weighing about 40g (1½oz). Using 2 spoons, shape each portion into a rough oval shape, then place in the freezer for 30 minutes to firm up.

9. When you are ready to cook and serve, place the beaten eggs in a bowl, the 50g (1¾oz) flour in another and the breadcrumbs on a tray. Pass the fritter portions through the flour, then the eggs and finally the breadcrumbs to coat.

10. Heat a deep-fat fryer to 180°C (350°F) or heat some sunflower oil in a deep, heavy-based pan (not filling more than two-thirds full). Fry the fritters for 2 minutes, in batches as necessary. Remove with a slotted spoon to drain on kitchen paper and season with salt.

11. Divide the soup among warmed soup bowls and place the fritters in the centre. Finish with the green olive tapenade, a few pieces of orange and some olive oil. Serve immediately.

Gurnard Curry
with Pineapple Chutney

Serves 4

200g (7oz) full-fat Greek yogurt
50g (1¾oz) fresh root ginger, peeled and grated
3 garlic cloves, finely grated
2 teaspoons garam masala
2 teaspoons ground cumin
1 teaspoon chilli powder
1 teaspoon ground turmeric
½ teaspoon sea salt
2 gurnard, 400–500g (14oz–1lb 2oz) each, gutted, scaled, skinned, filleted and pin-bones removed

For the pineapple chutney
2 tablespoons sunflower oil
1 small onion, finely chopped
1 teaspoon mustard seeds
2 red peppers, deseeded and finely sliced
3 red chillies, deseeded and finely sliced
2 garlic cloves, finely chopped
1 large ripe pineapple, peeled and finely chopped
a pinch of sea salt
200ml (7fl oz) white wine vinegar
100g (3½oz) caster sugar
2 sticks of lemongrass, crushed and halved
100ml (3½fl oz) water

For the curry sauce
2 tablespoons sunflower oil
2 teaspoons mustard seeds
1 teaspoon cumin seeds
1 large onion, finely sliced
4 garlic cloves, finely chopped
2 tablespoons peeled and finely chopped fresh root ginger
1 red chilli, deseeded and finely chopped
1 tablespoon Madras curry powder
2 teaspoons garam masala
600g (1lb 5oz) ripe, fresh tomatoes, chopped
400ml (14fl oz) can of coconut milk
400g (14oz) can of chickpeas, drained
100g (3½oz) baby spinach, washed and picked
a handful of coriander leaves

Gurnard is a perfect species for cooking in or serving with sauces, like curry. The balance of a meaty texture and the almost shellfish flavour doesn't get bullied by big flavours. This is a version of a dish I serve at Outlaw's Fish Kitchen; it's light enough to be served as starter rather than the usual main course. The pineapple chutney isn't authentic at all, it's something we created and think works well on the side. If there's lots left over, don't worry, it has multiple uses and lasts well in the refrigerator. I've been known to chuck it in a cheese sandwich – don't judge me, try it!

1. For the gurnard, mix the yogurt with the ginger, garlic, spices and salt. Add the fish and coat well in the yogurt mix. Leave to marinate for at least 2 hours.

2. For the chutney, heat a large pan over a medium heat and pour in the oil. When hot, add the onion, mustard seeds, peppers and chillies and sweat for 2 minutes, stirring occasionally. Add the garlic, pineapple and a pinch of salt, mix well and then add the vinegar, sugar, lemongrass and measured water. Bring to a simmer and cook for 10 minutes, or until the mixture becomes syrupy. Remove from the heat and leave to cool. Once cooled, discard the lemongrass.

3. For the sauce, heat the oil in a large pan over a medium heat. When hot, add the mustard and cumin seeds. Once they start to pop, add the onion and sweat for 5 minutes, stirring occasionally. You want the onion to start browning for flavour, but not burn. Add the garlic, ginger, chilli and spices and cook for 2 minutes, then add the tomatoes and cook for 6 minutes until they start to collapse. Reduce the heat and add the coconut milk and chickpeas. Bring to a simmer, then taste and season with salt. Keep warm.

4. For the rice noodles, heat a deep-fat fryer to 180°C (350°F) or heat some sunflower oil in a deep, heavy-based pan (not filling more than two-thirds full). Fry the dried noodles for 2 minutes in a few batches until bubbled up and crispy. Drain on kitchen paper and season with salt.

Ingredients & recipe continued overleaf

Round fish

Recipe continued

To serve
sunflower oil, for deep-frying
100g (3½oz) dried fine rice noodles
2 limes, cut into wedges

5. To cook the fish, preheat the grill to a high heat. Wipe off the excess yogurt marinade from the fish and lightly oil a grill tray. Place the fish under the grill and cook for 6 minutes until the fish is cooked through and no longer opaque.

6. Meanwhile, bring the curry sauce to a gentle simmer. Add the spinach and coriander and check the seasoning.

7. Divide the sauce between 4 warm bowls and top with the fish. Add the crispy rice noodles and serve the chutney and lime wedges on the side. You can serve with rice, but I think the chickpeas do the trick.

Grilled Haddock
with Braised Leeks & Anchoïade Sauce

Serves 4

2 tablespoons sunflower oil
4 x 120g (4¼oz) haddock fillet portions, scaled and pin-boned
1 sprig of thyme, leaves picked, plus more to serve
sea salt and freshly ground black pepper

For the sauce
2 large egg yolks
1 garlic clove, chopped
8 anchovy fillets in olive oil
juice of 1 lemon
250ml (9fl oz) olive oil
2 tablespoons double cream
4 tablespoons Roasted Fish Stock (see page 250)
1 tablespoon chopped chives
sea salt and freshly ground black pepper

For the leeks
olive oil
4 leeks, washed and cut into 3cm (1¼ inch) slices
1 sprig of thyme, leaves picked
2 garlic cloves, crushed
100ml (3½fl oz) dry white wine
100ml (3½fl oz) Roasted Fish Stock (see page 250)

When you get good haddock there's nothing nicer than a simply grilled fillet – the blistered, almost burnt skin goes so well with the soft sweet texture of the fish. This dish is very quick to put together. Once you understand the technique of making a warm mayonnaise sauce, you'll never look back. Anchoïade is traditionally a condiment used in Provence at the start of a meal; it gave me the inspiration to make a version of my own. The sauce with the haddock and leeks is delicious.

1. For the sauce, put the egg yolks, garlic, anchovies and lemon juice into a food processor and blend for 30 seconds. With the blades running, add the oil in a slow, steady stream. Season well with salt and pepper and transfer to a pan. Pour in the cream and fish stock and stir. Keep the sauce in the refrigerator until you cook the fish.

2. Preheat the grill to its highest setting.

3. To cook the leeks, heat a frying pan over a medium heat. Once hot, add a drizzle of oil. Place the leek slices, cut-side down, in the pan and cook for 3 minutes, turning occasionally, until golden brown. Season with salt and pepper and sprinkle over the thyme leaves. Add the garlic, then pour in the white wine and fish stock and bring to a simmer. Cover and cook for 8 minutes.

4. While the leeks are cooking, cook the fish. Oil and season a sturdy grill tray that won't buckle under the heat. Place the fish, skin-side down, onto the oiled tray and season with salt, pepper and thyme. Brush with more oil, then flip over. Slide the fish under the grill and cook for 5–6 minutes. When the fish is cooked, leave to rest for 2 minutes.

5. Warm 4 plates. Heat the sauce while constantly stirring to the point where steam rises from it. Do not boil!

6. Share the leeks equally between the warm plates. Add the chives to the sauce and drizzle it around the leeks. Top with the haddock, scatter with thyme leaves and serve.

Poached Haddock & Roasted Portobello Mushroom Rarebit

Serves 4

500ml (18fl oz) full-fat milk
2 bay leaves
1 sprig of thyme
400g (14oz) haddock fillet, skinned and pin-boned
sea salt and freshly ground black pepper

For the rarebit mix
25g (1oz) unsalted butter
25g (1oz) plain flour
100ml (3½fl oz) dry cider
150g (5½oz) mature Cheddar, grated
1 teaspoon Worcestershire sauce
1 teaspoon English mustard
sea salt, to taste
a pinch of cayenne pepper
1 sprig of thyme, leaves picked, plus extra leaves to serve

For the mushrooms
4 large portobello mushrooms, outer skins and stalks removed
1 shallot, chopped
1 sprig of thyme, leaves picked
a drizzle of olive oil
4 teaspoons white wine vinegar
40g (1½oz) unsalted butter, to serve

This is a lovely, comforting dish and would work really well with most white or even smoked fish, especially smoked haddock. You can make the rarebit in advance and bake the mushrooms too, but it's just as easy to make everything fresh. It's also great for breakfast. Haddock is a fish that deserves a bit more love.

1. To make the rarebit mix, place the butter in a saucepan and heat gently until melted. Add the flour and cook out for 2 minutes, then gradually add the cider, stirring all the time. Once all the cider has been incorporated, reduce the heat and cook for 5 minutes. Stir the cheese into the sauce until melted, then add the Worcestershire sauce and mustard. Taste for seasoning, adding salt, cayenne pepper and thyme. Mix well.

2. Line a baking tray with baking parchment and evenly spread the rarebit mix onto it, 1cm (½ inch) thick. Cover the surface with a sheet of baking parchment to stop a skin forming and leave to cool.

3. Preheat the oven to 180°C Fan (400°F), Gas Mark 6.

4. Place the mushrooms upside down in a baking dish. Sprinkle over the shallot and thyme and drizzle with olive oil and vinegar. Place a knob of butter on each mushroom and bake in the oven for 20 minutes. When cooked, leave to cool.

5. To poach the haddock, bring the milk to a simmer along with the bay leaves, thyme and a pinch of salt. Carefully add the haddock and poach for 5 minutes, then lift it out and place on a tray to cool until you can handle it.

6. Preheat the grill to a medium setting.

7. Flake the fish and place on top of the mushrooms. Cut out 4 circles of rarebit to the size of the mushrooms, then cover the fish with it. Season with black pepper. Place under the grill for 2–3 minutes until nicely coloured. Serve immediately, scattered with thyme leaves, perhaps with dressed salad leaves on the side.

Salt Hake Fishcakes
with Pickled Carrots & Béarnaise Mayonnaise

Serves 4

400g (14oz) hake fillet
4 tablespoons sea salt
1 tablespoon sugar
zest of 1 lime
zest of 2 lemons
1 large baking potato
olive oil
1 small leek (white and pale green part only), thoroughly washed and finely sliced
1 banana shallot, finely chopped
2 garlic cloves, finely chopped
2 tablespoons chopped flat-leaf parsley leaves
100g (3½oz) plain flour
2 eggs, beaten
150g (5½oz) panko breadcrumbs
sunflower oil, for deep-frying
sea salt and freshly ground black pepper

For the pickled carrots
2 carrots, peeled
1 banana shallot, finely sliced
1 garlic clove, finely chopped
75ml (2½fl oz) white wine
75ml (2½fl oz) white wine vinegar
75ml (2½fl oz) water
75g (2½oz) caster sugar
1 star anise
1 sprig of tarragon

For the Béarnaise mayonnaise
3 eggs
1 tablespoon white wine vinegar
zest and juice of 1 lemon
1 teaspoon English mustard
300ml (10fl oz) olive oil
2 tablespoons chopped tarragon

To serve
4 spring onions, sliced
a small handful of tarragon leaves
extra virgin olive oil

The natural moisture in hake ensures the mix for these fishcakes is just firm enough to allow a good coating of crumbs and stay intact once fried.

1. To salt the hake, mix the salt, sugar, lime zest and the zest of 1 lemon. Lay the hake in a tray and sprinkle the salt mix over every surface of the fish. Cover and refrigerate for 1 hour.

2. For the pickled carrots, slice them into fine ribbons, using a mandoline or vegetable peeler. Place in a bowl with the shallot and garlic. In a small pan, bring the wine, wine vinegar, water, sugar, star anise and tarragon sprig to a simmer, stirring until the sugar has dissolved, then pour over the carrots. Lay clingfilm over the surface to keep the carrots submerged and leave to cool.

3. Wash the salt mix off the hake fillets in cold water and pat dry. Chop into 5mm (¼ inch) pieces, then place in the refrigerator.

4. Preheat the oven to 180°C Fan (400°F), Gas Mark 6. Bake the potato for 1 hour until cooked.

5. Heat a frying pan over a medium heat, then add a drizzle of olive oil. Once hot, add the leek, shallot and garlic. Cook, stirring, for a few minutes, to soften the vegetables until they become translucent. Allow to cool.

6. Cut the baked potato in half and scoop out the flesh. Pass it through a potato ricer into a large bowl, or mash smoothly using a hand masher. Add the sweated vegetables, remaining lemon zest, chopped parsley and salt hake. Mix well, seasoning with salt and pepper to taste. Shape the mixture into balls the size of a golf ball, rolling them neatly. Place on a tray and allow to cool, then refrigerate for at least 30 minutes to firm up.

7. To make the mayonnaise, place the eggs, vinegar, lemon zest and juice and mustard into a food processor and blitz. With the blades running, gradually add the olive oil through the funnel, drip by drip to start with and then in a steady stream until it is all incorporated and you have a mayonnaise. Scrape into a bowl, season with salt and plenty of black pepper and fold in the tarragon. Cover and refrigerate.

8. To cook the fishcakes, have the flour, beaten eggs and panko breadcrumbs ready in three separate bowls. Heat a deep-fat fryer to 180°C (350°F) or heat some sunflower oil in a deep, heavy-based pan (not filling more than two-thirds full). Pass the balls through the flour, then the egg and finally the breadcrumbs to coat. Deep-fry in batches for 2–3 minutes until crispy. Drain on kitchen paper and season with salt.

9. To finish, drain the carrots from the pickling liquor, add some of the spring onions and tarragon leaves, season with salt and pepper and mix well.

10. Serve the fishcakes alongside a pile of pickled carrots. Dress with more spring onions, tarragon leaves and a drizzle of oil. Serve with the mayonnaise.

Hake & Mussels in a Bag
with Beer, Bacon & Leeks

Serves 4

- 4 x 150g (5½oz) skin-on hake portions
- 2 teaspoons coriander seeds, ground
- 20 live mussels, cleaned and beards removed
- 4 sprigs of thyme
- zest of 2 oranges
- 8 tablespoons wheat beer
- sea salt and freshly ground black pepper

For the leeks & bacon
- 100g (3½oz) unsalted butter
- olive oil
- 8 slices smoked streaky bacon, finely sliced
- 2 leeks, washed and shredded
- 2 garlic cloves, finely chopped
- 150ml (5fl oz) wheat beer

Cooking in paper is nothing new, but I think it's a super-simple way of serving fillets of fish. It's a very gentle way of cooking more delicate species. This recipes marries fish and shellfish with beer, which – I suppose – sounds a bit strange, but trust me, it works so well. I use a wheat beer because it is not too bitter but has a touch of acidity and freshness that works beautifully with the fish. I like to serve this with a bowl of chips.

1. To cook the leeks, heat a large pan over a medium heat and add the butter and a drizzle of oil. When the butter is bubbling, add the bacon and cook for 5 minutes, stirring occasionally. When the bacon has started to brown, add the leeks and cook for another 5 minutes. Season with salt and pepper. Now add the garlic and cook for 1 minute, then pour in the beer. Cook for about 5 minutes until the beer has reduced, then remove from the heat and leave to cool.

2. Preheat the oven to 200°C Fan (425°F), Gas Mark 7.

3. On a clean work surface, lay out 4 large sheets of baking parchment (roughly 30 x 30cm/12 x 12 inches). Divide the leek and bacon mix into 4 equal portions and arrange over one half of each sheet of parchment. Season the hake portions with salt, pepper and ground coriander seeds and place on top of the leeks together with 5 mussels in each parcel, a sprig of thyme and an equal share of the orange zest. Fold over the paper and crimp the edges so they are firmly sealed, leaving you with 4 parcels. Leave a small opening to allow you to pour 2 tablespoons of beer into each parcel. Seal the hole up by folding it down tightly. If the quality of the paper isn't great, you may need to use 2 sheets for each parcel or add a layer of foil on the outside. The aim is that the moisture inside doesn't escape – this is really important!

4. Place the hake parcels onto a baking tray or two and bake in the oven for 15 minutes. When the cooking time is up, remove the parcels and serve immediately. Allow whoever is eating to open their own parcel – that's the magic and the drama!

Smoky Hake Steak
with Sherry-Roasted Pepper Potatoes

Serves 4

4 hake steaks, cut from a 3–4kg (6lb 8oz–8lb 12oz) fish
2 teaspoons smoked paprika
2 sprigs of thyme, leaves picked
olive oil
juice of 1 lime
sea salt and freshly ground black pepper

For the pepper potatoes
olive oil
75g (2½oz) unsalted butter
1 banana shallot, finely sliced
2 red peppers, peeled, deseeded and finely sliced
1 green pepper, peeled, deseeded and finely sliced
1 yellow pepper, peeled, deseeded and finely sliced
2 garlic cloves, finely sliced
2 sprigs of thyme, leaves picked
2 bay leaves
75ml (2½fl oz) sherry vinegar
150ml (5fl oz) dry sherry
1 tablespoon caster sugar
2 large potatoes, peeled and thinly sliced
200ml (7fl oz) fish, vegetable or chicken stock

To serve
a handful of flat-leaf parsley leaves, chopped (optional)

Larger-sized hake are best to eat, as the smaller fish tend to be less flavoursome and dry out very quickly when cooked. In this recipe, I cut a large fish across the bone, creating what almost looks like a classic 'darne' cut. The pepper potatoes are a bit of work, but the process is worth it in the end. If you do decide to use fillets of fish for this recipe, just be aware that the fish cooking time needs to be reduced.

1. Preheat the oven to 160°C Fan (350°F), Gas Mark 4.

2. Start with the pepper potatoes. Heat a large pan and add a drizzle of olive oil and the butter. When the butter is bubbling, add the shallot and peppers. Season with salt and pepper and cook for 10 minutes, stirring occasionally. Add the garlic, thyme and bay leaves and cook for 1 minute. Add the vinegar, sherry and sugar and cook for another 10 minutes until the liquid has almost all reduced.

3. In a large baking dish, alternately layer the pepper mix with the sliced potatoes, seasoning with salt and pepper as you go. Pour in the stock, then cover with foil and bake for 30 minutes.

4. After this time, remove the foil, then return to the oven for 10 minutes until golden brown.

5. Meanwhile, preheat the grill. (If you need to switch your oven to grill, wait until the pepper potatoes are ready, then cover with foil and keep in a warm spot – it will stay hot enough while you cook the fish.)

6. Season the fish all over with salt, pepper, smoked paprika and thyme leaves. Oil a good grill tray and place the hake steaks on it without touching each other, if you can. If they touch, they will not cook evenly and may fuse together. Grill the fish on the middle shelf for 12 minutes, drizzling with more oil and a squeeze of lime juice halfway through. To check if the fish is cooked, insert a small knife or skewer into the thickest part. Hold it there for 5 seconds and touch it against the back of your hand – it should be warmer than warm, but not uncomfortably hot.

7. To serve, warm 4 plates and share the pepper potatoes among them. Add the grilled hake steaks and spoon over any cooking juices. Serve with a sprinkle of parsley, if using.

Baked Hake & Cauliflower Purée
with a Pine Nut, Smoked Chilli & Rosemary Butter

Serves 4

4 hake fillets, 140g (5oz) each, scaled and skinned
2 teaspoons chopped rosemary leaves
olive oil, for drizzling
sea salt and freshly ground black pepper
1 lime, zested, then peeled and segmented, to serve

For the pine nut, smoked chilli & rosemary butter
150g (5½oz) pine nuts
1 teaspoon chopped dried chipotle chilli, or ½ teaspoon chipotle chilli flakes
100g (3½oz) unsalted butter, softened
1 shallot, finely chopped
1 tablespoon chopped rosemary leaves

For the cauliflower purée
a drizzle of olive oil
80g (2¾oz) unsalted butter
1 large cauliflower, finely sliced
100ml (3½fl oz) water

This recipe works well when there's a bit of a chill in the air; it's a comforting dish, the softest of flakes from the hake and the richness, nuttiness and heat of the butter work together so well. Baking the hake this way is gentle enough not to dry the fish out, which is always a danger when you pan-fry or grill hake. The heat of the oven is just that little bit more subtle than the directness of a stove top or grill. Bear in mind that the cooking times I've given below for cooking are for lovely, thick fillets. I recently went into a fishmongers and the hake fillets were very thin, nothing wrong with this, just reduce the cooking time. I'd serve this with new potatoes and a green salad.

1. To make the pine nut butter, toast the pine nuts and chilli in a dry frying pan for a minute or 2, until golden all over. Leave to cool slightly, then transfer to a food processor and blitz until finely ground. While still slightly warm, mix with the butter, shallot and chopped rosemary and season with salt and pepper to taste. Spoon the butter onto a sheet of greaseproof paper and form into a long sausage shape. Place another sheet of greaseproof paper on top and roll to form a more even log. Wrap in the paper, twist the ends to secure, then chill in the freezer for an hour or so to firm up. (You will have more butter than you need, but it can be kept in the freezer to use on another day.)

2. To make the cauliflower purée, heat a medium pan with a tight-fitting lid over a medium heat. Add a drizzle of oil and the butter. Once bubbling, add the cauliflower, then season with salt and sweat for 3 minutes until beginning to soften. Pour in the measured water and put the lid on. Cook for 5 minutes, then stir well. Cook for another 5 minutes and then remove the lid. The aim is to cook the cauliflower fully and have as little liquid left as possible. Transfer the cauliflower to a food processor or blender and blitz for a few minutes until smooth. Taste and adjust the seasoning, if needed. Keep warm if using straight away, or cover and keep in the refrigerator until needed.

3. Preheat the oven to 180°C Fan (400°F), Gas Mark 6.

4. Season the hake all over with rosemary, salt and pepper. Line a baking tray or dish large enough to cook the fish in a single layer with greaseproof paper or foil. Oil the hake and lay it on the tray or dish, then bake in the oven for 5 minutes.

5. Meanwhile, slice enough of the pine nut butter to cover each portion. Remove the fish from the oven and lay the butter on top, then return it to the oven for 3 minutes to melt the butter.

6. Heat the cauliflower purée and spoon equally onto 4 warm plates. When the fish is cooked, serve alongside the purée. Arrange the lime segments on top of the fish and sprinkle over the zest.

Braised Fillets of John Dory
with Soy, Ginger & Celery

Serves 4

4 celery sticks, peeled and sliced
2 John Dory, 500g (1lb 2oz) each, filleted and skinned, each fillet cut into 3
6 spring onions, sliced
30g (1oz) fresh root ginger, peeled and finely chopped
1 green chilli, deseeded and finely sliced
sea salt and freshly ground black pepper

For the braising stock
200ml (7fl oz) fish stock
100ml (3½fl oz) white wine
100ml (3½fl oz) water
100ml (3½fl oz) soy sauce
50ml (2fl oz) white wine vinegar
20g (¾oz) caster sugar

To serve
1 orange, segmented
a handful of coriander leaves
2 spring onions, finely sliced
4 teaspoons toasted sesame oil

John Dory is a fish that varies in shape and size and can be tricky to get just right when you cook the fillets off the bone. I find it better to fillet the fish and then break it down into the natural 'mini fillets'. This gives you six nice pieces from one fish, especially if they're 1kg (2lb 4oz) plus, allowing you to check every piece of fish when cooking. Simply remove the smaller pieces as they're done, leaving the thicker pieces to continue cooking. The cooking technique with this dish is nice and gentle, allowing you to see what's going on. You can serve this as a starter or add some rice and extra vegetables for a main course.

1. Heat the ingredients for the braising stock in a large, wide pan with a tight-fitting lid. Stir until the sugar has dissolved.

2. Add the celery to the pan and simmer gently for 5 minutes.

3. Season the fish with salt and pepper, then add it to the pan along with the spring onions, ginger and chilli. Put the lid on and simmer gently for 5 minutes.

4. Warm 4 serving bowls. Once the fish is cooked, share it among the bowls and pour over a few spoonfuls of the braising stock along with a portion of the braised celery. Add an orange segment to each piece of fish, scatter over the coriander leaves and spring onions, drizzle with the sesame oil and serve.

Whole Baked Peppered John Dory
with White Bean & Lemon Aïoli

Serves 4

1 x 2kg (4lb 8oz) or 2 x 1kg (2lb 4oz) John Dory, trimmed of sharp spines and fins, scaled, head removed
a drizzle of olive oil

For the rub

2 teaspoons black peppercorns
2 teaspoons pink peppercorns
1 teaspoon Szechuan peppercorns
4 teaspoons sea salt
1 teaspoon dried thyme
2 teaspoons dried oregano

For the white bean aïoli

1 garlic bulb, broken into cloves, unpeeled
150ml (5fl oz) olive oil, plus extra to drizzle
1 x 400g (14oz) can butter beans, drained
2 egg yolks
zest and juice of 1 lemon
1 teaspoon dried oregano
sea salt and freshly ground black pepper

To finish

a handful of flat-leaf parsley leaves
a handful of mint leaves
2 teaspoons capers in brine, drained
1 large orange, peeled and segmented
1 tablespoon extra virgin olive oil

Baking fish whole is very simple and the more you do it, the more confident you'll become. A few tips that are important for success: 1 – take the fish out of the refrigerator at least an hour before cooking. 2 – just as you would do with meat, rest the fish after cooking (5 minutes is fine) as this will release the cooking juices which you can then spoon over the fillets once you have taken them off the bone. 3 – never discard the cooking juices – that's where the flavours are! I would serve this with some chips or potato wedges.

1. First, make the rub. Toast all the peppercorns in a dry frying pan over a steady heat for 2 minutes until fragrant. Remove from the heat and add the salt, thyme and oregano. Leave to cool slightly, then blend in a small food processor or spice grinder.

2. Cover the entire fish with the rub. Leave somewhere cool for 1 hour to raise the core temperature; this helps the fish to cook evenly. If you want to leave the rub for longer, omit the salt from the recipe, adding it just before cooking (the salt will cure the fish if left too long and will ruin the flesh).

3. Preheat the oven to 200°C Fan (425°F), Gas Mark 7.

4. To make the white bean aïoli, take a square of foil and scrunch up the sides. Put all the garlic cloves inside, sprinkle with salt and drizzle with olive oil. Seal the foil into a bag, place on a baking tray and roast for 25 minutes. Remove from the oven and leave to cool slightly.

5. Reduce the oven temperature to 180°C Fan (400°F), Gas Mark 6.

6. Peel the garlic and add it to a food processor along with the beans, egg yolks, lemon zest and juice and oregano. Blend to combine. With the blades still running, add the olive oil in a steady stream through the feeder tube. Once emulsified, season with salt and pepper. Blend for 1 minute, taste and adjust the seasoning. Spoon into a bowl and cover with clingfilm. Refrigerate unless serving immediately.

7. Line a baking tray or dish big enough for the fish with baking parchment. Oil the paper and lay the fish on top. Place in the oven and cook for 10 minutes. Remove the fish and check the thickest part with a skewer, holding it in place for 10 seconds and then removing it and holding it against the back of your hand. If it's cold, the fish needs 5 more minutes. Check again the same way until the skewer is warm to hot, but not so hot that it burns. Remove from the oven when cooked and leave to rest for a few minutes while you plate up.

8. Warm 4 plates and a platter for the fish. Put the herbs, capers, orange and some seasoning into a bowl and mix carefully. Spoon the aïoli into a dish and place the Dory on a platter. Serve immediately, drizzled with extra virgin olive oil, with the orange and herb salad on the side. The fish will come off easily with a knife and fork.

Crispy Ling
with Smoked Chilli Jam

Serves 4

400g (14oz) ling fillet, skinned and pinboned
2 tablespoons finely chopped fennel herb
zest of 1 lime
1 teaspoon fennel seeds, toasted and ground
100g (3½oz) gluten-free self-raising flour
130ml (4fl oz) dry sparkling cider
sunflower oil, for deep-frying
sea salt and freshly ground black pepper
1 lime, cut into 4 wedges, to serve

For the smoked chilli jam
1 red onion, finely chopped
2 red peppers, deseeded and finely sliced
1 red chilli, deseeded and sliced
2 dried chipotle chillies, chopped, or 1 teaspoon chipotle chilli flakes
2 garlic cloves, finely chopped
1 x 200g (7oz) can good-quality chopped tomatoes
150g (5½oz) soft light brown sugar
100ml (3½fl oz) red wine vinegar
1 lemongrass stick, smashed and bruised with the back of a heavy knife
a pinch of sea salt

This dish is probably the most popular nibble or small plate we've ever made at Outlaw's Fish Kitchen. I've slightly updated it with smoked chillies and the addition of fennel herb and seed. Ling is a good fish to deep-fry, because it has a firm texture that flakes well. Other white fish species will work here too. You will need some cocktail sticks to cook these.

1. To make the chilli jam, put the ingredients into a heavy-based pan (I use a cast-iron one) and bring to the boil, stirring to dissolve the sugar. Reduce the heat and simmer gently, stirring occasionally, for about 45 minutes until the jam is well reduced. Once it starts to catch on the bottom of the pan, stir constantly over the heat until it looks like bubbling lava. Transfer to a bowl and leave to cool.

2. Cut the ling into roughly 4cm (1½ inch) chunks. Mix the chopped fennel, lime zest, ground fennel seeds and a good pinch of salt together in a bowl. Add the ling pieces and toss to mix. Leave to marinate for 30 minutes.

3. To make the batter, mix the flour and cider together until smooth.

4. Heat enough oil for deep-frying in a deep-fat fryer to 180°C (350°F) or heat some sunflower oil in a deep, heavy-based pan (not filling more than two-thirds full). Season the fish with salt and pepper.

5. You will need to cook the fish in 2 or 3 batches. One at a time, prick each chunk with a cocktail stick and dip into the batter to coat, then carefully lower into the hot oil with the cocktail stick attached. Deep-fry for 3–4 minutes until cooked and crispy. Gently lift the fish out with a slotted spoon to drain on kitchen paper and pull out the cocktail sticks. Keep warm while you cook the rest.

6. Serve immediately on a platter or individual plates, with a bowl of the chilli jam and some lime wedges on the side.

Pan-fried Ling & Pancetta
with Braised White Cabbage & Apple

Serves 4

4 x 160g (5¾oz) skinless ling fillets
olive oil
12 sage leaves
16 slices pancetta
sea salt and freshly ground black pepper

For the white cabbage
2 tablespoons olive oil
1 onion, finely sliced
½ white cabbage, finely shredded
1 tablespoon fresh oregano leaves
100ml (3½fl oz) white wine vinegar
700ml (1¼ pints) white wine
1½ tablespoons honey
2 Granny Smith apples, peeled and grated
2 teaspoons chopped sage
2 teaspoons chopped chives

For the dressing
juice of 1 lemon
4 tablespoons extra virgin olive oil
1 green apple, peeled and finely chopped
2 tablespoons chopped chives

If you've not tried ling before, but you like fish such as cod and haddock, you'll love it. Don't get your frying pan too hot for this recipe as you want to fry it gently and patiently. The pancetta, white cabbage and apple accompaniment here is lovely; a great winter combination. I find creating wintery seafood dishes the hardest, due to availability of ingredients, but I'm particularly chuffed with this one.

1. Preheat the oven to 160°C Fan (350°F), Gas Mark 4.

2. To make the braised cabbage, heat a large ovenproof pan that has a tight-fitting lid over a medium heat. When the pan is hot, add the olive oil and onion and cook for 5 minutes, stirring occasionally until softened. Add the shredded cabbage, oregano, vinegar, white wine, honey and grated apple, seasoning well with salt and pepper. Cover with the lid and cook in the oven for 2 hours, or until the white cabbage is tender.

3. Remove the fish from the refrigerator 30 minutes before cooking to come up to temperature.

4. Remove the cabbage from the oven and transfer the pan to the stove over a medium heat. Uncover the pan and cook until the liquor reduces down and thickens. Keep warm.

5. Increase the oven temperature to 180°C Fan (400°F), Gas Mark 6.

6. Heat a large nonstick ovenproof pan (or seasoned cast-iron pan) over a medium–high heat. When the pan is hot, add a drizzle of olive oil and fry the sage leaves for 1 minute on each side. Drain on kitchen paper.

7. Lay out 4 pieces of pancetta and place a fish fillet on top. Season and add a crispy sage leaf, then wrap the pancetta slices around the fish. Repeat to make 4 parcels. Place the fish into the hot pan and gently fry for 3 minutes until the edges start to turn golden, then slide the pan into the oven and cook for 4 minutes. Carefully remove the pan from the oven and turn the fish over. The residual heat will finish the cooking.

8. While the fish is in the oven, warm 4 plates. Mix together the lemon juice, olive oil, apple, chives and some seasoning to make the dressing. Warm the cabbage, stirring in the chopped sage and chives.

9. Share the cabbage among the 4 plates and carefully place the fish alongside. Arrange the remaining sage leaves around, then finish with a few spoonsful of the dressing and serve.

Szechuan Cured Monkfish
with Mustard Mayonnaise & Cucumber Salad

Serves 4

100g (3½oz) sea salt
100g (3½oz) caster sugar
2 teaspoons black peppercorns
2 teaspoons Szechuan peppercorns
2 teaspoons fennel seeds
2 teaspoons yellow mustard seeds
500g (1lb 2oz) very fresh monkfish fillet, skinned and trimmed of any sinew (see pages 78–9)
200ml (7fl oz) dry white wine

For the mustard mayonnaise
2 egg yolks
2 teaspoons English mustard
juice of ½ lemon
250ml (9fl oz) olive oil
2 teaspoons wholegrain mustard
sea salt and freshly ground black pepper

To serve
1 cucumber, halved lengthways, deseeded and cut into thin batons
2 gherkins, cut into thin batons
a few sprigs of dill
a pinch of sea salt
a drizzle of extra virgin olive oil

This dish is from the menu at Outlaw's Fish Kitchen and is a great example of what the restaurant is about. It really belongs to Tim, my head chef there, and evolved from a conversation we had about classic salt-beef bagels! He takes a good-quality piece of monkfish and cures it with bold flavours, just enough so that it doesn't lose the monkfish characteristics. The mustard mayonnaise, gherkins and cucumber complement the fish so well. Note: you will need to cure the fish several hours in advance.

1. Place the salt, sugar and half the spices into a food processor and blitz thoroughly to a powder.

2. Lay the monkfish in a plastic container big enough to hold it in one layer. Sprinkle evenly with the salt mixture, turning the fish over a few times to ensure it's completely coated. Drizzle the white wine evenly over the fish, then cover and place in the refrigerator for 3 hours to cure, turning every hour.

3. When the time is up, take the fish out of the container and wash off the cure with cold water, then pat dry with kitchen paper. Put the fish back into a clean container and return it to the refrigerator for 1 hour to firm up.

4. Dry-roast the remaining spices in a pan until aromatic. Leave to cool, then grind in a mortar and pestle or spice grinder until fine. Sprinkle the fish with the spice mix, then wrap it tightly in clingfilm. At this point, you can freeze the fish for up to a month. I suggest you freeze the cured fish anyway for a short while, as it makes it easier to slice.

5. To make the mayonnaise, place the egg yolks, English mustard and lemon juice in a bowl and whisk together for 1 minute. Slowly add the oil, drop by drop to begin with, then in a steady stream, whisking constantly until the mixture is emulsified and thick. Alternatively, you can make the mayonnaise in a blender or food processor, blending the egg yolks, mustard and lemon juice for 1 minute and then adding the oil slowly through the funnel with the motor running. Season the mayonnaise and add the wholegrain mustard, then cover and refrigerate until ready to serve. It will keep in the refrigerator for a couple of days.

6. To slice the fish, take it from the freezer and leave on a chopping board for 5 minutes. As the fish slightly thaws you can slice it with a serrated or sharp knife. Be careful not to leave the clingfilm on! Lay the slices on a tray or straight onto serving plates.

7. To serve, mix the cucumber, gherkins and dill in a bowl with a pinch of salt and the olive oil. Share the cucumber mix between the plates and drizzle with any oil left in the bowl. Serve with the mustard mayonnaise.

Harissa-Roasted Monkfish
with Olive Hollandaise & Crispy Kale

Serves 4

This recipe is exactly what monkfish should be; roasted in the oven, on the bone, with bold flavours that work wonderfully with the meaty texture and add another dimension.

2kg (4lb 8oz) whole monkfish tail, trimmed of sinew and membrane removed (see pages 78–9), cut into 4 equal portions
olive oil
extra virgin olive oil, for drizzling
sea salt

For the harissa paste
2 teaspoons coriander seeds
2 teaspoons cumin seeds
2 teaspoons fennel seeds
2 teaspoons caraway seeds
1 red onion, chopped
10 garlic cloves, peeled
10 red chillies, deseeded and chopped
2 chargrilled peppers in brine, chopped
100ml (3½fl oz) olive oil
zest and juice of 1 lemon

For the crispy kale
100g (3½oz) kale, stalks removed
2 tablespoons olive oil
1 tablespoon ras el hanout

For the olive hollandaise
100ml (3½fl oz) olive oil
100ml (3½fl oz) clarified butter (ghee)
3 egg yolks
zest and juice of 1 lemon
2 tablespoons water
20 olives, pitted and finely chopped
1 tablespoon chopped flat-leaf parsley leaves
1 tablespoon chopped mint
freshly ground black pepper

1. For the harissa paste, toast all the seeds in a dry frying pan for 5 minutes over a medium–low heat until fragrant. Leave them to cool and then blitz in a small food processor or grinder.

2. Put the onion, garlic, chillies, grilled peppers and olive oil into a food processor and blitz to a paste. Season with salt.

3. Reheat the frying pan. When hot, add the paste and fry for 10 minutes, stirring occasionally. Stir in the spices and lemon zest and juice, then allow to cool. This makes more than you need, but it can be stored in the refrigerator for up to 1 week.

4. Spread 3 tablespoons of the harissa paste all over every surface of the monkfish. Cover and place in the refrigerator for 2 hours. Remove from the refrigerator to come up to temperature 1 hour before cooking.

5. Preheat the oven to 220°C Fan (475°F), Gas Mark 9.

6. Place the kale in a large bowl and toss with the olive oil to coat. Spread over a baking sheet and bake in the oven for 8 minutes, checking it after 6 minutes. Drain on kitchen paper and sprinkle with the ras el hanout.

7. To make the olive hollandaise, warm the olive oil and clarified butter in a pan until tepid, then remove from the heat. Place the egg yolks in a medium heatproof bowl and add the lemon zest, juice and water. Stand the bowl over a pan of gently simmering water and whisk until the mixture thickens enough to form a ribbon when the beaters are lifted. Remove the bowl from the pan and slowly whisk in the olive oil mixture in a thin, steady stream. Once all the oil is incorporated, season the hollandaise with salt and pepper to taste. Cover with clingfilm to prevent a skin forming and keep warm while you cook the fish.

8. Preheat the grill to its highest setting.

9. Line a baking tray with foil and drizzle over some oil. Lay the monkfish on the tray and season with salt. Slide it under the grill at least 10cm (4 inches) from the heat source and cook for 10 minutes. To check the monkfish, insert a skewer into the thickest part of the fish and hold it there for 10 seconds, then touch the skewer on the back of your hand. If it's cold, continue to cook for another 3 minutes and check again. The skewer should be be warm to hot, but not burn you. Remove the fish from the grill and leave to rest for 5 minutes.

10. Mix the olives and herbs into the hollandaise. Place place a portion of fish onto warmed plates with a big spoonful of hollandaise and some crispy kale. Drizzle with extra virgin olive oil and serve immediately.

Monkfish Karaage
with Seaweed Tartare Sauce

Serves 4

50g (1¾oz) fresh root ginger, peeled and finely grated
2 garlic cloves, grated
70ml (2½fl oz) soy sauce
70ml (2½fl oz) sake or white wine
2 tablespoons toasted sesame oil
2 teaspoons caster sugar
400g (14oz) prime monkfish fillet, trimmed of sinew and membrane (see pages 78–9)
sunflower oil, for deep-frying
100g (3½oz) cornflour
sea salt, for seasoning

For the seaweed tartare sauce
2 egg yolks
2 teaspoons wasabi
1 tablespoon yuzu juice
2 nori sheets, blended in a small food processor (save a pinch to serve)
2 teaspoons sesame seeds, toasted
a pinch of sea salt
250ml (9fl oz) sunflower oil
50ml (2fl oz) sesame oil
2 teaspoons capers in brine, drained
1 gherkin, finely chopped
4 spring onions, sliced
1 tablespoon chopped chives

To serve
a few pinches of bonito flakes
lime wedges
steamed rice

The word karaage means deep-fried the Japanese way. Usually, you see it with chicken coated in cornflour or potato starch, but it doesn't have to be chicken, so my thought was that monkfish would work well treated the same way – and it does. I marinate the fish first, which I think makes a big difference and is well worth the wait. The seaweed tartare sauce isn't Japanese – it's just a tasty tartare sauce with Japanese ingredients. This dish is perfect with a cold beer.

1. First, marinate the fish. Place the ginger, garlic, soy, sake, sesame oil and sugar into a suitable container and mix until the sugar has dissolved. Cut the fish into 8 equal pieces and leave to marinate for 1 hour.

2. To make the tartare sauce, add the egg yolks, wasabi and yuzu juice to a food processor and blend for 30 seconds. Add the nori, sesame seeds and salt, then blend. With the blades running, pour in the oils in a slow, steady stream until emulsified. Transfer the mayonnaise to a bowl and add the capers, gherkin, spring onions and chives. Mix well and taste. Refrigerate until needed.

3. Heat a deep-fat fryer to 160°C (320°F) or heat some sunflower oil in a deep, heavy-based pan (not filling more than two-thirds full). Mix the fish with the cornflour and tap off any excess. When the fryer is hot, fry the fish for 2 minutes, then remove with a slotted spoon to drain on kitchen paper. Increase the temperature of the oil to 190°C (375°F). Meanwhile, warm 4 plates.

4. When the oil is up to temperature, fry the fish again for another 2 minutes until crisp. Drain on kitchen paper and season with sea salt and a pinch of the blitzed nori.

5. To serve, divide the fish among the warm plates. Place the tartare sauce in small ramekins and serve alongside. Top with bonito flakes and serve with lime wedges and steamed rice.

Sticky Sweet & Sour Monkfish
with Cucumber, Carrot & Sesame Salad

Serves 4 as a starter

4 monkfish tails, 400–600g (14oz–1lb 5oz) each, trimmed of sinew (see pages 78–9), cut into chunks across the bone
100g (3½oz) cornflour
50ml (2fl oz) sparkling water
sunflower oil, for deep-frying
sea salt, to season

For the chilli rub
1 teaspoon chilli flakes
2 teaspoons fennel seeds
½ teaspoon black peppercorns
2 teaspoons chopped rosemary leaves
zest of 1 orange

For the glaze
45g (1¾oz) tomato purée
360ml (12fl oz) white wine vinegar
360ml (12fl oz) dry cider
180ml (6fl oz) soy sauce
180g (6oz) soft dark brown sugar
1 teaspoon chilli flakes

For the salad
4 spring onions, sliced
2 carrots, peeled and cut into matchsticks
a handful of coriander leaves
2 teaspoons toasted sesame seeds, plus 2 teaspoons extra to serve
a pinch of sea salt
juice of 1 lime

This is a firm favourite at Outlaw's Fish Kitchen, and the credit goes to head chef, Tim Barnes. He spent a while getting this exactly how he wanted it until it was just perfect. Cooking the monkfish on the bone this way is a great way to get the most out of this fascinating species. It's a very moreish recipe and a crowd-pleaser, too. This is great served with sticky rice.

1. To make the rub, dry-fry the ingredients in a hot frying pan until aromatic, about 3 minutes. Remove the pan from the heat, pour into a bowl and allow to cool, then blend in a small food processor or spice grinder until fine.

2. Roll the monkfish chunks in the chilli rub and leave for 1 hour.

3. Meanwhile, make the glaze. Place all the ingredients into a pan, bring to a simmer and cook to reduce by three-quarters. Leave to cool.

4. To make the salad, mix the spring onions, carrots, coriander and sesame seeds together with a pinch of salt and the lime juice. Divide among 4 plates.

5. Heat a deep-fat fryer to 180°C (350°F) or heat some sunflower oil in a deep, heavy-based pan (not filling more than two-thirds full).

6. Make a smooth paste of the cornflour, sparkling water and a pinch of salt. Pass the monkfish through the batter, coating well. Carefully lower the pieces into the hot oil and cook for 4 minutes (you may need to do this in 2 batches). Remove with a slotted spoon and transfer the cooked monkfish to the pan of glaze. Turn to coat well.

7. Divide the monkfish among the plates, sprinkle with sesame seeds and serve immediately.

Serves 4

a generous drizzle of olive oil
2 ray wings, weighing 500g (1lb 2oz) each, cut into equal halves
1 small red onion, sliced
2 garlic cloves, halved
60g (2¼oz) fresh root ginger, peeled and chopped
100ml (3½fl oz) white wine vinegar
100ml (3½fl oz) white wine
sea salt and freshly ground black pepper

For the beetroot
2 large beetroot, washed
100ml (3½fl oz) white wine vinegar
50g (1¾oz) fresh root ginger, peeled and sliced

For the dressing
zest and juice of 1 lime
6 tablespoons olive oil
2 teaspoons honey
1 teaspoon English mustard
1 small green chilli, deseeded and finely chopped

For the salad
1 frisée lettuce, washed and picked
4 spring onions, sliced
1 orange, peeled and segmented
a handful of coriander leaves

Soused Ray
with Beetroot, Orange & Ginger Salad

Sousing is always a winner, especially when the balance of acidity, sweetness and saltiness is spot on, and this style is great for ray. It's just right for being cooked and rested in a mixture of vinegar, wine and oil. The ray can be refrigerated but will become gelatinous; you'll need to warm it up carefully if you choose to go that way.

1. Start with the beetroot. Place the beetroot in a pan with the vinegar, ginger and enough water to cover, adding a good pinch of salt. Simmer until tender, 40–60 minutes depending on size and freshness. When the beetroot are cooked, leave to cool in the liquid until you can handle them comfortably. Rub off the skins and leave to cool completely, then cut into bite-sized chunks.

2. Preheat the oven to 180°C Fan (400°F), Gas Mark 6.

3. Heat a large nonstick ovenproof frying pan over a medium heat. Drizzle in some olive oil and season the ray with salt and pepper. Carefully place it into the pan and fry for 2 minutes on each side. Remove and set aside.

4. Add a drizzle more oil to the pan and fry the onion for 2 minutes until softened. Add the garlic and ginger and cook for another minute. Pour in the vinegar and wine and bring to a simmer, then return the fish to the pan, thickest side down, and transfer to the oven to cook for 6 minutes. (If you don't have a pan that's big enough or isn't ovenproof, use a baking dish.)

5. Meanwhile, make the dressing. Whisk the ingredients together and season, set aside.

6. Remove the fish from the oven and carefully turn it over, then transfer it to a platter and pour over the sousing liquid and onions.

7. To finish, place the lettuce, spring onions and beetroot into a large bowl with the dressing and gently mix. Taste and season as you wish. Add the orange segments and coriander just before serving.

8. To serve, share the salad among 4 plates and place the fish platter in the centre of the table for everyone to share.

Ray Scrumpets & Celeriac Salad
with a Mustard & Herb Mayonnaise

Serves 4

1 litre (1¾ pints) Roasted Fish Stock (see page 250)
2 ray wings, weighing 300g (10½oz) each, skinned
1 shallot, finely chopped
4 teaspoons capers in brine, drained
2 gherkins, finely chopped
2 tablespoons finely chopped flat-leaf parsley leaves
1 tablespoon finely chopped tarragon leaves
1 tablespoon wholegrain mustard
1 teaspoon English mustard
zest and juice of 1 lemon
100g (3½oz) plain flour
2 eggs, beaten
200g (7oz) breadcrumbs (I use blitzed focaccia)
sunflower oil, for deep-frying
sea salt and freshly ground black pepper

For the mustard & herb mayonnaise
3 egg yolks
1 tablespoon English mustard
1 tablespoon white wine vinegar
1 tablespoon chopped tarragon leaves
1 tablespoon chopped chives
300ml (10fl oz) sunflower oil

For the celeriac salad
1 celeriac, peeled, finely sliced and cut into matchsticks
2 tablespoons mustard mayonnaise (see above)
1 tablespoon chopped tarragon
1 tablespoon chopped chives
zest of 1 lemon

To serve
a few fronds of fennel herb
lemon wedges

Ray is a meaty fish, so when I was developing a dish that would work for either the beginning of a meal as a snack or as a hearty small plate, I wanted to use it for something a bit different. Earlier in my career, we did various slow-cooked meats fried in breadcrumbs called 'scrumpets'. I've researched the origins of these, but all I can find is, 'a term for meat that is breaded and fried'! Ray works so well in this recipe, especially paired with the mustard mayonnaise and celeriac salad. These can also be cut smaller and served as canapés. The cooked ray, once set, can be frozen for up to a month.

1. Preheat the oven to 180°C Fan (400°F), Gas Mark 6.

2. Heat the fish stock and pour it into a roasting tray large enough to hold the ray wings. Season the ray with salt and pepper and carefully lower into the stock. Cover the tray with foil and place in the oven for 15 minutes.

3. Remove the tray from the oven and carefully lift the ray wings onto another tray to cool slightly. When the ray is still hot but not uncomfortable to handle, pick the meat away from the cartilage and place into a bowl. Season the fish with salt and pepper, then add the shallot, capers, gherkins, herbs, mustards, lemon zest and juice, and 5 tablespoons of the poaching stock (leftover stock can be strained, cooled and frozen for other uses). Very carefully mix everything together, but try not to break up the lovely ray strands.

4. Line a 3cm (1¼ inch) deep tray with greaseproof paper. Put the ray mix into the tray and carefully but firmly press it down. Cover and put into the refrigerator to firm up. For best results, leave for 6 hours.

5. When the ray has set, remove it from the tray and cut into rectangles about 6 x 3cm (1¼ x 2½ inches). Return to the refrigerator until needed.

6. To make the mayonnaise, put the egg yolks, mustard, vinegar and herbs into a bowl and whisk together for 1 minute. Slowly add the oil, drop by drop to begin with, then in a steady stream, whisking constantly until the mixture is emulsified and thick. Season with salt and pepper to taste, then cover and refrigerate until needed.

7. To make the salad, mix all the ingredients together and season to taste.

8. Have the flour, beaten eggs and breadcrumbs ready in three separate bowls. Pass each ray scrumpet first through the flour, then the egg and finally the breadcrumbs to coat, making sure each is covered well.

9. Heat a deep-fat fryer to 180°C (350°F) or heat some sunflower oil in a deep, heavy-based pan (not filling more than two-thirds full). Carefully lower the scrumpets into the hot oil and fry for 3 minutes until crisp. Drain on kitchen paper and season with salt.

10. To serve, divide the celeriac salad among 4 plates and place a scrumpet next to each pile. Finish with the mayonnaise, some fennel herb and lemon wedges. Serve hot.

Serves 4

4 ray wings, weighing 160g (5¾oz) each, skinned and trimmed
zest of 1 lemon
2 sprigs of thyme, leaves picked
2 tablespoons olive oil, to serve
sea salt and freshly ground black pepper

For the cauliflower aïoli
½ cauliflower, cut into florets
2 egg yolks
2 tablespoons lemon juice
2 garlic cloves, chopped
200ml (7fl oz) light olive oil

For the cauliflower salad
½ cauliflower, finely sliced
1 green apple, peeled and cut into matchsticks
4 teaspoons small capers
2 tablespoons extra virgin olive oil
3 tablespoons crème fraîche
zest and juice of 1 lemon
2 tablespoons chopped flat-leaf parsley leaves

Steamed Ray
with Cauliflower & Apple Salad & Cauliflower Aïoli

When ray is at its freshest, steaming is the way to go if you want to understand the true character of the species. The gentle heat from the steam helps the ray stay moist, soft and delicious, and a touch of lemon zest and thyme complements it so well. Cauliflower aïoli is a nice recipe to make and something a bit different to serve with ray.

1. To make the aïoli, cook the cauliflower florets in salted boiling water until tender. Drain well and cool.

2. Weigh out 200g (7oz) of the cooked cauliflower and place in a food processor with the egg yolks, lemon juice and garlic. Blitz to combine, then add the rest of the olive oil in a slow, steady stream through the feeder tube, blending until fully incorporated. Season with salt and pepper to taste. Transfer to a bowl and leave to cool, then cover and place in the refrigerator (unless using straight away).

3. For the salad, mix everything together in a large bowl and taste for seasoning, adding more salt and pepper if needed.

4. To cook the ray, set up a bamboo steamer or turn on the steamer setting in your oven. Line 1–2 steamer trays with greaseproof paper. Season the fish with lemon zest, thyme leaves, salt and pepper, then place into the steamer and cook for 6 minutes. Remove and leave to rest for 3 minutes while you plate up.

5. Warm 4 plates and share the salad among them. Place the fish next to the salad and spoon on some of the cauliflower aïoli. Drizzle with olive oil, then serve hot.

Grilled Butterflied Red Mullet
with a Tomato, Anchovy, Mint & Basil Salad

Serves 4

olive oil
4 red mullet, about 300–400g (10½–14oz) each, scaled, gutted and butterfly-filleted
1 tablespoon dried oregano
sea salt and freshly ground black pepper

For the dressing
2 very ripe plum tomatoes, chopped
1 red pepper, deseeded and chopped
12 basil leaves
1 garlic clove, roughly chopped
1 teaspoon caster sugar
200ml (7fl oz) extra virgin olive oil

For the salad
4 handfuls of watercress, washed
20 mixed heritage tomatoes, halved widthways
2 tablespoons good-quality capers
20 pickled anchovies, halved lengthways
a small bunch of basil, leaves picked
2 tablespoons mint leaves

Red mullet is the perfect-sized fish for butterflying and grills beautifully. It's a sunshine fish and works well with sunshine flavours. The tomato dressing is delicious and well worth making with the red mullet. Get the tastiest tomatoes you can, it will make the difference.

1. First, make the dressing. Using a freestanding or stick blender, blitz the tomatoes and pepper with the basil, garlic, sugar and olive oil in a bowl or jug until smooth. Line another bowl or jug with muslin, pour in the dressing and squeeze the muslin to extract as much liquid as possible, leaving the solids in the cloth to be discarded. Season the dressing with salt and pepper to taste.

2. To assemble the salad, place the salad ingredients in a large bowl, pour over the dressing and mix. Divide the salad among 4 bowls. There will be a lot of dressing, but that's fine.

3. Preheat the grill to medium-high and oil a grill tray large enough to hold all 4 butterflied red mullet.

4. Oil the fish and season all over with oregano, salt and pepper. Lay skin-side up on the grill tray and grill for 4 minutes. Try to get some nice colour and blistering of the skin (this not only looks good, it also gives the skin great flavour). Leave the fish to rest on the tray for 2 minutes; save any juices that collect in the grill tray.

5. Top the salad with the red mullet and drizzle over the cooking juices. Serve along with crusty bread to mop up the dressing.

Spiced Pan-Fried Red Mullet
with Mushroom Soup & Lime Cream

Serves 4

olive oil
2 red mullet, weighing 500–600g (1lb 2oz–1lb 5oz), scaled, gutted, filleted and pin-boned
sea salt and freshly ground black pepper
4 tablespoons extra virgin olive oil, to serve

For the seasoning mix
2 teaspoons coriander seeds
2 teaspoons cumin seeds

For the soup
olive oil, for cooking
1 onion, finely chopped
350g (12oz) button mushrooms, sliced
100ml (3½fl oz) double cream
400ml (14fl oz) full-fat milk
juice of 1 lime

For the lime cream
100ml (3½fl oz) double cream
100ml (3½fl oz) crème fraîche
zest and juice of 1 lime
2 teaspoons chopped tarragon

Pan-fried red mullet fillets are very simple to cook, just make sure you don't get the pan too hot. What you are after is a medium to hot pan and be patient! Also, before cooking, make sure you get the skin on the fillets nice and dry, as this will help it become lovely and golden. Mushroom soup is one of my favourite soups to make and eat. This recipe uses button mushrooms, but you can use any mushrooms. The touch of coriander seed, cumin and lime flavours elevate this recipe and help the marriage with the red mullet.

1. For the seasoning mix, grind together the coriander and cumin seeds in a mortar and pestle or spice grinder.

2. First, make the soup. Heat a little olive oil in a large saucepan, add the onion and cook over a medium heat for 1 minute, without colouring. Add the sliced mushrooms and cook, stirring now and again until they release their liquid and start to colour and roast in the pan; this should take about 10 minutes. Pour the cream and milk onto the mushrooms and season with a little salt and 2 teaspoons of the seasoning mix. Bring to the boil, then remove from the heat and tip the mixture into a blender. Add the lime juice and blend until smooth. Pass through a sieve and pour back into the pan. Taste, adjusting the seasoning if necessary.

3. To make the lime cream, whisk everything together and season to taste with salt and pepper. Now whisk until firm and chill in the refrigerator.

4. Meanwhile, reheat the soup and warm 4 bowls.

5. To cook the red mullet, drizzle some olive oil into a large nonstick frying pan. Season the red mullet with salt, pepper and 2 teaspoons of the seasoning mix and lay it skin-side down in the pan. Place over a medium-high heat and cook the fish for 2–3 minutes until the edges of the skin start to turn golden. Carefully turn the fish over, then take the pan off the heat and leave for about 30 seconds to finish cooking in the residual heat.

6. Share the soup among the bowls and place a fillet of red mullet in the centre. Finish with a spoonful of the lime cream and a drizzle of extra virgin olive oil.

Orange & Fennel Pan-Fried Grey Mullet
with Roasted Carrots & Carrot & Fennel Seed Vinaigrette

Serves 4

100g (3½oz) green beans (about 16 in total)
1 grey mullet, about 1.5kg (3lb 5oz), scaled, filleted and pin-boned, portioned into 4
2 teaspoons fennel seeds, toasted and ground
finely grated zest of 1 orange
olive oil
sea salt and freshly ground black pepper

For the carrot & fennel seed vinaigrette
200g (7oz) carrots, peeled and chopped
1 tablespoon pastis
2 tablespoons orange juice
1 teaspoon fennel seeds, toasted and ground
1 tablespoon cider vinegar
4 tablespoons extra virgin olive oil

For the roasted carrots
100g (3½oz) salted butter
2 teaspoons fennel seeds
4 carrots, peeled and halved lengthways
1 banana shallot, sliced
1 garlic clove, finely chopped
10 green olives, pitted and halved
50ml (2fl oz) cider vinegar
small handful of fennel herb, fennel fronds or carrot tops (optional)

When grey mullet is at its best, it's a fantastic fish for pan-frying. The skin on a grey mullet, when scaled with care and dried thoroughly, will reward you by becoming beautifully crisp. The natural oil that comes out as you carefully cook it is a point of difference from any other species and makes it unique. The carrot, fennel seed and olive combination in the rest of the dish complement that uniqueness perfectly.

1. To make the vinaigrette, place the chopped carrots, pastis, orange juice, fennel seeds and vinegar in a small blender and blitz finely, then transfer to a sieve lined with muslin set over a bowl and squeeze out as much juice as possible. Put 4 tablespoons of the juice into a bowl, whisk in the olive oil and season with salt to taste. Set aside.

2. Blanch the green beans in a pan of boiling water for 3 minutes, then drain and chill in the refrigerator.

3. Preheat the oven to 170°C Fan (375°F), Gas Mark 5.

4. For the roasted carrots and olives, place all the ingredients, except the fennel herb or fronds, into a roasting tray or dish. Season with salt and pepper and cook in the oven for a total of 30 minutes, stirring every 10 minutes. When the carrots are roasted, remove from the oven, add the fennel herb (if using) and mix well. Keep warm.

5. To cook the fish, season it with fennel seeds, orange zest, salt and pepper. Heat a nonstick pan over a medium heat and add a drizzle of olive oil. Once hot, place the fish skin-side down into the pan and cook gently for 4 minutes until the skin is golden. Turn the fish over and cook for 30 seconds, then turn off the heat. The residual heat will finish the cooking.

6. Warm 4 plates. Add the beans to the carrots and warm for 1 minute, then share the vegetables among the plates. Dress with the vinaigrette and place the fish on top, then serve.

Hot-Smoked Grey Mullet Pâté
with Rosemary Crackers & Beetroot Ketchup

Serves 4

300g (10½oz) grey mullet fillet, skinned and pin-boned
100g (3½oz) sea salt
50g (1¾oz) caster sugar
100ml (3½fl oz) white wine
4 sprigs of thyme, leaves picked
oak chips

For the rosemary crackers
90g (3¼oz) unsalted butter
2 teaspoons finely chopped rosemary leaves
1 tablespoon baking powder
1 teaspoon sea salt
175g (6oz) wholemeal flour
175g (6oz) plain flour
140ml (4½fl oz) water

For the beetroot ketchup
500g (1lb 2oz) raw beetroot, peeled
2 shallots, finely chopped
2 Granny Smith apples, peeled and chopped
250ml (9fl oz) cider vinegar
1 red chilli, deseeded and chopped
2 cloves
50g (1¾oz) caster sugar
1 litre (1¾ pints) good apple juice

For the pâté
100g (3½oz) full-fat Greek yogurt
100g (3½oz) full-fat cream cheese
zest and juice of 1 orange
1 tablespoon creamed horseradish
2 tablespoons chopped flat-leaf parsley leaves
sea salt and freshly ground black pepper

Hot-smoking is a nice way to cook grey mullet. The oiliness of the fish mingles so well with the smoke. I cure my smoked fish with wine and herbs first, but you could just salt the fish. If you are not a fan of smoke, or you don't have a hot smoker, you can cure the fish and bake it in the oven for the same time; it will still be delicious. The beetroot ketchup is great with the pâté, and with lots of other things too, so maybe make more, it's worth it!

1. To cure the mullet, mix together the salt, sugar, white wine and thyme. Place the fish in a container and pour the salt mixture all over it. Cover and chill in the refrigerator for 3 hours, turning every hour.

2. Wash the salt mixture off the fish in cold water, then pat dry. Keep in the refrigerator until you are ready to cook.

3. To make the crackers, combine all the ingredients in a mixer until a dough forms. Transfer to a bowl, cover with a tea towel and refrigerate for 1 hour.

4. Preheat the oven to 180°C Fan (400°F), Gas Mark 6.

5. Cut the dough in half and roll out as thinly as possible (I find using a pasta machine the best way to do this), then cut into your desired shapes (I like triangles). Place on a nonstick baking sheet and bake for 12 minutes. Cool on a wire rack and store in an airtight container until required.

6. To make the ketchup, place everything into a pan and simmer for 1 hour, stirring occasionally. When the liquid has reduced and the mixture starts to catch, reduce the heat to the lowest possible and cook for another 10 minutes. Transfer everything to a food processor and blitz until smooth. Pass the mixture through a fine sieve and allow the ketchup to cool. Keep refrigerated for up to 2 weeks.

7. Set up your hot smoker with the oak chips and get it smoking. Place the cured fish on the smoking rack and cook for 8 minutes. Remove the heat source and leave for another 4 minutes, then remove the fish from the smoker and leave to cool.

8. To make the pâté, flake the cured mullet into a bowl and add the yogurt, cream cheese, orange zest and juice, horseradish and parsley. Give everything a good mix, then taste and season as desired. Keep in the refrigerator if making in advance, but it's nicer served straight away.

9. To serve, place the pâté in a bowl on a sharing platter with the ketchup and crackers on the side.

Gin-Cured Trout
with Juniper-Pickled Cucumber & Gin Salad Cream

Serves 4

1 side of farmed trout, weighing 600g (1lb 5oz)

For the cure
250g (9oz) sea salt
250g (9oz) caster sugar
150ml (5fl oz) gin

For the juniper-pickled cucumber
100ml (3½fl oz) white wine vinegar
1 shallot, finely chopped
1 green chilli, deseeded and finely chopped
50g (1¾oz) caster sugar
6 juniper berries, crushed
a pinch of sea salt
1 cucumber, peeled and cut into matchsticks

For the gin salad cream
2 egg yolks
2 teaspoons Dijon mustard
½ teaspoon caster sugar
2 tablespoons lemon juice
3 tablespoons gin
200ml (7fl oz) olive oil
50ml (2fl oz) double cream
sea salt

For the dressing
4 tablespoons extra virgin olive oil
4 teaspoons chopped sweet cicely, plus a few fancy leaves for garnish (alternatively, use tarragon or chervil)
sea salt and freshly ground black pepper

The trout we use comes to us fresh from a farm that is 15 miles away in Boscastle. It's a lovely farmed fish and is produced as ethically as possible. This dish is perfect for a dinner party. All the work is done in advance, so all you need to do is plate up.

1. For the cure, put the salt and sugar in a bowl and mix. Lay the trout on a tray and sprinkle evenly with the salt-sugar mixture, then pour over the gin and turn the fish over a few times to ensure it is coated all over. Place in the refrigerator to cure for 4 hours, turning every hour.

2. Wash the cure off the fish with cold water and pat dry with kitchen paper. Wrap the fish tightly in clingfilm and place back in the refrigerator for 1 hour to firm up. (At this stage, you can freeze the fish for up to a month.)

3. To pickle the cucumber, put all the ingredients except the cucumber into a pan and bring to a simmer. Remove from the heat and leave to cool fully. Once cold, add the cucumber and leave for 1 hour to do its magic.

4. To make the salad cream, whisk the egg yolks, mustard, sugar, lemon juice and gin together in a bowl for 1 minute, then gradually whisk in the oil, a little at a time, until fully incorporated. To finish, slowly whisk in the cream and season with salt to taste. Cover and refrigerate until required.

5. For the dressing, drain off three-quarters of the liquor from the cucumber and mix with the olive oil, chopped sweet cicely and seasoning.

6. To serve, slice the cured trout into 1cm (½ inch) thick pieces and divide among 4 plates. Dot the salad cream equally on each plate and lay some pickled cucumber over the fish. Finish with the dressing and some sweet cicely leaves.

Pan-Fried Trout on Baked Aubergine
with Olive Tapenade & Lemon Mayonnaise Sauce

Serves 4

2 tablespoons olive oil
4 x 120–140g (4–5oz) trout fillet portions
1 teaspoon thyme leaves, plus extra to garnish
sea salt and freshly ground black pepper
200g (7oz) green beans, trimmed, to serve

For the rosemary & lemon oil
zest of 1 lemon
400ml (14fl oz) olive oil
2 rosemary sprigs, tender leaves picked

For the aubergine
2 aubergines
2 garlic cloves, chopped
3 tablespoons extra virgin olive oil
zest and juice of 1 lemon

For the tapenade
200g (7oz) mixed pitted black and green olives
1 tablespoon capers in brine or salt
1 garlic clove, finely chopped
1 teaspoon finely chopped thyme leaves
2 tablespoons extra virgin olive oil

For the lemon mayonnaise sauce
2 egg yolks
1 teaspoon English mustard
zest and juice of 1 lemon
300ml (10fl oz) olive oil
3½ tablespoons double cream
100ml (3½fl oz) fish stock

Pan-fried trout with a crispy skin is a delightful thing. It's a good, forgiving fish that is perfect just slightly pink in the middle. Make sure you cook the fish gently and be patient. Don't let the pan get too hot or you will scorch the edges and they will taste dry. The aubergine and olive combination works so well here, because the oily nature of trout loves sunshine flavours.

1. For the rosemary and lemon oil, put the lemon zest into a blender with the oil and rosemary leaves and blitz for 2 minutes. Pour the oil mixture into a jug and leave to infuse and settle for 24 hours. Strain the oil into a sterilized bottle, then keep in the refrigerator. Use within a month.

2. Preheat the grill to its hottest setting.

3. Pierce each aubergine a few times with a small, sharp knife, then place on a grill tray and grill, turning every 3–4 minutes, until each one is burnt all over and starting to collapse. This will take about 35 minutes. When the aubergines are cooked, leave them to cool until you can handle them, then slice in half and scoop out the flesh onto a chopping board. Don't worry if you get a few black bits in the mix. Add the garlic, olive oil and lemon zest and juice, then chop together. Taste and adjust the seasoning.

4. For the tapenade, place all the ingredients in a small food processor and blitz until well blended but not super-fine; keep it a little chunky. Taste and season with salt and pepper.

5. For the mayonnaise sauce, whisk the egg yolks with the mustard, lemon zest and juice, then slowly add the oil, drop by drop to begin with. As the mixture begins to thicken, add the rest of the oil in a steady stream, whisking constantly until emulsified. Stir the cream into the mayonnaise, then thin down with the fish stock. Season to taste. Keep cool until ready to serve.

6. Simmer the beans in a pan of salted water for 3 minutes, then drain and set aside. Heat a nonstick pan over a medium heat and drizzle in the oil. Season the trout with salt, pepper and thyme leaves. Place the fish into the pan skin-side down and cook for 3 minutes until the skin is golden. While this is cooking, warm up your sauce (don't boil it) and the aubergine. Flip the fish over carefully, then remove the pan from the heat.

7. Place the green beans into the fish pan to warm through.

8. Spoon the aubergine in the centre of 4 plates. Lay the beans next to it and place the fish on top. Spoon the sauce around, then add a spoonful of the tapenade on top of the fish. Drizzle with the rosemary and lemon oil to finish.

4

Oily fish

Anchovies, Bluefin Tuna, Herring, Mackerel, Pilchards/Sardines, Smoked Fish

Anchovies

Anchovies are fantastic fish, the basis of so many international dishes. They're incredible simply grilled when fresh, but when preserved they become a flavour bomb with magical abilities to take something from delicious and transform it to outrageously delicious.

A resilient species, anchovies can sustain relatively high levels of fishing pressure. In the Bay of Biscay in the early 2000s, fishing for anchovies was put on hold due to the decline in stocks. This was successful and stocks have come back stronger and are seemingly being monitored in a more sustainable way.

They're related to herrings and a have a short life of about 3 years. They swim in large shoals feeding on plankton and small fish larvae. Found mainly around the Mediterranean and off the coasts of Spain, Portugal and France, they swim nearer the sea surface in the summer months and go deeper in the winter.

The anchovies I use are caught by ring netters at the same time as they are targeting herring and sardines, but they are also caught using pelagic trawling and purse seine netting, none of which have an impact on the seabed.

Notes
The anchovies I buy travel up from the south of the Atlantic and in the summer are around the Bay of Biscay, then they swim past the English Channel and into the Celtic Sea.

The main spawning happens April–November in estuaries and saltwater lakes.

Best time to eat
Late summer and early autumn.

Cooking & serving
- My favourite ways to eat anchovies are: salted anchovies, simply on toast with butter; or boquerones (anchovies marinated in oil and vinegar) in a tomato salad.

- It's quite rare to see them fresh, but if you do, buy them and simply cook them under a hot grill.

- Preserved anchovies are readily available and should always be in your kitchen cupboard ready for action.

Bluefin Tuna

In the UK, tuna has been around in good numbers for a while now, but it wasn't until a few years ago that the evidence of growing numbers was becoming clear and consistent. Bluefin tuna fishing could genuinely become a brilliant, sustainable fishery, creating jobs and futures for young fisherfolk. For that reason, it's worth going steady and not decimating the stocks.

There are two main stocks of tuna in the Atlantic that swim in different areas and mature at different times: the eastern stock is made of up fish that swim in the Mediterranean and up the east Atlantic coast; the west Atlantic stock swim in the Gulf of Mexico and up the west Atlantic coast. They are same species, but maturity happens at different rates. The eastern stock fish that I see mature at 25kg (55lb), which is roughly 4 years old, but western stock matures at 145kg (320lb) and 9 years old. Northern Atlantic bluefin tuna can grow as big as 600kg (1,323lb) and live to 40 years old! Tuna is a serious predator, and when they are around in our oceans the other fish know about it.

When it comes to sustainability, the fish have slightly different guidelines according to the location of each stock. Current information collected on bluefin tuna points towards an increase in stocks, which is incredible considering they almost collapsed in the 1980s and '90s. The importance of the fishery is massive. It is imperative we look after them – if we do, there will be a great fishery for generations to come.

Having bluefin tuna in UK waters is probably the most exciting development since I've been cooking fish. Quite simply, it's an incredible species with so much potential, and when creating new dishes it gives so many different options.

Notes
At the time of writing, the Marine Management Organization has granted 15 licences for catching blue-fin tuna in the UK. They must only be caught by rod and line with lures, and according to a closely monitored system that ensures the fisherman report what they've caught, when and where, recording as much information as possible. The only other way blue-fin tuna can be landed is by the ring-netters which catch oily fish, such as herring and sardines. They are allowed 1 fish per day, per trip, as bycatch.

I tend to buy fish that weigh between 70–100kg (154–220lb), but you can get 200kg (440lb) or more – I wouldn't have a chopping board big enough for a fish like that, and often these bigger fish are damaged due to the difficulty in handling them.

Best time to eat
July–December.

Cooking & serving
- Due to its size, the preparation of bluefin tuna is specialist, and you can buy it in different cuts. I look at the fish as I would if I were breaking down an animal: loins, tail, belly, head, offal, etc.

- If planning to eat bluefin tuna raw, ask for a cut from the top part of the main loin fillet, closest to the spine. Essentially, the meat further inside the fillet is more tender, and as you go closer to the skin it gets tougher. For cooking, ask for fillet closer to the tail (but not the tail itself).

Herring

Herring is, unfortunately, a species that has been overfished for years – I would avoid them from large suppliers. It's such a shame, because herring is one of my favourite species to use on menus and I adore them. However, as I have seen with other species, if you leave them alone for a while, they can come back. For this reason, I've not included any specific recipes for them in this book.

Herring swim in large shoals of similar age, and spawn in shallow waters on an annual cycle. They're caught using specially designed herring ring nets which take the majority of the shoal. Due to overfishing, I'd say unless you find a small fisherman who has some, leave them alone.

Notes
Nicknamed 'silver darlings', you'd understand why if you saw them in the sea or caught one; they sparkle and shimmer in the water in a unique and remarkable way.

Best time to eat
Fresh herring can be eaten all year, but are at their best through the autumn.

Cooking & serving
- The best size herring to use are 400–500g (14oz–1lb 2oz).

- Oil-rich, this small fish is delicious and versatile.

- In my opinion, it must be eaten very fresh, ideally as soon as it's landed.

- Herring is also great preserved or smoked (see page 172), most famously pickled as rollmops or smoked as kippers.

- I'm partial to the creamy roe, or 'milts', on toast.

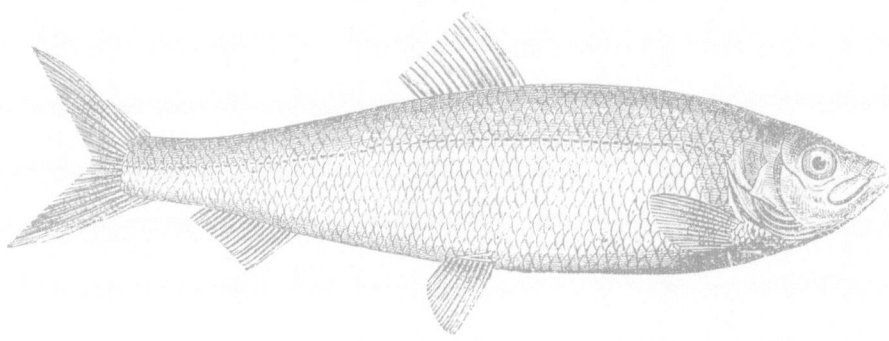

Mackerel

Mackerel is my favourite fish and I love nothing more than catching, cooking and eating it. I have several favourite ways of preparing mackerel, which are very different, but that just shows how versatile it is. Ideally, for me, a freshly caught mackerel screams out to be cooked on the beach over coals the moment it is landed, and eaten there and then!

Beautiful to look at, due to its fantastic markings, and impressive in the sea – mackerel is closely related to tuna. Basically, it's a speed machine; it zooms through the water at a great pace in large shoals, hunting down small fry during the summer. When winter comes, it's off to the deep to virtually hibernate and wait until things warm up again.

Mackerel mature at about 3 years old, increasing in size rapidly and piling on weight during the first and second year. When fishing, line-caught with feathers offers the best quality. Currently, the minimum landing size is 20cm (8 inches), but the fish mature at 28cm (11 inches), so perhaps this should be increased to allow as many as possible to get to spawning age? Seems sensible to me.

Notes
Mackerel is amazingly good for you, particularly as it's packed with beneficial omega-3 fatty acids.

Best time to eat
July–March.

Cooking & serving

- Freshness is key with mackerel, you really need to cook and eat it within a few hours of it being caught.

- When buying, look for hand-line-caught fish – these are the best quality and most sustainable choice due to the low-impact fishing method.

- When very fresh, it's fantastic raw (see page 163), but you'll need to be delicate with your touch when preparing it, because the flesh is fragile.

- When grilled over wood or coals, whole or butterflied, the fat in the fish just does something magical with the live fire and gives lovely, crispy skin (see page 171).

- If mackerel has been hanging around for a couple of days, I'd opt to cure and smoke it instead (see pages 172).

Oily fish

Pilchards/Sardines

'Sardine' or 'pilchard', which should it be? In fact, these are the same fish – it's the age and size that determines the name. After 2 years, a sardine becomes known as a pilchard and can go on to live well into double figures if it avoids its many predators. They're an exciting species that are caught together with anchovies; if you see them, buy them. Sardine and pilchard stocks are presently healthy and are checked by an annual survey to ensure stocks stay strong.

A migratory fish, pilchards/sardines travel according to the temperature of the sea and availability of food, arriving off our shores from summer until early winter when they swim off to warmer waters. Caught using ring nets, a modern take on a purse seine net, the fish are drawn in as the net is pulled in; once alongside the boat, they are scooped into iced holds to keep the quality as high as possible.

Notes

In Cornwall, we now call pilchards 'Cornish sardines', because it helps them sell on menus. For some reason, the public have an issue with the word 'pilchard', but don't mind 'sardine'! It beats me, but if it helps these healthy, tasty little fish sell, then I'm all for it.

No recipes are included in this book as, at the time of writing, no pilchards/sardines had arrived in Cornish waters!

Best time to eat

Summer and through until early winter.

Cooking & serving

- 150–200g (5½–7oz) is a good size for eating.

- Rich in omega-3 fatty acids, they're a very healthy fish to eat. As an added bonus, the bones in sardines are so small and unnoticeable that you can eat them, too.

- My favourite way to eat sardines is straight off the barbecue, butterflied or whole.

- They are also lovely cured and pickled (see page 167).

Smoked fish

I adore good-quality smoked fish and sometimes smoke it myself. The words 'smoked fish' can conjure for me images of those nasty vacuum-packed smoked kippers with the strange star-shaped butter pat on top, or unnaturally bright yellow smoked haddock with a definite whiff of fish that's past its best! However, nowadays, even if home-smoking isn't an option, you can buy good-quality smoked fish.

Obviously, the calibre of a smoked fish is largely determined by the freshness and quality of the original catch, but the curing process plays a major role as well. Back in the old days, smoking was a way of preserving your catch and making it go further through the year. Now, smoked fish is enjoyed purely for its special flavour, and there's a lot of work involved in getting a top-quality product which also brings a higher price tag.

If possible, source your smoked fish from the excellent artisan smokeries dotted around the country. Or consider investing in your own hot or cold smoker and experiment with different cures and woods for smoking. Expect a degree of trial and error to begin with; in time, you'll find you can successfully smoke pretty much anything you buy or catch yourself.

So, what is the difference between hot- and cold-smoked fish? With cold smoking, the temperature barely reaches 25°C (77°F). The curing process of salting the fish draws out excess moisture and firms up the flesh, then the smoking dries the fish and imparts flavour, but the fish remains raw. Hot smoking actually cooks the fish and could be described as roasting with the addition of smoky aromas. The pre-salting or brining is much less, as the intention is to eat the fish straight away, unlike cold-smoked fish, which keeps for longer. Hot smoking is more suited to oily fish, as white fish are inclined to dry out with the higher temperature, but with skill it can be done.

My favourite smoked fish is smoked mackerel. It is such a great convenience food and the oiliness of the mackerel works well and stops the fish drying out.

If you find a good smokehouse, I would encourage you to support it. It isn't easy to make a living from smoking fish and this ancient tradition needs to be protected. A life without smoked haddock and a poached egg would be a sad life!

Best time to eat

Standard smoked fish is available all year around.

Cooking & serving

- For a special treat, seek out some top-grade, small artisanal smokers who buy the fish when it's bang in season so that the important characteristics, such as oil levels and firmness of fillet, are just right. The difference is incredible and an art in itself.

- Smoked fish is one of the best convenience foods ever created, I think. Smoked mackerel is perhaps the best example: you don't even have to cook it, put it straight into a salad or flake it on to a jacket potato, delicious!

- My favourite ways to use smoked fish are: smoked mackerel – beetroot and horseradish salad; smoked haddock – kedgeree; smoked trout – with scrambled eggs; smoked mussels – breaded and deep-fried.

Serves 4 as a side

Anchovies with Crispy Potato Wedges
with Lemon & Garlic Crème Fraîche

Boquerones are fresh, white anchovy fillets that are marinated in olive oil and vinegar. I can't get enough of them, eating them like sweets! Traditionally, in Spain, they are served as tapas and usually finished with garlic and parsley. With that in mind, and with my love of chips, this side dish was born. A simply grilled fillet of white fish with a bowl of these anchovy potatoes and a green salad is my idea of heaven. My take on dirty fries!

4 large baking potatoes
12 garlic cloves, separated; 1 clove finely chopped, the rest left with skins on
½ tablespoon olive oil
zest and juice of 1 lemon
5 tablespoons full-fat crème fraîche
sunflower oil, for deep-frying
24 boquerones (anchovies in vinegar)
3 tablespoons finely sliced flat-leaf parsley
sea salt and freshly ground black pepper

1. Preheat your oven to 200°C Fan (425°F), Gas Mark 7.

2. Cook the baking potatoes for 1½ hours, turning them at the halfway point.

3. Meanwhile, place the skin-on garlic cloves on a large piece of foil. Season with salt and the olive oil, then scrunch the foil over to make a bag. Place into the oven for 15 minutes, then remove and set aside.

4. In a small serving bowl, mix the lemon zest and juice with the crème fraîche and chopped garlic, then season with salt and pepper. Set aside in the refrigerator.

5. When the potatoes are cooked, cool slightly and cut into fat wedges.

6. Heat a deep-fat fryer to 180°C (350°F) or heat some sunflower oil in a deep, heavy-based pan (not filling more than two-thirds full). Fry the potato wedges for 3–4 minutes until crisp and golden. Drain on kitchen paper and season with salt and pepper.

7. Add the baked garlic cloves to the fryer and cook for just 30 seconds, then remove and drain on kitchen paper.

8. Divide the potato wedges among 4 plates or bowls and drape the anchovies over them. Scatter over the fried garlic and sliced parsley. Serve hot, with the cold lemony crème fraîche alongside.

Raw Tuna in Chilled Cucumber, Mint & Pea Soup

Serves 4 as a starter

300g (10½oz) bluefin tuna, diced
sea salt and freshly ground black pepper

For the soup
300g (10½oz) cucumber, peeled and sliced
10g (¼oz) mint leaves, chopped
10g (¼oz) tarragon leaves, chopped
100g (3½oz) fresh peas, podded
100g (3½oz) spinach, washed and coarse stems removed
1 green chilli, deseeded and chopped
50g (1¾oz) whole almonds, roasted
60g (2¼oz) full-fat Greek yogurt
100g (3½oz) stale white bread, crusts removed
2 tablespoons white wine vinegar
1 garlic clove, sliced
50ml (2fl oz) olive oil
200ml (7fl oz) water

To serve
4 tablespoons Mint Oil (see page 251)
1 tablespoon chopped mint leaves
1 tablespoon chopped tarragon leaves
4 tablespoons fresh peas, podded and cooked
½ cucumber, peeled, deseeded and finely chopped to the size of the peas
juice of 1 lime

This is a simple recipe that works well with the rich tuna. The combination of flavours in this soup scream 'summer' to me and are so refreshing on a hot day. I use 'fatty tuna' – meat from the belly, which is the fattiest part. This is a great dish for a party as everything can be done in advance, with the exception of a bit of mixing at the end. If you can't get hold of tuna, use raw hand-dived scallops or cooked crab meat in the same way – I've served both before.

1. For best results, mix all the ingredients for the soup the day before serving and leave them to mingle and get to know one another in a bowl. Cover and refrigerate.
2. The next day, place all the soup ingredients in a blender or food processor and blend for 2 minutes until smooth. Chill the soup for a minimum of 2 hours.
3. To prepare the tuna, place it in a bowl with 2 tablespoons of the mint oil and half of the chopped herbs, and season with salt and pepper to taste. Spoon the mixture equally into 4 chilled bowls.
4. Mix the remaining mint oil and herbs with the peas and cucumber in a bowl and add the lime juice. Adjust the seasoning.
5. Taste the soup again now that it's chilled and adjust the seasoning adding salt and pepper if needed – you want it to be well balanced. Pour the soup into each bowl around the tuna. Finish with a spoonful of the peas and cucumber and serve immediately, chilled.

Griddled Tuna Belly
with Aubergine Purée, & Tomato, Olive & Cumin Dressing

Serves 4

400g (14oz) tuna belly, cut into 4 equal pieces
olive oil
sea salt and freshly ground black pepper

For the aubergine purée
2 aubergines
100g (3½oz) smoked almonds
juice of 1 lemon
1 teaspoon ground cumin
1 garlic clove, finely chopped
1 tablespoon extra virgin olive oil
1 tablespoon toasted sesame oil

For the rub
2 teaspoons cumin seeds, toasted and ground
2 teaspoons pink peppercorns, toasted and ground
4 teaspoons chopped fresh oregano leaves
4 teaspoons sea salt

For the dressing
4 tablespoons extra virgin olive oil
1 teaspoon cumin seeds
1 teaspoon thyme leaves
2 ripe tomatoes, peeled, deseeded and chopped
12 black olives, pitted and sliced
1 tablespoon small capers in brine, drained
2 tablespoons sherry vinegar
2 tablespoons shredded coriander leaves
20 mint leaves, shredded
sea salt

When a whole bluefin tuna arrives in the kitchen, it really is a special occasion. The belly is always the part everyone is excited to see – I think it's the cross-section of fat that amazes when seeing it prepped. We've found that tuna belly benefits from a good searing on each side of the slice, which intensifies the uniqueness of the tuna flavour. In this recipe, the mixture of Mediterranean ingredients really brings out the best of the tuna belly. The aubergine purée is delicious, too.

1. To prepare the aubergine purée, heat the grill to its highest setting. Pierce the skins of the aubergines in a few places and place them on a grill tray. Grill, turning them every few minutes, until they are soft, almost collapsing, and the skins have blackened. Allow to cool for a minute or so, then cut them in half lengthways and scoop out the flesh.

2. Blitz the aubergine flesh in a food processor with the smoked almonds, lemon juice, cumin and garlic, then add the olive and sesame oils and season with salt and pepper. Blend until smooth. Transfer the aubergine purée to a bowl and allow it to cool. Cover and refrigerate if you are not using it straight away.

3. To make the rub, mix all the ingredients together.

4. To get the tuna ready for cooking, take it out of the refrigerator about 30 minutes before to bring it to room temperature and season with 4 teaspoons of the rub.

5. For the dressing, warm the extra virgin olive oil in a pan over a low heat along with the cumin seeds and thyme. Keep warm while you cook the fish.

6. Heat a large nonstick griddle pan over a high heat. Once hot, add a good drizzle of olive oil. Carefully place the tuna in the pan and cook for 1 minute on each side.

7. While the fish is cooking, add the tomatoes, olives, capers, vinegar and a little salt to the dressing.

8. Place the tuna on 4 warmed plates with a spoonful of aubergine purée alongside. Stir the shredded coriander and mint through the tomato and olive dressing and spoon it on top of the fish and around the plates. Serve immediately.

Tuna Fishballs in Tomato Sauce
with Pesto & Parmesan

Serves 4

200g (7oz) lean tuna trimmings
200g (7oz) fatty tuna (belly) trimmings
2 shallots, finely chopped
2 teaspoons garlic powder
1 teaspoon ground cumin
1 teaspoon ground coriander
1 tablespoon chopped thyme leaves
1 egg, beaten
100g (3½oz) breadcrumbs
olive oil
sea salt and freshly ground black pepper

For the pesto
1 tablespoon pine nuts
1 garlic clove, finely chopped
4 tablespoons extra virgin olive oil
1 bunch of basil
1 tablespoon grated Parmesan

For the tomato sauce
2 tablespoons olive oil
2 small shallots, chopped
3 garlic cloves, finely chopped
6 salted anchovy fillets in oil, drained
2 tender rosemary sprigs, leaves picked and chopped
4 teaspoons caster sugar
100ml (3½fl oz) sherry vinegar
500g (1lb 2oz) canned tomatoes
500ml (18fl oz) tomato passata
20 basil leaves, sliced
2 tablespoons chopped flat-leaf parsley leaves

To serve
50g (1¾oz) Parmesan, for grating
4 tablespoons extra virgin olive oil

When you buy a whole tuna, it's the same as buying a whole animal – you want to, and should, use it all. You're left with a surprising amount of what you could call 'top-grade fish trimmings'. There's nothing wrong with them apart from being trimmings, the quality is still as good as the prime cuts. I wanted to come up with a few dishes to use these trimmings. This is one of them and it's absolutely delicious and the perfect way to do that. Actually, it's my longstanding head chef Tim Barnes' recipe. My role was to give him the idea… and eat it (someone has to do the tough jobs)! Tim tinkered with the recipe for a while until he got it spot on and now it's one of my favourite ways to eat tuna. These fishballs are also great served like tapas or folded through pasta.

1. To make the tuna fishballs, first mince or chop the tuna finely, then mix it with the shallots, spices, thyme, egg and breadcrumbs in a bowl. Season with salt and pepper and mix again. Fry off a little piece of the mixture in an oiled pan and taste, then adjust the seasoning of the mixture if necessary.

2. Using your hands, shape the mixture into even golf ball-sized balls. Place on a tray in the refrigerator to rest.

3. To make the pesto, gently cook the pine nuts and garlic in a pan with the olive oil over a medium heat until golden, then cool. When the mixture is cold, transfer to a food processor along with the basil and blend for 30 seconds. Scrape down the sides of the food processor, add the Parmesan and season. Blitz for 30 seconds, then transfer to a container and refrigerate until required.

4. Meanwhile, make the tomato sauce. Heat a large frying pan or flameproof casserole dish over a medium heat and add the olive oil. Once hot, add the shallots and cook for 4–5 minutes until they become translucent. Add the garlic, anchovies and rosemary and cook for 2 minutes, then add the sugar and sherry vinegar and cook for another 2 minutes. Pour in the tomatoes and passata, adding a good pinch of salt. Simmer for 20 minutes.

5. Blitz the tomato sauce with a hand blender or in a food processor, then pass it through a sieve into a pan and keep warm.

6. Heat a little olive oil in a nonstick frying pan and fry the tuna fishballs over a medium heat for 8–10 minutes, turning every 2 minutes.

7. Warm the sauce for 1 minute and add the basil and parsley. Taste for seasoning and adjust if necessary.

8. Divide the sauce and fishballs among 4 bowls and finish with the pesto. Grate over the Parmesan and drizzle with extra virgin olive oil, then serve.

Serves 4 as a starter

Poached Tuna & Pickled Shallots on Toast
with Green Beans & Black Olive Mayonnaise

400g (14oz) bluefin tuna, prime or trimmings
500ml (18fl oz) water
2 teaspoons cider vinegar
50ml (2fl oz) white wine vinegar
sea salt and freshly ground black pepper

For the black olive mayonnaise
2 egg yolks
1 teaspoon English mustard
20 black olives, pitted and finely chopped
1 garlic clove, finely chopped
300ml (10fl oz) olive oil

For the pickled shallots
2 tablespoons olive oil
2 banana shallots, finely sliced
2 sprigs of thyme, leaves picked and chopped
1 teaspoon caster sugar
75ml (2½fl oz) sherry vinegar

To serve
160g (5¾oz) green beans, trimmed
extra virgin olive oil
2 tablespoons finely chopped chives
1 tablespoon finely chopped tarragon leaves
4 slices of focaccia

Another dish that was created from buying whole bluefin tuna and using the trimmings. We waste nothing! At home, I doubt you'll be buying whole bluefin tuna, but not to worry – a lovely piece of loin or steaks will work well with this dish. I really enjoy eating dishes like this, lots of different textures and delightful flavours that work together so well. You could substitute poached trout or even a grilled mackerel fillet.

1. To make the mayonnaise, place all the ingredients apart from the oil into a food processor. Blend for 30 seconds, then stop and scrape down the sides of the processor bowl. Continue to blend and slowly add the oil in a steady stream until the mayonnaise thickens. Season with salt and pepper and blend for 10 seconds, then transfer to a bowl and place in the refrigerator until ready to serve.

2. For the shallots, heat a frying pan over a medium heat and add the oil. Once hot, add the shallots and cook for 5 minutes without colouring, stirring occasionally. When the shallots are softened and collapsing, add the thyme, sugar and vinegar and season with salt and pepper, then reduce the heat and cook for 5 minutes. Remove from the heat and leave to cool.

3. Bring a pan of salted water to the boil and have ready a bowl of ice-cold water. Blanch the beans for 2 minutes, then drain and plunge into the iced water. When they are cold, drain and set aside until ready to serve.

4. To cook the tuna, combine the measured water, vinegars and 2 teaspoons of salt in a pan and bring to a simmer. Season the tuna well, then lower it into the pan and poach for 2 minutes. Remove from the liquid and allow the tuna to cool.

5. When cool enough to handle, carefully slice or flake the tuna and dress with extra virgin olive oil, salt, pepper, the chives and tarragon.

6. To finish the dish, heat a griddle pan. Once hot, oil the focaccia slices and griddle until well-coloured. Dress the beans with extra virgin olive oil and salt and pepper, mixing well. Take 4 plates and place a slice of grilled focaccia on each one. Drizzle the bread with more extra virgin olive oil and a sprinkle of salt. Top with the beans, then add the tuna. Finish with the shallots and a dollop, or fancy drizzle, of the mayonnaise. Serve at room temperature.

Mackerel Tartare
with Beetroot & Apple

Serves 4 as a starter

2 very fresh large mackerel, gutted, filleted, pin-boned and skinned
½ shallot, finely chopped
1 green apple (any acidic variety), peeled and diced
1 tablespoon small capers in brine
1 tablespoon chopped tarragon leaves
1 tablespoon cider vinegar
sea salt and freshly ground black pepper

For the beetroot
2 large beetroot, washed
100ml (3½fl oz) cider vinegar
2 sprigs of tarragon
a drizzle of extra virgin olive oil
½ shallot, finely chopped

To serve
6 tablespoons extra virgin olive oil
2 handfuls of watercress, washed

If you fancy giving a raw dish a go at home, this one is a great place to start. The hardest part will be getting the mackerel at its best, but – with prior warning – a good fishmonger should be able to get you some.
If not, this dish would work well with bass or bream. If you don't happen to be a beetroot lover you can substitute it for fennel or cucumber.

1. To cook the beetroot, place in a saucepan and cover with water. Add the vinegar, tarragon and 2 teaspoons of salt, then bring to a simmer and cook for 30–40 minutes until tender. Insert a small knife into the beetroot to see if it's cooked. Leave to cool in the water.

2. When cool enough to handle, remove the skin and cut 4 thin slices from one beetroot. Finely chop the rest. Lay the slices out on a tray, season with salt and pepper then drizzle with the extra virgin olive oil. Leave to cool completely.

3. For the tartare, cut the mackerel fillets lengthways, then cut into rough dice. Place all the fish in a bowl with the shallot, apple, capers and tarragon. Season with salt, pepper and the vinegar. Mix well, but with a light touch.

4. To serve, take 4 cold plates and place a slice of beetroot on each. Share the mackerel tartare alongside. Mix the chopped beetroot with the shallot and the 6 tablespoons of extra virgin olive oil, then add to the plates with some watercress.

Oily fish

Mackerel Pickled in Pastis
with Pickled Rhubarb & Orange Dressing

Serves 4 as a starter

1 red onion, sliced
2 garlic cloves, crushed
½ teaspoon chilli flakes
10 fennel seeds, crushed
2 bay leaves
300ml (10fl oz) white wine vinegar
100ml (3½fl oz) Pastis
200g (7oz) caster sugar
zest of 1 orange
4 very fresh mackerel, gutted and filleted
sea salt
chervil or tarragon leaves, to garnish (optional)

For the pickled rhubarb
75ml (2½fl oz) white wine
4 teaspoons pastis
75ml (2½fl oz) white wine vinegar
50g (1¾oz) caster sugar
75ml (2½fl oz) water
1 teaspoon fennel seeds
160g (5¾oz) rhubarb, peeled and thinly sliced

For the dressing
100ml (3½fl oz) extra virgin olive oil
1 orange, peeled and segmented

As soon as I know we can get some great-quality mackerel, we bring out our pickled mackerel recipes. Pickled or soused fish can strike fear into the hearts of some people, maybe because they have had bad experiences in the past. Fear not, follow this recipe and you'll have a whole new excitement for pickled fish! You'll need to pickle the mackerel the day before you want to serve this dish.

1. Put the red onion, garlic, chilli flakes, fennel seeds and bay leaves into a saucepan. Add the vinegar, pastis, sugar and orange zest and bring to a simmer for 2 minutes, then add 4 teaspoons of salt. Remove from the heat and allow to cool.

2. Meanwhile, lay the mackerel fillets side-by-side in a dish that is big enough to hold them snugly and contain the pickling liquor. Add salt to the fillets, as if you are seasoning them before cooking. Leave in the refrigerator for 1 hour.

3. Once chilled, wash the mackerel fillets in ice-cold water and pat dry. Pour the cooled pickling liquor over the mackerel fillets and cover with clingfilm, pushing the fish down to keep them submerged. Place in the refrigerator and leave for 24 hours before eating.

4. For the pickled rhubarb, pour the wine into a large pan with the pastis, vinegar, sugar, measured water, fennel seeds and a pinch of salt, and bring to a simmer. Put the rhubarb in a suitable container and pour the pickling liquor over. Submerge the rhubarb in the liquid and leave to cool.

5. When ready to serve, remove the pickled fish from the refrigerator. Discard the pickling liquor but reserve the onions.

6. Measure 50ml (2fl oz) of the rhubarb pickling liquor to make a dressing and mix it with the red onion slices from the fish pickling liquor, then add the extra virgin olive oil and orange segments. Season with salt to taste.

7. Slice the mackerel fillets into bite-sized pieces and arrange on a serving platter with the rhubarb. Spoon over the orange and red onion dressing, then garnish with chervil or tarragon leaves if using. Serve with sourdough and salted butter.

Salt & Vinegar-Cured Mackerel
with Sesame Sauce

Serves 4 as a starter

2 large mackerel, gutted, filleted and pin-boned
4 tablespoons sea salt

For the vinegar cure
300ml (10fl oz) rice wine vinegar
150ml (5fl oz) water
50g (1¾oz) caster sugar

For the sesame sauce
1 tablespoon caster sugar
3 tablespoons water
50g (1¾oz) fresh root ginger, grated
2 tablespoons dark soy sauce, or to taste
4 teaspoons lime juice
4 tablespoons sesame paste or tahini
2 teaspoons sesame oil

To serve
1 cucumber, peeled, halved lengthways, deseeded and sliced
1 tablespoon blitzed nori seaweed sheets
8 breakfast radishes, thinly sliced
1 tablespoon rice wine vinegar
sea salt and freshly ground black pepper

This is my take on the classic Japanese *shime saba* preparation. Having such fresh fish in the restaurant, it's automatic to consider how you can showcase a certain species without losing its unique characteristics. There are a lot of similarities in my thoughts about cooking and serving seafood to that of Japanese cuisine. I've never been to Japan and I've never worked in a Japanese restaurant, but I think because I work with the seasons and the best fish available to me, my mind is in the same zone. In Japan, the sesame sauce is known as *goma dare* and is used as a dipping sauce or even salad dressing.

1. Lay the prepared mackerel in a tray and sprinkle the salt evenly all over. Leave in the refrigerator for 45 minutes.

2. Heat the ingredients for the vinegar cure in a saucepan until the sugar has dissolved, then leave to go cold.

3. For the sesame sauce, place the sugar, water and ginger into a pan and heat until the sugar has dissolved. Add the soy sauce, lime juice, sesame paste and sesame oil and blend with a stick blender until incorporated. Taste and add a little more soy if it's not salty enough. Set aside.

4. Wash the salt from the mackerel and pat dry. Place the mackerel into the cold vinegar cure, making sure it's submerged. Leave in the refrigerator for 45 minutes.

5. Mix the cucumber in a bowl with the nori, radishes and rice wine vinegar, and season with salt and pepper.

6. To fnish, remove the mackerel from the vinegar cure and pat dry. Using a sharp knife, slice the mackerel fillets into thin slices and arrange equally on 4 plates. Divide the sesame sauce into 4 small bowls to dip the fish into. Alternatively, pour it over the fish if you wish. Arrange the cucumber and radishes on and around the mackerel, then serve.

Breaded Butterflied Mackerel
with an Anchovy, Saffron & Lemon Mayonnaise Sauce

Serves 4

4 mackerel, gutted, butterflied (see page 77) and pin-boned
100g (3½oz) plain flour
2 eggs, beaten
200g (7oz) breadcrumbs (I like to blitz up focaccia or ciabatta)
150ml (5fl oz) clarified butter or ghee

For the rub
2 teaspoons fennel seeds
1 teaspoon black peppercorns
zest of 1 lemon
2 teaspoons sea salt

For the anchovy, saffron & lemon mayonnaise sauce
3 egg yolks
a pinch of saffron threads
1 teaspoon English mustard
zest and juice of 1 lemon
2 garlic cloves, chopped
8 salted anchovies
1 red chilli, deseeded and chopped
2 tablespoons chopped flat-leaf parsley leaves
300ml (10fl oz) sunflower oil
100ml (3½fl oz) vegetable stock
sea salt and freshly ground black pepper

For the salad
1 fennel bulb, finely sliced and placed in cold water
12 breakfast radishes, washed and thinly sliced
2 Baby Gem lettuce, leaves separated and washed
3 tablespoons finely chopped chives
zest and juice of 1 lemon
4 tablespoons extra virgin olive oil

Mackerel butterflied and breaded is a lovely way to prepare and cook them. This is great for lunch served with the punchy anchovy and lemon sauce. If you don't have a pan big enough and the breadcrumbing is a faff, just grill the fish. Mind you, if you do have the time, the breadcrumbs really make the dish and give it an extra dimension that works well and will wow!

1. For the rub, toast the spices, lemon zest and salt in a frying pan for 3 minutes until aromatic. Leave to cool, then blitz in a mortar and pestle or spice grinder. Transfer to a container until required.

2. Season the mackerel well all over with the rub. Arrange the flour, eggs and breadcrumbs in 3 separate large bowls or trays. Pass each mackerel through the flour, then the egg and finally the breadcrumbs. Keep in the refrigerator until needed.

3. For the sauce, put the egg yolks, saffron, mustard, lemon zest and juice, garlic, anchovies, chilli and parsley into a food processor and blend together for 1 minute. Scrape down the sides of the food processor bowl and slowly add the oil, drop by drop to begin with, then in a thin, steady stream, blitzing constantly, until the mixture is emulsified and thick. Season the mayonnaise with salt and pepper to taste, then add the vegetable stock and blend. Transfer to a pan and set aside.

4. For the salad, drain the fennel from the water and place in a bowl with the radishes, lettuce leaves, chives and lemon zest and juice. Drizzle in the extra virgin olive oil and season with salt and pepper. Mix well.

5. To cook the fish, heat a large, deep frying pan over a medium heat and add the clarified butter. When the butter is hot, carefully lay the mackerel in the pan skin-side down and cook for 2 minutes until the breadcrumbs are golden. Carefully turn the fish over and cook for another 2 minutes. You may need to add the butter and cook the mackerel in batches, depending on the size of your pan and the fish. Drain on a plate lined with kitchen paper.

6. Heat 4 plates and gently warm the sauce, stirring continuously – do not allow it to boil – it's ready when warm, not hot. Place the fish on the plates, pour the sauce around and serve the salad on the side.

Barbecued Whole Mackerel
with Asparagus & Smoked Chilli Sauce

Serves 4

4 large mackerel, gutted

For the rub
2 teaspoons chilli flakes
1 tablespoon fennel seeds
1 teaspoon black peppercorns
zest of 2 oranges
1 tablespoon sea salt
1 tablespoon chopped thyme leaves

For the smoked chilli sauce
a drizzle of olive oil
1 shallot, chopped
3 garlic cloves, chopped
2 smoked chillies, chopped
2 thyme sprigs, leaves picked and chopped
1 tablespoon fennel seeds
zest of 1 orange
50g (1¾oz) soft dark brown sugar
75ml (2½fl oz) red wine vinegar
100ml (3½fl oz) freshly squeezed orange juice
200g (7oz) good-quality canned plum tomatoes
sea salt and freshly ground black pepper

To serve
16 asparagus spears, trimmed
12 spring onions, trimmed
2 small oranges, halved

I am often asked, 'What is your favourite cooked fish dish to eat?' Well, barbecued mackerel is the one for me. There's something about the smell, texture, crisp bits and the smoke from the coals and wood that makes me very happy. This recipe is my very favourite way to eat it, and I love the smoked chilli sauce here that's served with it.

1. To prepare the rub, toast the spices in a dry pan over a medium heat for a minute or so until fragrant and starting to crackle. Add the orange zest, salt and thyme and heat for 30 seconds. Grind in a mortar and pestle or spice grinder until fine, then leave to cool.

2. Slash the skin of the mackerel 3–4 times on each side and place the fish on a tray. Sprinkle all over with the spice mixture, rubbing it into the slashes. Leave to marinate in the refrigerator for 1 hour.

3. To make the chilli sauce, heat a frying pan over a medium heat and add the olive oil. When hot, add the shallot, garlic and chillies and sweat for 3 minutes. Stir in the thyme, fennel seeds and orange zest and cook for another minute. Add the sugar and wine vinegar and stir until the sugar has dissolved, then bubble and reduce until syrupy. Add the orange juice and tomatoes. Bring to a simmer and bubble until the liquid has reduced by half again. Taste, then season with salt and pepper, as required.

4. Tip the contents of the pan into a food processor and blitz for 3 minutes. Strain the sauce through a fine sieve into a bowl and leave to cool.

5. Light your barbecue 1 hour before you plan on eating.

6. When the coals are white hot, place the mackerel on the barbecue rack and cook for 3 minutes on one side, then carefully turn the fish over and cook on the other side for 3 minutes. (Alternatively, you can cook the mackerel under a hot grill.) Grill the asparagus, spring onions and orange halves until golden.

7. Carefully lift the fish onto a serving platter, using a big fish slice (not tongs – mackerel is too delicate for those). Serve immediately, with the chilli sauce, asparagus, spring onions and orange halves on the side.

Hot-Smoked Mackerel Salad
with Sweet Potatoes & Raspberries

Serves 4

4 mackerel, gutted, filleted and pin-boned
8 tablespoons sea salt
zest of 1 lemon
zest of 1 orange
2 sprigs of thyme, leaves picked
oak chips, for smoking

For the dressing
zest and juice of 1 orange
200ml (7fl oz) olive oil
1 tablespoon white wine vinegar
1 teaspoon English mustard
1 teaspoon honey
sea salt and freshly ground black pepper

For the salad
2 sweet potatoes, peeled and diced into 2cm (¾ inch) cubes
a drizzle of olive oil
1 red onion, finely sliced
50ml (2fl oz) red wine vinegar
2 heads chicory, separated into individual leaves
16 raspberries
1 orange, peeled and segmented
1 punnet mustard cress, cut

I know what you're thinking… raspberries and fish? When I first heard the combination, I thought the same. I was in Barcelona and ate a smoked duck salad with raspberries that blew me away, it was super delicious. Straight away, I was thinking about how I could make a similar salad? The hot-smoking technique in this recipe is great for fish, because it cooks so quickly. The same technique would work equally well with pilchards/sardines, anchovies or herring.

1. To cure the mackerel, mix the salt, zests and thyme together. Place the mackerel in a container and sprinkle the cure over them, making sure the salt mixture is coating the fish well. Cover and place in the refrigerator for 2 hours.

2. After this time, wash the salt off the fish in ice-cold water and pat dry. Keep refrigerated.

3. To smoke the fish, set up a smoker with the oak chips inside and get them smoking over a medium heat. (This recipe also works well on a barbecue if you don't have good extraction in your home kitchen.) Place the fillets on a smoking rack and smoke them for 10 minutes, then remove from the heat but leave the fish in the smoker for another 2 minutes. Remove the fish from the smoker and leave to cool. Flake the fillets from the bones and place in a large salad bowl.

4. For the dressing, whisk together all the ingredients and season to taste. Set aside.

5. Preheat the oven to 180°C Fan (400°F), Gas Mark 6.

6. Place the sweet potato cubes on a baking tray, drizzle with olive oil and season with salt and pepper, then roast in the oven for 20 minutes. Transfer them to the bowl with the mackerel.

7. For the salad, mix the sliced red onion with the vinegar in a bowl and season. Add them to the mackerel bowl along with the chicory and mix to combine. Season with salt and pepper to taste, then arrange on a platter. Finish with the raspberries, orange segments and mustard cress, then drizzle over the dressing. Serve immediately.

Smoked Mackerel & Baked Red Onions
with Mint, Tarragon & Caper Crème Fraîche

Serves 4

4 mackerel, gutted, filleted and pin-boned
4 tablespoons sea salt
1 tablespoon caster sugar
4 tablespoons dry cider
oak chips, for smoking

For the baked onions
4 large red onions, peeled
2 sprigs of thyme, leaves picked and chopped
2 garlic cloves, finely chopped
1 tablespoon soft light brown sugar
100g (3½oz) unsalted butter
2 tablespoons red wine vinegar
sea salt and freshly ground black pepper

For the mackerel mix
1 shallot, finely chopped
1 tablespoon small capers in brine
2 tablespoons chopped tarragon leaves
zest and juice of 1 lemon

For the mint, tarragon & caper crème fraîche
6 tablespoons full-fat crème fraîche
1 tablespoon chopped mint
1 tablespoon chopped tarragon
2 tablespoons small capers, chopped

To serve
mustard cress
1 tablespoon chopped fresh tarragon leaves
a few fresh mint leaves, finely sliced

In this recipe I've given you the process for smoking your own mackerel, but if you have a good supply of smoked mackerel from a reliable smokehouse, you could skip that bit and make your life easier. Smoking your own fish is a nice thing to do and you can use it for so many other dishes, a personal favourite being a simple beetroot and smoked mackerel salad.

1. To cure the mackerel, lay the fillets skin-side down in a snug container. Mix the salt, sugar and cider together and spread over the fillets, making sure they are completely covered. Cure for 1 hour in the refrigerator.

2. After this time, wash off the cure in cold water and pat the fillets dry with kitchen paper.

3. To smoke the fish, set up a smoker with the oak chips inside and get them smoking over a medium heat. This works well on a barbecue if you don't have good extraction in your home kitchen. Place the fillets on a smoking rack and smoke them for 10 minutes, then remove from the heat but leave the fish in the smoker for another 10 minutes. Remove the fish from the smoker and leave to cool.

4. Preheat the oven to 200°C Fan (425°F), Gas Mark 7.

5. Put the red onions into a saucepan, pour over enough water to cover and add a good pinch of salt. Bring to the boil, then cook at a steady simmer for 15 minutes. Drain well and cut them across their equators. Transfer to a baking dish and sprinkle with the thyme, garlic, sugar and some salt and pepper. Add the butter and wine vinegar to the dish. Bake in the oven for about 25 minutes, basting occasionally with the buttery juices, until they are tender and well coloured. Allow to cool.

6. Dice the smoked mackerel and mix it with the shallot, capers, tarragon and lemon zest and juice. Season with salt and pepper. Take the centres from the onions and stuff the cavities with the mackerel mixture, getting as much in as possible. Lay the centres in the baking dish too and bake in the oven for a further 10 minutes.

7. While they're finishing, mix the crème fraîche with the herbs and capers, then season with salt and pepper. Warm 4 plates. Serve the onions with a spoonful of the cooking juices over the top and the crème fraîche on the side, scattered with mustard cress, chopped tarragon and mint.

Oily fish

Smoked Haddock Fritters with Cheese Sauce

Serves 4

400ml (14fl oz) milk
2 garlic cloves, finely chopped
300g (10½oz) smoked haddock, fillet, skinned and chopped
150g (5½oz) unsalted butter
200g (7oz) plain flour
5 large eggs, beaten
50g (1¾oz) mature Cheddar, grated
2 tablespoons chopped curly parsley leaves
2 teaspoons English mustard
3 spring onions, finely sliced
sunflower oil, for deep-frying
sea salt and freshly ground black pepper

For the cheese sauce
800ml (27fl oz) full-fat milk
45g (1¾oz) unsalted butter
1 tablespoon extra virgin olive oil
60g (2¼oz) plain flour
2 teaspoons English mustard
2 tablespoons chopped chives
150g (5½oz) mature Cheddar, grated

To serve
4 spring onions, finely sliced
1 teaspoon sweet smoked paprika
50g (1¾oz) Parmesan, finely grated

Smoked haddock is a perfect fish for giving that lovely smoked flavour to a hearty dish like this. The fritters are simply delicious and will become a favourite once you've made them. I've successfully made the recipe with smoked mackerel before, and crab too, so maybe try putting your own spin on this one.

1. To make the fritter mixture, bring the milk and garlic to a simmer and poach the chopped haddock for 3 minutes. Remove the haddock from the milk and measure out 250ml (9fl oz) of the strained poaching milk into another pan, leaving the garlic behind. Add the butter to the milk and, when it has melted, add the flour to the mixture and mix until it has combined and looks like a smooth dough. Reduce the heat and cook for 5 minutes, stirring occasionally.

2. Transfer the dough to a mixer or bowl and leave to cool for 2 minutes. Whisk in the beaten egg a little at a time until it is all incorporated. Fold in the haddock, cheese, parsley, mustard and spring onions and season with salt and pepper. Transfer to a container and refrigerate.

3. To make the sauce, warm the milk in a saucepan. In another pan, heat the butter and olive oil until the butter is melted and bubbling, then add the flour. Cook, stirring, for 2 minutes, then stir in the warmed milk, a ladleful at a time, until it is incorporated. Bring to a simmer, then reduce the heat as low as possible and cook for 20 minutes, stirring occasionally to ensure the sauce doesn't catch. Add the mustard, chives and cheese to the sauce and whisk until the cheese has melted and fully combined. Taste for seasoning, adding salt and pepper to taste. Keep warm.

4. To cook the fritters, heat a deep-fat fryer to 180°C (350°F) or heat some sunflower oil in a deep, heavy-based pan (not filling more than two-thirds full). Preheat the oven to 100°C Fan (250°F), Gas Mark ½.

5. When the oil is hot, take a spoonful of the fritter mix. Using 2 spoons, shape the mix between the spoons to create a rough-looking rugby ball shape. Carefully drop, one dollop at a time, into the fryer and cook for 3 minutes until golden. I'd suggest frying no more than 6 at a time.

6. Drain the fritters on a plate lined with kitchen paper and keep warm in the low oven while you cook the remaining mixture. When all the fritters are cooked, heat the sauce and share a few spoonfuls among 4 plates. Top with the fritters and sprinkle with the spring onions, smoked paprika and Parmesan. Serve hot.

5

Shellfish & cephalopods

Cockles, Clams, Mussels,
Scallops, Crab, Lobster, Langoustine,
Squid, Cuttlefish, Octopus, Oysters

Cockles

My first taste of cockles was on Hastings seafront in southeast England. My grandad bought them from a fish stall and, of course, we had them with malt vinegar and white pepper. Since then, I've used them in many different ways; my favourite being freshly steamed in a sauce to serve alongside a fish dish.

There are over 200 living species of cockles around the world. An edible, marine bivalve mollusc, true cockles are part of the *Cardiidae* family. The common cockle is the cockle we find in the UK.

Cockles are common around the UK and sustainable. Commercially, they can be dredged, but gathering with rake and bucket by hand is best. Mature cockles for eating are generally 2–3 years old; occasionally they live to 5 years, but these become a little tough to eat.

Notes
Cockles live happily anywhere and are quite easy to gather yourself with a rake and a bucket, but check the quality of the water is good enough for cockling before going ahead. Be aware that foraging in areas where cockles usually live often involves fast tidal water, so check the tides before venturing out.

Best time to eat
Available all year, but I suggest avoid them during the spring and summer months.

Cooking & serving
- When you get your cockles home, it's best to purge them in a mixture of salt and water overnight to get rid of all the sand and mud before cooking them.

- Make sure you throw away any that are open, as they will be dead.

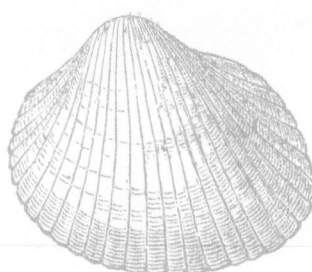

Clams

Tasty, succulent clams can be found all around our UK coastline. Manila, surf and razor clams – all of which taste fantastic – are the most common varieties, but you might also come across the imaginatively named carpet shells, sand gapers, hard shells, warty venus and other varieties at the right time of year. Local knowledge is the key.

Clams live in sandy, muddy and pebbly areas. Some varieties are native, while others have arrived on our shores and settled. You will find them in various sizes according to variety and age.

Clams can be dredged, but hand-gathering is always best due to both sustainability and reduced chance of damage.

Notes
It's always worth checking out where the clams you are buying are from. Razor clams, in particular, should be hand-gathered and over 10cm (4 inches), because under that size they will not have had time to reproduce.

When buying clams, always buy them live. Never seal them in a bag or container or they will suffocate and die.

Best time to eat
September–February.

Cooking & serving

- With the exception of razor clams, which need to be treated slightly differently owing to their very different shape, clams can be cooked in the same way as mussels and cockles.

- Thoroughly mix 60g (2¼oz) of sea salt with 2 litres (3½ pints) of cold water until the salt dissolves, then put the clams in the water and leave them for 3 hours. This will purge out the sand. Carefully lift the clams from the water and give them another rinse – they will now be ready to cook.

- Sometimes, you will still get a grain of sand and it's best to just accept this and not let it ruin your enjoyment of these beauties.

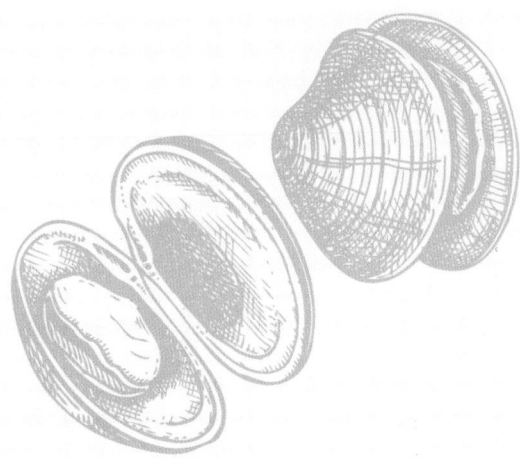

Shellfish & cephalopods

Mussels

I'm fortunate to have an abundance of fantastic mussels, both wild and farmed, growing all around the coast of Cornwall where I live, but it's rare to find wild mussels in the shops nowadays. You can gather wild mussels yourself at the beach, provided you take some precautions to avoid ghastly food poisoning.

Mussels can filter up to 1 litre (1¾ pints) of seawater per hour, but that water needs to be clean. If gathering them yourself, stick to beaches and rocky areas with fast-running tides, well away from any sewage outlets and harbours.

Farmed mussels are safest to eat – they are held in clean seawater and treated with ultraviolet light for 48 hours to eradicate nasty bacteria before being sold.

The common wild mussel has a lot to contend with while clinging to rocks, seaweed and other mussels in shallow waters near rocks. Constantly threatened by predators, they also need to survive extremes of temperature and a fair amount of battering when conditions get rough.

Farmed mussels are harvested, while wild ones are hand-collected. They can be various sizes according to age.

Notes
Mussels are an excellent, sustainable seafood and easy to prepare. Farmed mussels are probably one of the most sustainable seafoods you can eat in the UK, so fill up your bowls!

Best time to eat
Avoid collecting wild mussels in hotter months when bacteria grows at a faster rate.

Cooking & serving
- Before cooking, check that the mussels are in good condition and the shells are closed. Tap any open mussels sharply – they will close if alive – otherwise discard them.

- Throw away any mussels with cracked or damaged shells.

- Always pull away the hairy 'beard' attached to one end of the mussel.

- Farmed mussels should only need a quick rinse to clean them without washing away flavour, but if mussels are sandy or dirty you'll need to give them a more thorough wash or a quick soak for a few hours in cold, salty water (see page 181).

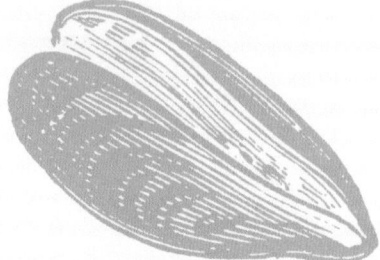

Scallops

Like mussels and oysters, scallops are filter feeders, but unlike their relatives they're mobile, swimming and moving around the ocean at different times of the year. With rows of many eyes arranged along the edge of their shells, on sensing danger scallops can swim off at an impressive speed. A flock of scallops swimming through the sea is an amazing sight!

There are two types of scallops in the UK: the king and the queen. King scallops will grow up to 15cm (6 inches) across, while queens never reach more than 10cm (4 inches). Scallops can live well into double figures, but they are best harvested and eaten when 3–5 years old.

You'll find scallops in sandy or pebbly areas and in open beds, anywhere they can hide.

Hauling a huge net attached to a beam over the seabed to catch scallops causes a lot of devastation, as it takes everything and breaks things in its path, meaning other species are often wiped out in the search for prized scallops. However, scallop divers can adversely affect sustainability too, as they tend to pick out the larger scallops, which are at their peak for reproduction and should really be left alone. However, properly done, scallop diving is the most sustainable way to catch these shellfish, far preferable to the commercial dredging method.

Scallops make wonderfully succulent and sweet eating. With respectful fishing, we should be able to enjoy them as an occasional treat with a clear conscience.

Notes
You can tell the age of a scallop by the rings on its shell, with each ring roughly representing a year.

The colour of a scallop's shell changes according to its surroundings; darker shells suggest it's from rocky coastlines whereas lighter shells are found in sandy locations.

Best time to eat
December until late spring.

Cooking & serving
- See page 193 for preparation advice.

- Serve raw (see page 215) or in ceviche (see page 219).

- They can also be pan-fried or baked in the shell (see page 216).

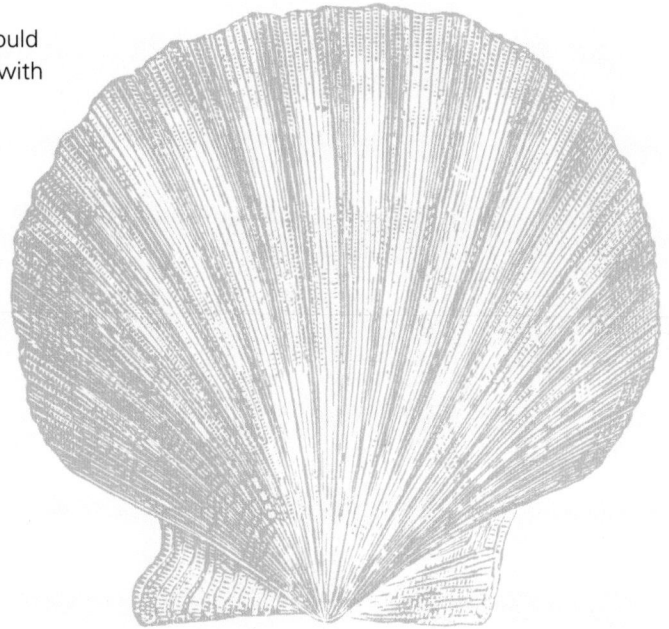

Crab

We see a variety of edible crabs in UK waters:

Common brown crab – this is by far our most popular variety, with succulent, tasty flesh that's easy to pick from the shell. The first brown crabs of the season are available to me in late March or early April, when Calum, my crab and lobster man, puts his pots back out after the rough winter weather has passed. A brown crab is a thing of beauty and should be celebrated when it's about, so treat it with care, cook it simply, savour its unique taste and enjoy.

Velvet crab – Unfortunately, we don't appreciate these enough and most of the velvet crabs caught in our waters go abroad, where they proudly sit on a *fruits de mer* platter or are made into fantastic pasta dishes.

Shore crab – These are the ones mussel farmers fear, because they have the capacity to wipe out young mussel beds in a very short time.

Spider crab – If you've ever seen a spider crab walking across the rocks at very low tide, you'll know how fascinating these alien-seeming creatures are to watch, and they're very tasty too. From May, they are everywhere for a couple of months, becoming a nuisance to most crab fisherman as they crowd the pots. From a boat at low tide, I've seen the seabed almost consumed by spider crabs covering every inch of sand and rock in a breeding frenzy. They then swim off into the deep, returning again the following May in their thousands.

Brown crabs and spider crabs hide out in small caves when the sea is rough and to stay away from predators, but they're pretty awesome predators themselves with strong claws that will grab your fingers if you're not careful. Younger brown crabs regularly burst out of their shell to grow a bigger one, leaving them temporarily vulnerable until the soft shell hardens to armour again. Shore crabs tend to live in estuaries and in seaweed where they can hide. Velvets swim and are often found in lobster and crab pots. Of the various crabs around our coastline, you are most likely to get pinched by the small, fast, aggressive velvet crab. With its red eyes, super speed and super strength, for something so small, it's pretty scary.

UK crab is not in a good position at the moment and something needs to be done. As I write, stocks of edible brown crab are not great due to overfishing by big industrial boats and a slight sea warming. However, on the bright side, pregnant females must be returned to the sea by law, which is helping.

Spiders, velvets and shore crabs, however, are plentiful in numbers. They deserve to be eaten more in the UK, although females with eggs should be avoided.

Notes

Generally, all crabs are caught by potting or netting.

The larger, brown cock crabs are the first to be caught around late March/early April. Around for 8–10 weeks, they then magically disappear, often overnight. From July until October, I get the smaller hen crabs, which are just as tasty but don't yield as much meat.

According to species, the best sizes to use are:
Brown – 2kg (4lb 8oz)
Velvet – the bigger the better
Shore – any size
Spider – 1.5kg (3lb 5oz)

Best time to eat

Brown – Cock crabs: late March–late June;
Hen crabs: July–October.
Velvet – all year.
Shore – all year.
Spider – May–July (best early in the season).

Cooking & serving

- Keep live crabs in a large container in the refrigerator, covered with a damp cloth and in the dark, and they'll last longer.

- See pages 196–7 for preparation advice.

- Brown – These are perfect for salads (see page 225), sandwiches, crab cakes and risotto.

- Spider – Also perfect for salads, sandwiches, croquettes (see page 223) and risotto. I make the most of these tasty crabs in the short time they are available. Towards the end of the season though, you do get the odd one that is watery – a consequence of the crab shedding its shell and devoting its energy to growing a new one.

- Velvet – If you want to make a special shellfish soup, these are the crabs to use. They don't yield much in the way of meat, but they do have fantastic flavour, especially when roasted.

- Shore crabs – The kind we catch on crab lines as kids have negligible meat yield and are only suitable for making stock or soup (see page 220). However, it's well worth doing this as often as you can, as they yield a tasty broth, and you'll be doing those mussel farmers a favour.

Lobster

I am extremely lucky to be based in Port Isaac, because it's one of the best places to source lobster in the UK and home to my restaurants. I only buy from experienced lobster fishermen and only ever using pots, the lowest impact on the environment you can get when fishing (except possibly free-diving, but you'd be crazy to do that for lobster – far too costly!). We're always kept well stocked from late spring until autumn with only the best specimens… if the weather is good.

Lobsters deserve a lot of respect and they certainly get it in our kitchens, where we cook them with care and simplicity. Their flavour and texture is so good, the less you do to them the better.

Lobsters live in rocky areas and under cliffs, anywhere they can hide. They will take any opportunity to feed, eating pretty much anything if it gets within their grasp. Sounds like me!

It has been suggested that lobsters can live up to 100 years old and grow up to 1m (3¼ft) long! The lobsters we serve are usually from 8–12 years old. In my opinion, they are at their tastiest at around 600–700g (1lb 5oz–1lb 9oz). I must admit, I once bought a very big lobster I saw for sale just to put it back in the ocean. When they get to a certain size above 1.5kg (3lb 5oz), I don't think they're worth eating, they're just tough. Leave them in the sea to reproduce, I say.

Lobsters are caught by potting and should always be put back when undersized. In Cornwall, the Cornwall Inshore Fisheries & Conservation Authority manage our lobster fisheries closely through minimum landing sizes and limiting the number of shellfish licenses for vessels. However, there isn't a limit on the amount of lobster caught, so there's always a risk of overfishing, which is crazy.

A voluntary scheme that fisherman have been participating in over the past decade has been played out using a technique called 'V notching'. Female lobsters are identified individually by fishermen with a section of the tail being marked to show that she's been put aside to reproduce and carry eggs for roughly 3 years until the notch grows out. This process massively increases the

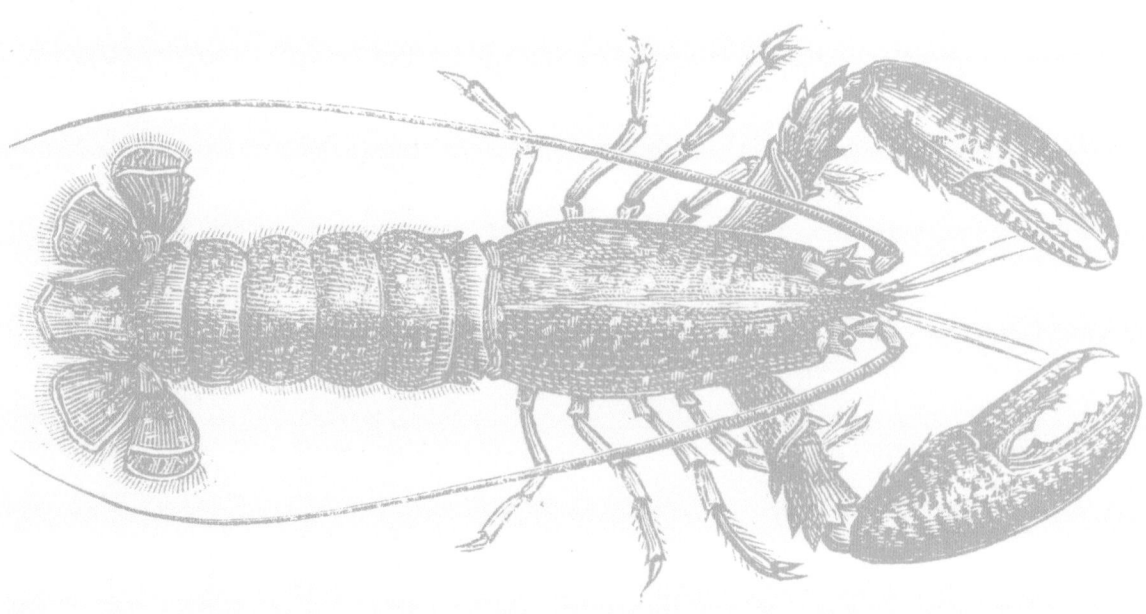

chances of the survival of juvenile lobsters, as fishermen and food establishments caught in possession of a V-notched lobster will be prosecuted. This scheme alone, with the awareness promoted by the National Lobster Hatchery, has increased lobster stocks and is a lesson in sustainability for the rest of the world. On a visit to our local National Lobster Hatchery in Padstow, you can witness and fully appreciate the battles and adventures a lobster must endure, even fighting with each other, to stay alive. The careful nurturing within the Lobster Hatchery is vital to keep this most beautiful of sea creatures going strong.

Notes
If you ever catch a lobster yourself and find it's a female with attached eggs (berries), carefully return it to the sea – by law, you must do so. Incredibly, the mother will carry those eggs for nearly a year, which when you consider the threats from predators and the forces of nature, is a miracle in itself.

Best time to eat
Late spring until autumn, provided they're not 'berried'.

Cooking & serving
- See page 194 for preparation advice.

- Boiled/poached; in salads (see page 227).

- Whole, grilled.

- Make sauce or soup with the shells (see page 232).

Shellfish & cephalopods

Langoustine (or Dublin Bay prawns or scampi)

Celebrated worldwide, langoustines are mainly found off the east and west coasts of Scotland. However, there is a small window in the year when you can find them off Cornwall too, but it will be the Scottish fisherman that catch them because their boats are set up with the correct equipment to do so.

They inhabit cold water and can grow up to 500g (1lb 2oz) in weight, but are super expensive at this size. Generally, you'll see them at around 200g (7oz).

Notes
To store, they're best kept alive in a dark place in the refrigerator.

Best time to eat
June–October.

Cooking & serving
- Peel the tail, blanch and pan-fry.

- Split and grill.

- The heads and claws make a great soup or stock.

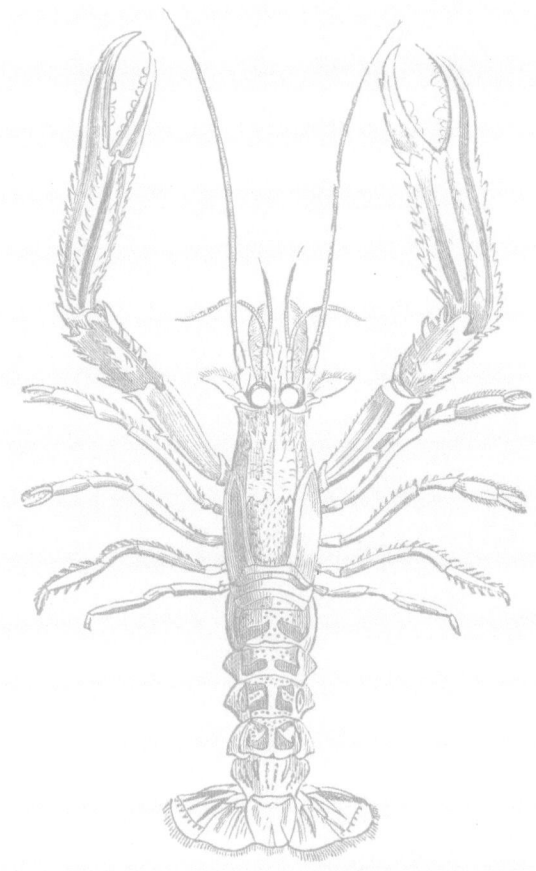

Squid

The squid is a fascinating creature – the ultimate hunting machine. It shoots through the water, steered by its large fins, siphoning water through its body to create what can only be described as 'jet power'. It can change colour to match its surroundings, switch direction in the water instantly, and shoot ink into the path of any prey or predator to cause confusion.

A cephalopod, it is loosely classified as shellfish as it has an internal shell called a quill. Swimming in shoals in shallow coastal areas, it can also be found to a depth of 500m (1,640ft).

Squid is very sustainable – aided by a fast life cycle; it has a one-year breeding season. It is caught by potting, jigging (a form of hook and line angling – this gives the best quality) or by getting caught up in nets.

Notes
When buying squid, check that the body and tentacles have no signs of pinkness, which indicates that it has been out of the sea for too long.

In my experience, frozen squid is often more tender than fresh, because the freezing process helps to tenderize the flesh.

Best time to eat
Late winter to early spring.

Cooking & serving
- See page 198 for preparation advice.

- The best size for quick cooking is around 200g (7oz).

- The best size for slow cooking is around 700g (1lb 9oz).

- The bigger the squid, the tougher they get.

Cuttlefish

My pet budgie learned to appreciate cuttlefish long before I tried it; when I was a kid, Burt the budgie always had a cuttlebone in his cage to keep his beak busy. Now I can see what the fuss was all about!

Probably one of the most intelligent creatures in the sea, like squid, camouflage is one of this cephalopod's most impressive attributes, enabling it to blend into any situation, whether hiding or hunting. They are loosely classified as shellfish as they have an internal shell – a cuttlebone.

One of our local fishermen once brought me a cuttlefish that had got caught in his lobster pot. Not realizing it was alive, I grabbed it and got a nasty clip from its beak. I certainly wouldn't want to be a fish engaged in battle with a cuttlefish!

Cuttlefish live for a few years and breed inshore, where most of them are caught either by trap or trawl.

Notes
A little under threat, try to find those that have been caught in traps, as they're more sustainable.

Best time to eat
May–February.

Cooking & serving
- The larger ones are nicest to eat, around 600–800g (1lb 5oz–1lb 12oz).

- I enjoy cuttlefish slow-cooked or braised (see page 235).

- I am also a big fan of cuttlefish ink, which has more flavour than squid ink and there is always more of it

Octopus

In Cornwall, there are two main species of octopus. Until recently, the most common was the curled octopus with its single row of suckers on each tentacle, the native species around the UK. However, due to the warmer weather and the attraction of more food to prey on, the Mediterranean octopus has arrived and is becoming somewhat of a nuisance. Fast, clever and ruthless hunters, they devour shellfish, getting in and out of lobster pots and clearing them of the catch in no time. Mind you, some are caught in the pots, which is to our advantage!

I wasn't a fan of eating octopus until recently; I think they are fascinating, but when you cook the native curled octopus it is rubbery and not very good to eat at all. However, the Mediterranean octopus with its double suckers on each of the eight tentacles makes good eating, and since their invasion I have been able to come up with some lovely recipes.

Octopus are fast-growing and short-lived, and feed on crustaceans and other shellfish. Within 2 years they are mature, the females producing over 30,000 eggs each, which they protect until hatched, at which point the adult females die. The baby octopuses are carried away by ocean currents. This makes the octopus a highly reproductive creature and therefore quite resilient to fishing.

Notes
Even if you buy fresh octopus I recommend you freeze it before cooking, because this tenderizes the flesh.

Best time to eat
May– February (but see Notes above).

Cooking & serving
- You'll see in my recipes that I dunk the octopus a couple of times before cooking; this helps to separate the tentacles so they don't stick together during cooking.

- My favourite way to cook octopus is to braise it carefully and when tender, grill it, or fry until it crisps up (see pages 244 and 248).

- Another favourite is to make croquettes using the braising stock, with the octopus chopped though it, then breaded and deep-fried.

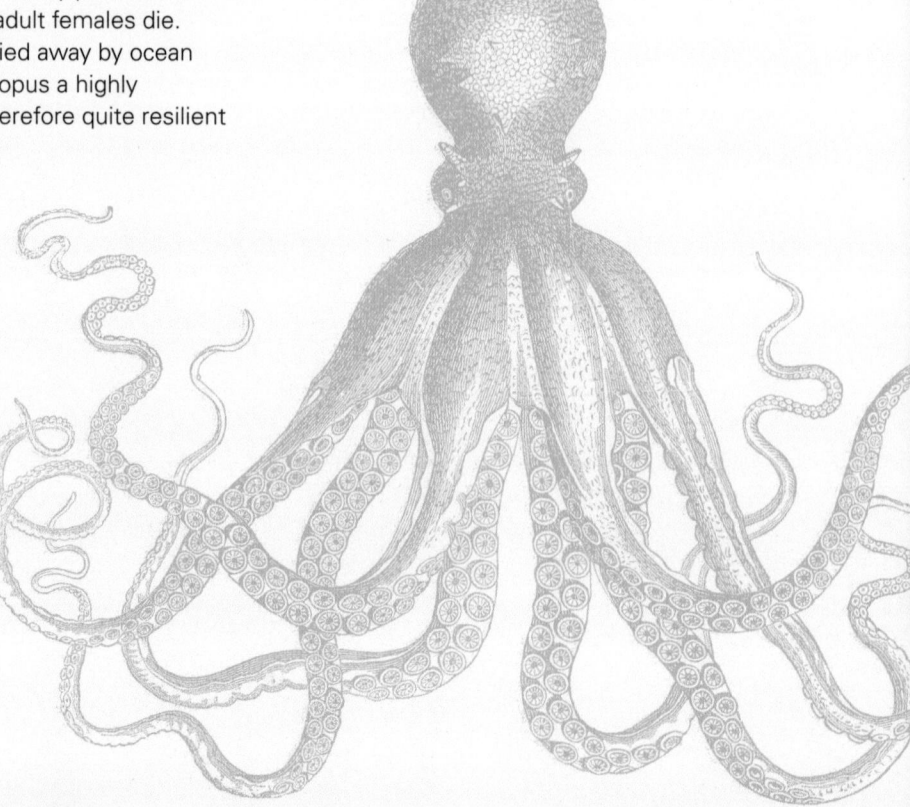

Oysters (native & farmed)

I like to use two types of oyster: farmed Pacific and wild native. To me, the wild native oyster is a treasure to be respected... and never, ever cooked. Just open and eat – as simple as that! I feel differently about farmed oysters. Yes, eat them raw, but I also think they have a special quality when cooked. The texture changes, but they're still wonderful.

All oysters draw in seawater, filtering up to 6 litres (10½ pints) a day and extracting the oxygen and nutrients they need to live and grow, so it goes without saying that water quality is a vital consideration. Wild natives inhabit estuaries and shallow water, hiding in muddy or sandy beds, so always check where they've been gathered from.

A hundred years ago, natives were abundant, cheap and eaten by rich and poor people alike. Nowadays, partly because of the damaging effects of pollution, natives are much rarer and considered a luxury food. A protected species, they can only be harvested outside of their spawning season. In many parts of the UK, the native oyster is listed as 'threatened', so if you happen to find one, double check before helping yourself; you could be breaking the law!

Pacific farmed oysters have been breaking loose for years and growing happily (and quite quickly) in wild waters, becoming invasive and causing problems in some areas.

Notes

Oysters have a reputation for only being good when there is an 'R' in the month, but this isn't entirely true. With wild native oysters you're certainly best sticking to this rule, because outside of this they are spawning and not good to eat. However, farmed Pacific oysters can be eaten at any time of the year – the main change during spawning time being that they become milky, but this won't hurt you. When they are like this we cook them breaded and fried, and they go down a treat. By eating farmed oysters you are eating seafood that is very sustainable.

Never eat an oyster that is open – it will be dead.

Best time to eat

October–December.

Cooking & serving

- Farmed oysters are best to eat when they are of a medium size for raw preparation, but if you are cooking them, the larger ones are best.

- See page 192 for preparation advice.

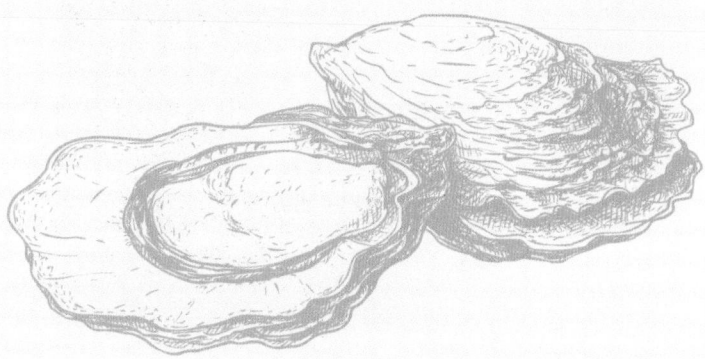

Shellfish & cephalopods

Preparing oysters

1. Using an oyster knife or sturdy butter knife, hold the oyster flat-side up in a folded tea towel. Insert the knife into the hinge of the oyster and wiggle it until you hear a popping sound.

2. Run the knife along the roof of the flat side to cut the attaching muscle from the top shell.

3. Cut away the same muscle from the bottom shell and flip the oyster over in the shell, taking care to retain the juices.

4. The shelled oyster.

Preparing scallops

1. Check the scallop is alive: either closed or will close when tapped. Hold the scallop between the fingers and thumb with the flat side facing up.

2. Insert the tip of a small, strong knife between the shells at the corner of the hinge and twist to break it.

3. Bring the knife down between the shells and pull off the top one.

4. Using a thin spoon, scrape around the scallop to release it from the shell. Grab the scallop, roe and skirt in your fingers and find the white muscle. Use your thumb and forefinger to prise the scallop meat from the muscle.

5. Carefully remove the membrane, separating the roe if you want, to leave the white scallop meat.

Shellfish & cephalopods

Preparing cooked lobster

1. A cooked lobster. Raw lobster is blue/black.

2. First remove the claws. Hold the body firmly in one hand and with the other, take the claw firmly at the base then twist and pull.

3. Hold the body firmly at the point where the tail connects to the head then twist and pull to remove the tail.

4. Turn the tail upside down and pull it out flat.

5. Hold the end of the tail fin and twist firmly to remove.

6. Once the tail is free, crack the shell by pushing down on it with force until you hear it crack.

7. Using both hands, grab the underside of the tail and pull out to separate the shell from the meat. Remove the shell and keep it for use in stocks, sauces and bisques.

8. Hold the tail meat in front of you and cut slightly off centre so you don't cut through the intestinal tract.

9. Continue until you have cut through the tail meat completely.

10. Carefully remove the intestinal tract. It should only be on one side.

11. Cut the tail meat into equal pieces. This is easier if you use the markings where the tail joints were.

12. Break the lobster claws into three pieces.

13. Using the handle of a spoon, remove the lobster meat from the knuckles.

14. Crack the claw by using a heavy knife and giving it a good, confident whack. The meat may fall out naturally; if not, use a spoon or crab pick to prise it out gently.

15. The meat you should get from one lobster.

Shellfish & cephalopods

195

Preparing cooked crab

1. Once cooked and cool enough to handle, remove the legs. Hold them firmly at the base then pull them away from the body and towards you.

2. Repeat the same process with the claws.

3. Firmly hold the body with the shell towards you. Using your thumbs, push away from the top to release the carapace.

4. Pull on the carapace to release it.

5. Carefully pull the carapace out to take it apart.

6. Remove the 'dead man's fingers'. They aren't poisonous but are unpleasant to eat.

7. Remove the membrane from inside the top of the shell.

8. Using a spoon, remove the brown meat from the top shell. Hen crabs will always give more meat than cock crabs.

9. Break the claws at the joints. They snap easily.

10. Remove the pincer from the claw to make it easier to remove the meat.

11. Using the back of a heavy knife or a mallet, hit the claw shell with one good, firm whack to crack it. Repeat this on all the other joints too.

12. Using the handle of a spoon or a crab pick, remove the meat from the claw

13. This is how the claw meat should look.

14. Repeat the same process with the crab's legs.

15. Cut across the carapace to reveal little channels filled with the white meat. Use the back of a spoon or a crab pick to remove all the meat.

16. Top left, brown meat; top right, shells (for stocks, bisques or sauces); bottom left, white meat; bottom right, bits to discard.

Shellfish & cephalopods

Preparing squid

1. Pull out the quill from the main body. Discard the quill as it's inedible.

2. Hold the body in one hand, grab the head and pull it firmly and carefully. The innards and ink sac will come away with it.

3. You should be left with the main body and fins or 'wings'.

4. Pull the fins or 'wings' away from the sides of the body.

5. Chop the tentacles off below the eyes to remove them.

6. Hold the tentacles and squeeze to remove the sharp beak/mouth – pull it away and discard, as this is inedible.

7. The three main parts of the squid (the body, tentacles and fins or 'wings' can now be rinsed, ready to cook. Some chefs remove the reddish skin from the fins/wings, but I leave it on because I like the taste and it sometimes crisps up, which is obviously delicious. The squid skin also adds a lovely colour to braises or stews when you slow cook it.

Cider-Pickled Cockles
with Fennel, White Cabbage & Apple Salad

Serves 4 as a starter

1kg (2lb 4oz) live cockles, washed well (check for open cockles and discard)
200ml (7fl oz) dry cider
200ml (7fl oz) cider vinegar
50g (1¾oz) caster sugar
2 shallots, finely chopped
2 garlic cloves, crushed
4 bay leaves
1 sprig of rosemary
sea salt and freshly ground black pepper

For the salad
1 fennel bulb, trimmed and finely sliced on a mandoline
¼ white cabbage, finely sliced on a mandoline
1 apple, peeled and grated
2 tablespoons chopped chervil, plus extra to serve
3 tablespoons cold-pressed rapeseed oil, plus extra to serve

Out of all the small shells that I get to cook, cockles are my favourite. When at their best, they're wonderful; plump and full of flavour. Other than simply steaming them and eating them as they are, I like to pickle them lightly and mix them through a salad. It makes a salad very interesting with those little bursts of sweet-and-sour cockle. You can do this same process with any shellfish, but cockles are best for me.

1. To steam the cockles open, heat a large pan with a tight-fitting lid over a medium heat. Once hot, add the cockles and cider and place the lid on immediately. Steam for 3 minutes and give the pan a shake. Place a colander over a bowl to catch the cooking liquid and pour the contents of the pan into the colander.

2. When the cockles are cool enough, pick out the meat and discard the shells. Place into another bowl.

3. Strain the cooking liquid through a piece of muslin or a very clean tea towel. This will ensure that any sand has been removed. Pour the strained liquid onto the cockle meat and give them a careful stir. Gently lift the cockle meat from the liquid into another bowl and refrigerate.

4. Strain the cooking liquid again into a pan and add the cider vinegar, sugar, shallots, garlic, bay and rosemary. Bring the mixture to a simmer and season with salt and pepper. Cool the liquid completely until cold, then place the cockle meat in the liquid and leave in the refrigerator for at least 6 hours (best overnight). They will last for 4 days in the refrigerator.

5. To make the salad, place the fennel and white cabbage into a bowl and season. Scrunch the vegetables with clean hands for 1 minute. Leave for 30 minutes, then drain off the excess water. Add the apple, chervil and rapeseed oil and mix well.

6. Take the cockles from the refrigerator and drain, reserving the liquid. Add 6 tablespoons of the reserved liquid to the salad. Place the cockles in the salad and mix with care, then share among 4 plates. Finish with a few chervil sprigs, a drizzle of cold-pressed rapeseed oil and serve. Bread and butter for mopping is advised!

Poached Clam Wontons
in Mushroom Broth

Serves 4

1kg (2lb 4oz) live clams, rinsed off and any open ones discarded
100ml (3½fl oz) white wine
sunflower oil
1 banana shallot, finely chopped
1 garlic clove, finely chopped
1 large carrot, peeled and finely chopped
1 celery stick, peeled and finely chopped
300g (10½oz) button mushrooms, finely chopped
2 tablespoons dark soy sauce
1 tablespoon fish sauce
zest and juice of 1 lime
2 tablespoons chopped coriander
200g (7oz) packet wonton pastry or gyoza wrappers
sea salt and freshly ground black pepper

For the broth
1 litre (1¾ pints) water
1 tablespoon instant dashi flakes
2 tablespoons white miso paste
50g (1¾oz) dried ceps
50ml (2fl oz) light rapeseed oil, plus extra for oiling
6 spring onions, finely sliced (white and green parts separated)
175g (6oz) mixture of shimeji, king oyster, shiitake or chestnut mushrooms
1 garlic clove, finely chopped
juice of 1 lime

To serve
4 spring onions, finely sliced
a handful of coriander leaves

Clams are great made into fillings for wontons and dumplings, and it's a good way to encourage people to eat them. Obviously, there's nothing wrong with them simply steamed open and served, but sometimes that's a bit boring. Using clams in this dish shows them off in a different mode. You could use any seafood in these wontons – a prawn version would be great!

1. To make the clam filling, heat a large pan with a tight-fitting lid over a medium heat. Once hot, add the clams and the white wine and place the lid on immediately. Steam for 2 minutes and give the pan a shake.

2. Place a colander over a bowl to catch the cooking liquid, then pour the contents of the pan into it. When the clams are cool enough, pick the meat and discard the shells. Strain the cooking liquid through a piece of muslin or a clean tea towel. This will make sure that any sand has been washed off. Pour the strained liquid onto the picked clam meat and stir.

3. Lift the clam meat out with a slotted spoon and reserve 4 tablespoons of the cooking liquid (discard the rest). Place the clams onto a board and chop finely, then put into a container and refrigerate.

4. Heat a frying pan over a medium heat and add a drizzle of sunflower oil. Once hot, add the shallot, garlic, carrot and celery. Season with salt and cook over a medium heat for 5 minutes, stirring occasionally. Add the button mushrooms and continue to cook for 10 minutes, stirring occasionally. Season with the soy sauce, fish sauce and the lime zest and juice. Stir well, then transfer to a tray to cool. When cool, add the vegetables to the clams along with the chopped coriander. Mix well.

5. To make the wontons, take a wonton wrapper and place 1 teaspoon of the clam filling in the centre. Wet the edges with water and fold two opposite corners together to make a triangle. Bring together the 2 lower points and pinch to make the dumpling. Repeat until you have 20 wontons. As you make them, cover them with a tea towel to stop them drying out. Set aside.

6. To make the broth, put the water, reserved clam juice and dashi into a saucepan and bring to a simmer, then whisk in the miso paste and dried ceps. Cover, remove from the heat and leave to stand for 10 minutes.

7. Meanwhile, heat a frying pan over a medium heat and add the rapeseed oil. When hot, add the white spring onions and the remaining mushrooms. Cook for 3 minutes, then add the garlic. Season with salt and pepper to taste and add the lime juice, stirring to deglaze the pan. Set aside.

8. Strain the miso liquor into a large clean pan with a lid, discarding the ceps, and bring to a simmer. Place the wontons into the broth, then cover and steam for 4 minutes.

9. Heat 4 soup bowls and share the spring onions, mushrooms and coriander leaves equally between them. Remove the lid from the pan and carefully lift 5 wontons into each bowl. Ladle the broth over the top and serve hot.

Mussel Pâté & Cider Jelly
with Soda Bread

Serves 4

1kg (2lb 4oz) live mussels, washed and de-bearded
100ml (3½fl oz) water
1½ bronze gelatine leaves
a drizzle of olive oil
1 banana shallot, sliced
2 tablespoons brandy
200ml (7fl oz) double cream
a pinch of cayenne pepper
2 tablespoons lemon juice
sea salt, to taste

For the cider jelly
100ml (3½fl oz) dry cider
100ml (3½fl oz) apple juice
a pinch of sea salt
2 bronze gelatine leaves

For the soda bread
120g (4¼oz) self-raising flour, plus extra for dusting
210g (7½oz) wholemeal flour
50g (1¾oz) light rye flour
20g (¾oz) bicarbonate of soda
100g (3½oz) organic oats
1 teaspoon fine salt
20g (¾oz) pumpkin seeds
20g (¾oz) sunflower seeds
80g (2¾oz) natural yogurt
80g (2¾oz) treacle
320ml (11fl oz) dry cider

To serve
a few red radishes, finely sliced
1 green apple, sliced and cut into matchsticks
tarragon leaves
extra virgin olive oil, to drizzle
sea salt and freshly ground black pepper

This recipe is a firm favourite with my customers – someone once said it was like 'eating luxury'; I like that! When you blend the cooked mussels, they take on a parfait-like texture, completely transforming this great, sustainable protein. The cider jelly adds a touch of acidity, and the little salad provides some freshness. The soda bread is so easy to make and will probably be more than you need. Well, we'll see, it's surprising how much we can eat when something's delicious, and this certainly is that!

1. To make the mussel pâté, heat a large pan with a tight-fitting lid and add the mussels. Pour in the measured water, cover and steam for 3 minutes until the mussels open and are cooked. Drain into a colander with a bowl underneath, reserving the liquid. Strain the liquid through a fine mesh sieve.

2. Pick the mussels from their shells and place in the strained cooking liquid – this will wash out any sand or grit that may be present. Carefully lift mussels from the liquid and discard it.

3. Soak the 1½ leaves of gelatine in a small bowl of cold water until soft.

4. Heat a medium pan over a medium heat and add a drizzle of olive oil. Once hot, add the shallot and sweat for 2 minutes until translucent and soft. Add the cooked mussels, brandy and cream and cook for 1 minute. Season with salt, the cayenne and lemon juice. Remove from the heat.

5. Squeeze the excess water from the gelatine and add to the mussel mixture. Transfer to a blender and blitz for 1 minute until smooth. Pour into a bowl and place in the refrigerator to set for at least 3 hours.

6. To make the jelly, heat the cider and apple juice and season with salt. Soften the 2 leaves of gelatine in a small bowl of cold water. Squeeze the excess water from the gelatine and stir into the hot liquid. Allow the liquid to cool, pour it into a bowl and refrigerate until set.

7. Preheat the oven to 200°C Fan (425°F), Gas Mark 7. Line a baking tray with a nonstick mat or baking parchment.

8. To make the soda bread, mix all the dry ingredients in one bowl and all the wet ingredients in another. Once both mixes are well mingled, mix them both together until there is no dry mixture visible and they have incorporated to make a dough. Flour your work surface and scrape the mixture onto it. Using floured hands, divide the mix equally and roll into 2 loaf shapes. Transfer to the prepared tray and slide into the oven to bake for 10 minutes.

9. Reduce the oven temperature to 160°C Fan (350°F), Gas Mark 4 and continue to bake for a further 20 minutes. Remove from the oven and cool on a wire rack.

10. To serve, chop the jelly and arrange on 4 plates. Using a warm spoon, portion the mussel pâté and place on top of the jelly. Arrange the radishes, apple matchsticks and tarragon on top. Season with salt and pepper, then finish with a drizzle of olive oil. Slice the soda bread and serve on the side.

Serves 4

Steamed Mussels in White Bean & Apple Soup
with Curry Oil

a drizzle of Curry Oil (see page 251)
1 garlic clove, crushed
50g (1¾oz) fresh root ginger, peeled and sliced
2 teaspoons curry powder
8 curry leaves
1kg (2lb 4oz) live mussels, washed and de-bearded
100ml (3½fl oz) dry cider

For the white bean & apple soup
sunflower oil
50g (1¾oz) unsalted butter
1 onion, chopped
3 garlic cloves, finely chopped
50g (1¾oz) fresh root ginger, peeled and finely chopped
6 curry leaves
300g (10½oz) canned haricot blanc or cannellini beans, drained
500ml (18fl oz) vegetable stock
1 green apple, peeled and chopped
100ml (3½fl oz) double cream
sea salt

To finish
1 green apple, peeled and finely chopped
1 tablespoon chopped fresh coriander
2 tablespoons Curry Oil (see page 251)

It seems to me that mussels have a perfect connection with Indian flavours. I always enjoy adding spices to mussel dishes, I think it brings out the best in them. Mussels are a good value and very sustainable seafood that you can eat with a smile on your face. The farming of mussels, especially the rope-grown ones, is getting more and more popular. This dish is a winter warmer and that's great, because winter's when mussels are at their best. Serve with bread or, even better, a naan.

1. To make the soup, heat a saucepan over a medium heat and add a drizzle of oil and the butter. Once hot and the butter is bubbling, add the onion and cook for 3 minutes, stirring occasionally, until soft. Add the garlic, ginger and curry leaves and cook for 2 minutes, then add the beans, stock and apple and cook for about 10 minutes until the apple is soft. Taste and season with salt, then add the double cream.

2. Transfer the soup to a blender and carefully blend (it's hot) for 2 minutes until smooth. Strain through a sieve into another pan, cover and keep warm if you are using it straight away. Alternatively, leave it to cool and chill in the refrigerator for up to 3 days.

3. To steam the mussels, heat a large pan with a tight-fitting lid over a medium heat. When the pan is hot, add a drizzle of curry oil, then the garlic, ginger, curry powder and curry leaves and cook for 1 minute. Add the mussels and cider and place the lid on immediately. Steam for 3 minutes and give the pan a shake. Place a colander over a bowl to catch the cooking liquid, then pour the contents of the pan into it.

4. To finish, warm the soup gently over a medium heat and give it a final taste, season if necessary. Mix the cooked mussels with the finely chopped apple, chopped coriander and curry oil. Ladle the hot soup into 4 warm bowls and share the mussels equally among them.

Steamed Oysters
with a Ginger Beurre Blanc

Serves 4 as a starter

20–24 live medium Pacific oysters
4 teaspoons finely chopped fresh root ginger
4 spring onions, finely sliced lengthways

For the ginger beurre blanc
2 small shallots, finely chopped
50g (1¾oz) fresh root ginger, peeled and finely chopped
100ml (3½fl oz) white wine
50ml (2fl oz) double cream
250g (9oz) unsalted butter
1 tablespoon chopped coriander
2 tablespoons diced peeled cucumber
sea salt and freshly ground black pepper

To serve
dampened sea salt, to sit the oyster shells on

Cooking oysters is a brilliant way to introduce people to them and their unique flavour. The texture becomes firmer and more of a pleasure to eat, in my opinion. This is a simple way of cooking oysters and a delicate method, too. The buttery ginger sauce pairs very well here, it's a combination that just works.

1. Open the oysters (see page 192) and reserve the juices.

2. To make the ginger beurre blanc, put the shallots, ginger, wine and reserved oyster juices in a pan and cook until the wine has almost completely reduced. Add the cream and reduce the heat to low. Now add the butter, piece by piece, whisking all the time; do not allow the sauce to boil or it will split. Once all the butter is incorporated, season with salt and pepper to taste. Strain the sauce through a sieve into a bowl and cover the surface with clingfilm or baking parchment to prevent a skin forming. Keep warm.

3. Set up a bamboo steamer or turn your oven to the steam setting. Scrunch up some foil and lay it into the steamer or steamer tray and arrange the oysters so that they are level on the foil. Into each oyster put a pinch of chopped ginger and a few pieces of spring onion. Steam for 3 minutes.

4. Meanwhile, arrange 4 piles of wet salt on 4 plates. Gently warm the sauce – don't allow it to boil – and add the chopped coriander and cucumber. When the oysters are cooked, arrange 5–6 on each plate and pour in a spoonful of sauce. Serve immediately.

Serves 4 as a starter

Deep-Fried Oysters in a Seeded Crumb
with a Barbecue Sauce

12 live medium Pacific oysters
100g (3½oz) plain flour
2 eggs, beaten
2 teaspoons sesame seeds
2 teaspoons pumpkin seeds
2 teaspoons poppy seeds
2 teaspoons sunflower seeds
100g (3½oz) breadcrumbs
sunflower oil, for deep-frying
sea salt and freshly ground black pepper

For the barbecue sauce
olive oil
½ onion, chopped
2 garlic cloves, chopped
½ green chilli, deseeded and chopped
1 smoked chilli, chopped
1 red pepper, deseeded and chopped
1 oregano sprig, leaves picked and finely chopped
1 teaspoon hot smoked paprika
1 tablespoon fennel seeds
zest and juice of ½ orange
50g (1¾oz) caster sugar
200g (7oz) good-quality canned chopped tomatoes
75ml (2½fl oz) red wine vinegar
50ml (2fl oz) apple juice
1 teaspoon English mustard

To serve
dampened sea salt, to sit the oyster shells on
¼ iceberg lettuce, shredded

Crispy oysters are a firm favourite with our customers at the restaurants. The texture is so good and, let's face it, if you breadcrumb something, nine times out of ten it's delicious! The barbecue sauce is a great recipe to have made up for other uses too, but with these crispy oysters it works a treat.

1. To make the barbecue sauce, heat a frying pan over a medium heat and add a drizzle of olive oil. When hot, add the onion, garlic, chillies and red pepper and sweat for 2 minutes. Add the oregano, smoked paprika, fennel seeds and orange zest and cook for another minute. Next, add the sugar, tomatoes and wine vinegar, stir until the sugar is dissolved, then bubble to reduce until syrupy. Add the orange juice, apple juice and mustard. Bring to a simmer and bubble until the liquid has reduced by half. Taste and season with salt and pepper as required.

2. Tip the contents of the pan into a food processor and blitz for 2 minutes. Strain through a sieve into a bowl and leave to cool. This sauce will keep in the refrigerator for 1 week.

3. Shuck the oysters and reserve the shells (see page 192). Clean the oyster shells, then mix some sea salt with a little water to the texture of wet sand. Place little piles of wet salt on a platter with an oyster shell on each one.

4. When you are ready to serve, put the flour into a bowl and season with salt and pepper. Have the beaten eggs ready in a separate bowl. In a third bowl mix the seeds with the breadcrumbs.

5. Heat a deep-fat fryer to 180°C (350°F) or heat some sunflower oil in a deep, heavy-based pan (not filling more than two-thirds full). One by one, pass the oysters through the flour, then the egg and finally the seeded breadcrumbs to coat thoroughly, laying them out on a tray ready to cook. Deep-fry the oysters for 1 minute until crisp, then drain on kitchen paper.

6. To serve, place some shredded lettuce into each oyster shell, add a crispy oyster and spoon a little barbecue sauce on top. Serve hot.

Champagne-Pickled Oysters
with Apple & Grape Relish

Serves 4 as a starter

12 live medium Pacific oysters
100ml (3½fl oz) Champagne vinegar
1 banana shallot, finely chopped
1 celery stick, finely chopped
50ml (2fl oz) extra virgin olive oil, plus extra for dressing
1 Granny Smith apple
1 lemon, peeled and segmented, and each piece cut into 4, reserving any juice
12 seedless, white grapes
1 tablespoon chopped chives

To serve
dampened sea salt, to sit the shells on
lemon slices
1 bottle of chilled Champagne (obviously!)

Champagne and oysters have always been served together, and here they are again, but with a slightly different twist. Oysters really take to being pickled this way, the texture firms up and almost intensifies that earthy, sweet and salty character. I really enjoy oysters served this way. The apple and grape combo brings freshness to the dish.

1. Open the oysters (see page 192) and strain their juices through a sieve lined with muslin into a measuring jug. Keep the shells.

2. Pour 100ml (3½fl oz) of the oyster juice into a bowl and add the Champagne vinegar, shallot and celery. Add the oysters and mix gently. Cover with clingfilm, pushing it down onto the surface to keep the oysters submerged. Leave to pickle for a minimum of 2 hours and up to 24 hours.

3. When ready to serve, clean and dry the oyster shells thoroughly, then place them on a bed of salt to hold them steady. Peel and core the apple and finely chop. Place in water with the reserved lemon juice to stop the apples turning brown. Cut the grapes into slices.

4. Remove the oysters from the pickling bowl and place one in each shell. Combine the chopped chives, drained diced apple and grape slices, then place a generous spoonful on top of each oyster with some lemon slices and a drizzle of extra virgin olive oil. Serve immediately, with a glass of Champagne.

Raw Scallops
with Cicely, Apple, Lemon & Roe Mayonnaise

Serves 4 as a starter

8 large hand-dived scallops, or 12 medium scallops, shucked and cleaned, saving the roes (see page 193)
1 green apple, peeled, sliced and cut into matchsticks
1 lemon, peeled and segmented
24 sweet cicely leaves (for the glamour!), optional, alternatively use tarragon or chervil
sea salt
extra virgin olive oil, to serve

For the roe mayonnaise
8 scallop roes
2 tablespoons sea salt
2 teaspoons smoked paprika
60g (2¼oz) egg yolks
juice of ½ lemon
1 teaspoon English mustard
300ml (10fl oz) olive oil

A complete no-cook scallop dish; probably the favourite scallop dish I've created in my career so far. We get our scallops hand-dived and they are something else. When a product is so good, it's best to let it speak for itself. I like the roes, but a lot of people don't use them. This is a great way of using them, as they're not as challenging when made into a mayonnaise. If you can't get scallop roes, any good-quality fish roe will work the same, but depending on size you will have to cure in salt for longer. Seafood doesn't get much simpler than this dish.

1. To make the mayonnaise, place the roes in a bowl with the salt and paprika and leave for 1 hour in the refrigerator. After this time, wash off the salt and pat the roes dry with kitchen paper.

2. Place the roes, egg yolks, lemon juice and mustard into a small food processor. Blend for 30 seconds, then slowly pour in the oil in a steady stream until the mayonnaise is thick. Scrape the sides of the food processor down, season with salt and pepper and blitz again for 30 seconds. Transfer to a disposable piping bag. Keep in the refrigerator for up to 3 days.

3. To finish the dish, take 4 plates and place them in the refrigerator. Using a very clean chopping board and a sharp knife, slice each scallop into 3 slices if large, 2 slices if medium. Lay 6 scallop slices onto each plate and season with sea salt. Pipe a small dot of mayonnaise onto each scallop, then top with a few apple matchsticks, a lemon segment and a sweet cicely leaf, if using. Finish with a drizzle of extra virgin olive oil and serve.

Baked Scallops on Squash Purée
with a Spiced Hazelnut Butter

Serves 4 as a starter

12 fresh scallops, shucked and cleaned, shells reserved (see page 193)
240ml (8¾fl oz) dry cider
seaweed or sea salt, to serve (optional)

For the squash purée
1 small butternut squash, peeled, deseeded and sliced
a drizzle of olive oil
75g (2½oz) unsalted butter
½ teaspoon cayenne pepper
1 teaspoon ground cumin
1 teaspoon ground coriander
100ml (3½fl oz) water
sea salt and freshly ground black pepper

For the crumbs
100g (3½oz) crustless good-quality brown bread
1 tablespoon chopped flat-leaf parsley leaves
40g (1½oz) Parmesan, finely grated

For the spiced hazelnut butter
100g (3½oz) blanched hazelnuts
150g (5½oz) unsalted butter, cut into cubes and softened
½ banana shallot, finely chopped
½ garlic clove, finely chopped
1 teaspoon ground cumin
a small pinch of cayenne pepper
1 teaspoon ground coriander
1 tablespoon chopped flat-leaf parsley leaves

I do adore a baked scallop. There's something special about scallops that have been baked in the shell with a tasty compound butter. I think it's the aroma of the hot shell and the sizzling butter and hazelnuts that get me with this dish. Feel free to play around with the butter recipe – the possibilities are endless with the different combinations of nuts or spices you could use.

1. To make the squash purée, heat a large pan with a tight-fitting lid over a medium heat. Once hot, add a drizzle of oil and the butter. When the butter starts to sizzle, add the squash and sweat for 3 minutes in the pan, stirring occasionally. Add the spices and season with salt and pepper. Pour in the measured water and stir, then cover and cook for 10 minutes, stirring every minute or so. When the squash has collapsed and there is nothing raw visible, continue to cook until the mixture has no excess water. Carefully transfer to a food processor and blitz for 2 minutes until smooth. Cover and set aside.

2. Preheat the oven to 180°C Fan (400°F), Gas Mark 6. Clean the scallop shells, dry well and reserve for cooking.

3. To make the crumbs, blitz the bread and parsley in a food processor until it is reduced to crumbs. Add the cheese and blitz for 30 seconds. Tip onto a tray and set aside.

4. To make the butter, tip the hazelnuts onto a baking tray and roast in the oven for 5 minutes until golden. Remove and leave to cool.

5. Put the softened butter into a bowl with the shallot, garlic, spices and chopped parsley. Mix well to combine and season with salt and pepper to taste. Chop the hazelnuts until fine, add to the butter and mix well. Set aside until ready to cook.

6. Increase the oven temperature to 220°C Fan (475°F), Gas Mark 9.

7. Place 2 teaspoons of squash purée into each scallop shell and 1 scallop on top. Pour 4 teaspoons cider into each shell and top with 20g/¾oz (roughly a heaped tablespoon) of the spiced hazelnut butter. Scatter the crumbs evenly over the top and place the scallops on a large baking tray (you may need to use 2 trays). Bake in the oven for 6–8 minutes. To check that they are cooked, insert a small knife into the centre of a scallop and hold it there for 10 seconds. Pull the knife out and touch it to the back of your hand; if the blade feels hot, they are ready. It should not be piping hot.

8. Serve the scallops straight away on a bed of seaweed or sea salt mixed with a drop of water.

Serves 4 as a starter

8 large hand-dived scallops, shucked and cleaned (see page 193)
4 teaspoons finely chopped red onion
½ green chilli, deseeded and finely chopped
100g (3½oz) cucumber, deseeded and finely chopped
100g (3½oz) watermelon, peeled and finely chopped
zest of 1 lime and the juice of 2 limes
a handful of coriander, leaves picked and chopped, reserving a few whole leaves for garnish
sea salt and freshly ground black pepper

To serve
100ml (3½fl oz) soured cream
extra virgin olive oil, to drizzle

Scallop Ceviche
with Watermelon, Cucumber & Avocado

There are many species of seafood that you can serve in a ceviche style, but scallops, for me, have to be the finest. I think it's the way the scallop meat takes on the citrus marinade and really gets infused with the flavours. Just make sure when you are doing preparations like this one, that you are super-careful with your hygiene and also buy the best quality you can afford. It will make a difference.

1. Cut the scallops into small dice and place in a bowl with the red onion, chilli, cucumber, melon, lime zest and juice. Season with salt and add the chopped coriander. Toss well to mix, then cover and leave to cure in the refrigerator for 10 minutes.

2. Divide the ceviche among 4 plates. Top each with a dollop of soured cream, a drizzle of olive oil and a coriander leaf. Serve immediately.

Shore Crab Soup
with Steamed Crab Dumplings

Serves 4

1kg (2lb 4oz) live shore crabs, placed in the freezer 1 hour before cooking
olive oil
100ml (3½fl oz) dry sherry
1 onion, finely chopped
2 carrots, peeled and sliced
4 garlic cloves, chopped
2 sprigs of thyme, picked
1 tablespoon tomato purée
thinly pared zest of 1 large orange, chopped
1 tarragon sprig
5 ripe plum tomatoes, chopped
50ml (2fl oz) brandy
2 litres (3½ pints) water
100ml (3½fl oz) double cream
sea salt and freshly ground black pepper
extra virgin olive oil, for drizzling

For the dumplings
a drizzle of olive oil, plus extra for oiling
1 shallot, finely chopped
1 green chilli, deseeded and finely chopped
300g (10½oz) gurnard fillet, pin-boned, skinned and chopped
1 egg, beaten
200g (7oz) crab meat, picked and checked for shell
1 tablespoon finely chopped flat-leaf parsley leaves
1 tablespoon finely chopped tarragon leaves

A good crab soup will always impress, and when you add a few of these crab dumplings, you're laughing. I think shore crabs make the best crab stock, but they can be substituted for velvet crab, or prawn or lobster shells. The finished soup, before adding the cream, freezes well and will be good for a few months – just add the cream when you defrost. You can use any white fish for the dumpling base, but gurnard is best for me.

1. Preheat the oven to 180°C Fan (400°F), Gas Mark 6.

2. Put the shore crabs in a large roasting tray and drizzle them with olive oil. Roast for 20 minutes, then turn them over and return to the oven for a further 20 minutes. Take the tray from the oven and gradually pour in the sherry, stirring to deglaze and scraping up the sediment from the bottom. Gently crush the crabs with the end of a rolling pin or a kitchen mallet.

3. Place a large saucepan over a medium heat. When hot, add a good drizzle of olive oil. Once hot, add the onion, carrots, garlic and thyme. Cook, stirring occasionally, for 3 minutes. Add the tomato purée and cook for 5 minutes, then add the orange zest, tarragon and tomatoes and cook for another 5 minutes. Now add the roasted crabs with the brandy and the measured water. Bring to a simmer and cook gently, uncovered, for 45 minutes, skimming off any impurities that rise to the surface from time to time.

4. While the soup is cooking, make the crab dumplings. Heat a frying pan over a medium heat and add a drizzle of oil, followed by the shallot and chilli. Sweat for 2 minutes to soften without colouring, then tip out onto a tray to cool.

5. Put the gurnard into a food processor and blitz for 30 seconds. Scrape down the sides of the food processor and season the mixture with salt and pepper, then blend for another 30 seconds. Transfer the mixture to a cold bowl and add the cooled shallot mixture, beaten egg, crab meat and herbs. Mix well with your hands, then shape into golf ball-sized pieces and place on a tray. Refrigerate.

6. Once the soup is cooked, pour the contents of the pan into a blender carefully (as the soup will be hot), pulse to break up the shells, then blend for 2 minutes. Strain through a fine sieve into a clean pan. Add the cream and bring to a gentle simmer. Taste and correct the seasoning. Keep warm.

7. Prepare a steamer basket over a pan of simmering water. Take the dumplings from the refrigerator, oil them all over and season with a little salt. Line your steamer with silicone paper. Place the dumplings in the steamer, cover and cook for 5 minutes.

8. To serve, ladle the soup equally into 4 warm bowls and share the dumplings among them. Drizzle with extra virgin olive oil and serve at once.

Spider Crab Croquettes
with Sweetcorn Sauce

Serves 4 as a starter

olive oil
1 onion, finely chopped
2 garlic cloves, finely chopped
1 fennel bulb, trimmed and finely chopped
150ml (5fl oz) white wine
400ml (14fl oz) fish stock
120g (4¼oz) unsalted butter
100g (3½oz) plain flour, plus an extra 50g (1¾oz) for coating
150g (5½oz) cooked spider crab claw meat
150g (5½oz) cooked spider crab brown meat, sieved
4 spring onions, finely sliced
2 tablespoons finely chopped tarragon leaves
50g (1¾oz) Parmesan, grated
2 eggs, beaten
100g (3½oz) dried breadcrumbs
sunflower oil, for deep-frying
sea salt and freshly ground black pepper

For the sweetcorn sauce
4 corn on the cob
150ml (5fl oz) fish stock
1 red chilli, deseeded and finely chopped
zest and juice of 1 lime
2 tablespoons chopped chives
1 tablespoon chopped tarragon leaves

To serve
30g (1oz) Parmesan, grated
1 lime, cut into 4 wedges

Spider crab (or Cornish king crab) is a good option when it comes to sustainability. When they're in season they're plentiful. If you're lucky enough to have a fishmonger who stocks picked spider crab meat, then this recipe is simple. If you need to cook and pick it yourself, it's more time-consuming, but very rewarding. You can substitue with any crab, lobster or prawns in this dish, all of which I have used with success.

1. To make the croquettes, heat a sauté pan over a medium heat and drizzle in some oil. Once hot, sweat the onion, garlic and fennel for 5 minutes, stirring occasionally until the vegetables start to soften, but not colour. Remove the vegetables from the pan and set aside.

2. Heat the white wine and stock in a separate pan until simmering.

3. Wipe out the first pan, reheat over a medium heat and add the butter. When it starts to bubble, add the 100g (3½oz) flour, stir and cook for 2 minutes. Now add the hot liquid, a ladleful at a time, stirring constantly to keep it smooth. Reduce the heat and simmer for 20 minutes, stirring.

4. After this time, add both the crab meats, the spring onions, tarragon and Parmesan and stir in. Remove from the heat and season with salt and pepper to taste. Tip into a tray lined with greaseproof paper and cool, then refrigerate for at least 1½ hours until set.

5. To make the sweetcorn sauce, grate the kernels from the corn cobs, collecting all the juices as you do so.

6. Put the grated corn and juices into a pan with the fish stock. Add a pinch of salt and cook over a medium heat for 10 minutes, stirring continuously. Push the mix through a sieve into a bowl to remove the kernel skins.

7. Pour the sweetcorn sauce into a pan with the chilli and lime zest and juice and warm through. Taste, adding salt and pepper, if necessary. Spoon into a container and leave to cool. Refrigerate until needed.

8. Using a spoon, divide the set crab mixture into 35g (1¼oz) pieces and roll into balls. Have the beaten eggs ready in one bowl, the 50g (1¾oz) flour in another and the breadcrumbs on a tray. Pass the crab croquettes through the flour, then the eggs and finally into the breadcrumbs to coat. Set aside until ready to cook.

9. Heat a deep-fat fryer to 180°C (350°F) or heat some sunflower oil in a deep, heavy-based pan (not filling more than two-thirds full). Fry the crab croquettes, in batches as necessary, for 2–3 minutes. Remove with a slotted spoon to a plate lined with kitchen paper and season with salt.

10. Meanwhile, gently warm the sauce and stir in the herbs.

11. Serve the croquettes on small plates along with the sauce, with grated Parmesan over the top and lime wedges on the side.

Crab with Apple & Carrot Salad
with a Curried Brown Crab Dressing

Serves 4

1 live brown crab, weighing about 1kg (2lb 4oz), placed in the freezer 1 hour before cooking
sea salt and freshly ground black pepper

For the apple & carrot salad
2 carrots, peeled, finely sliced and cut into matchsticks
2 Granny Smith apples, peeled and cut into matchsticks
1 tablespoon chopped mint leaves
1 tablespoon chopped coriander leaves
zest and juice of 1 lime

For the curry dressing
2 egg yolks
zest and juice of 1 lime
250ml (9fl oz) Curry Oil (see page 251)
75ml (2½fl oz) good-quality apple juice
4 tablespoons crème fraîche
1 tablespoon chopped coriander

To serve
a small handful of watercress, picked and washed
coriander leaves

This salad is really refreshing and simple to put together once you have mastered the crab cooking and picking. Of course, you could buy the crab meat to make it even simpler. The dressing with this dish is extremely yummy. When hen crabs are available in autumn, this dish goes to another level because the brown meat in the female crabs is particularly good. The curry oil is a useful storecupboard ingredient to have, so don't worry if there's some left over – it can be used as a simple salad dressing or to cook a lovely pan-fried fillet of fish.

1. To cook the crab, bring a large pan of water to the boil and season it generously with salt (make it very salty). Plunge the crab into the boiling water and cook for 15 minutes. As soon as it is cooked, lift out onto a tray and leave until cool enough to handle.

2. Prepare the crab (as described on page 196), extracting all the white meat from the body, claws and legs, and the brown meat from the top shell. Don't forget to discard the dead man's fingers, stomach sac and hard membranes from the body. When you have extracted all the meat, go through it carefully a couple of times with your fingers to check for fragments of shell and cartilage. You can refrigerate the crab meat or freeze it at this point, but I prefer to eat it straight away. You'll need 100g (3½oz) of white crab per portion and 4 tablespoons of brown crab for the dressing. The rest will freeze well for another day.

3. To prepare the salad, mix the carrots, apples, herbs, lime juice and zest in a bowl. Season with salt and pepper to taste. Set aside.

4. For the dressing, whisk together the egg yolks, lime zest and juice. Slowly pour in the curry oil, whisking continuously until all the oil is incorporated. Season with salt and pepper and taste.

5. Add 1 tablespoon of the dressing to the white crab meat and fold in well. Season with salt and pepper.

6. Add 4 tablespoons of the brown crab meat, the crème fraîche and coriander to the remaining dressing and mix well.

7. To finish, spoon the white crab meat neatly onto 4 plates and pile the salad alongside. Drizzle over a few spoonfuls of the dressing and finish with some watercress and coriander. Serve the rest of the dressing in a bowl on the side.

Lobster Cocktail Flatbreads
with Orange & Basil

Serves 4

2 live lobsters, about 600g (1lb 5oz) each, placed in the freezer 30 minutes before cooking
2 tablespoons mayonnaise
4 spring onions, finely sliced
12 basil leaves, finely sliced
sea salt and freshly ground black pepper

For the flatbread
250g (9oz) self-raising flour, plus extra for dusting
2 teaspoons sea salt
200g (7oz) full-fat Greek yogurt
10 basil leaves, shredded
1 teaspoon fennel seeds
20g (¾oz) Parmesan, grated
olive oil, for greasing and drizzling

For the salad
1 baby gem lettuce, leaves separated, washed and dried
1 red chicory, leaves separated, washed and dried
2 tablespoons extra virgin olive oil
2 tablespoons red wine vinegar

To serve
1 large orange, segmented
4 spring onions, finely sliced
a few small basil leaves
extra virgin olive oil

This combination of flavours has been very faithful to me over the years. I first paired lobster with orange and basil back when I created a recipe for lobster risotto (see page 231) at my first restaurant, The Black Pig. Raised eyebrows were seen from the guests – fruit with lobster, in a risotto? Little did they need to worry – this is a combination that delivers, and thank goodness those customers agreed. The recipe here is a lovely lunchtime dish or can be a starter for a swanky dinner. The flatbread recipe is very easy to make and the combinations of ingredients you could add is endless.

1. First, make the flatbread dough. Place all the ingredients, except the olive oil, in a bowl and mix well until evenly combined and the mixture forms a dough. Turn out onto a lightly floured work surface and knead for 2 minutes. Cover with a clean, damp tea towel.

2. Preheat the oven to 200°C Fan (425°F), Gas Mark 7 and oil 2 large baking sheets with olive oil.

3. Divide the dough into 8 equal portions and shape each into a ball. Roll each one into a round, about 3mm (1/8 inch) thick and lift onto the oiled trays. Slide the flatbreads into the oven and bake for 12–14 minutes until nicely coloured and crispy at the edges. As you take them from the oven, drizzle with a little olive oil. Place on a wire rack to cool.

4. Bring a pan of salted water to the boil over a high heat. Once the water is boiling, quickly take the lobsters from the freezer, place on a board and firmly insert the tip of your knife into the cross on the head to kill each one instantly. Plunge the lobsters straight into the boiling water and cook for 11 minutes. Remove from the water and place on a tray to cool down. When cool enough to handle, carefully extract the meat (see page 194). Cover and refrigerate if not using straight away.

5. To make the cocktail, chop the lobster into 1cm (½ inch) pieces. Put the mayonnaise, spring onions and basil into a bowl and mix well. Add the lobster pieces and mix carefully so as not to break them up. Season with salt and pepper to taste.

6. For the salad, put the lettuce and chicory leaves into a bowl and dress with the oil, vinegar and some salt and pepper.

7. To serve, share the salad and lobster cocktail equally among the flatbreads. Top with the orange segments, spring onions and basil leaves and drizzle with extra virgin olive oil.

Lobster Kedgeree
with Turmeric Poached Eggs

Serves 4

50ml (2fl oz) olive oil
50g (1¾oz) unsalted butter
1 onion, finely chopped
1 leek, finely chopped
1 celery stick, finely chopped
1 fennel bulb, finely chopped
1 carrot, finely chopped
1 garlic clove, finely chopped
50g (1¾oz) fresh root ginger, peeled and finely chopped
650ml (22fl oz) Lobster Stock (see page 250)
300g (10½oz) basmati rice, washed and drained
1 teaspoon saffron threads
1 tablespoon medium curry powder
2 teaspoons ground turmeric
2 cooked lobsters, meat flaked into chunks (see page 194)
a handful of coriander, chopped
20 mint leaves, chopped
4 teaspoons chopped chives
2 spring onions, finely sliced
sea salt and freshly ground black pepper
1 lemon, cut into 4 wedges, to serve

For the turmeric poached egg
75ml (2½fl oz) white wine vinegar
2 teaspoons ground turmeric
4 large eggs

You can't beat a good bowl of kedgeree, so I thought why not try it with lobster instead of smoked fish and it worked so well. At our guesthouse, we serve kedgeree freshly made at every service and it goes down a treat. I used to serve it with the traditional boiled egg, but I found that a poached egg eats together with the rice dish so much better. I've been told that the actual Indian version of kedgeree is made with lentils, as well as rice. That sounds delicious to me, and of course lobster with lentils works too. First though, give this a try – you won't be disappointed, I promise.

1. Preheat the oven to 180°C Fan (400°F), Gas Mark 6.

2. Place an ovenproof pan over a medium heat. When hot, add the oil and butter. When the butter is bubbling, add the onion, leek, celery, fennel, carrot, garlic and ginger and cook, stirring, for 2 minutes to soften but not colour. In a separate pan, bring the lobster stock to a simmer. Add the rice to the vegetable pan and cook, stirring, for 1 minute. Add the saffron, curry powder, turmeric and some salt and pepper. Pour over the lobster stock and bring the rice to the boil, then cover with a lid or some foil. Place the pan in the oven and cook for 10 minutes until tender.

3. To poach the eggs, fill a large pan with some water and add the vinegar and turmeric. Bring to a simmer ready to cook the eggs.

4. Take the rice pan out of the oven and lift the lid. Add the lobster and fold through the rice carefully. Put the lid back on while you cook the eggs.

5. Carefully crack the eggs into the simmering water and cook for 4 minutes. Drain the poached eggs on a plate lined with kitchen paper.

6. Gently fold the herbs and spring onions through the rice and season with salt and pepper to taste. Serve the kedgeree straight from the pan into warmed bowls, place the a poached egg in the centre of each bowl and serve with lemon wedges on the side.

Lobster Risotto
with Spring Onions, Orange & Basil

Serves 4

1 large live lobster, or 2 smaller ones, placed in the freezer 30 minutes before cooking
2 litres (3½ pints) Lobster Stock (see page 250)
50ml (2fl oz) olive oil
100g (3½oz) unsalted butter
2 shallots, finely chopped
2 garlic cloves, halved and germ removed
200g (7oz) carnaroli risotto rice
8 spring onions, finely sliced
100g (3½oz) Parmesan, grated
1 large orange, peeled, segmented and sliced
sea salt and freshly ground black pepper

For the basil oil
60 basil leaves
400ml (14fl oz) olive oil

For the foam
400ml (14fl oz) Lobster Stock (see page 250)
100ml (3½fl oz) double cream
300ml (10fl oz) full-fat milk

This is the dish that gained me national attention, and the recipe I've cooked most often in all my restaurants. When I first cooked it at my restaurant The Black Pig in Rock, Cornwall I was a virtual unknown and had to gain customers' trust… I couldn't afford to serve a whole lobster, but this risotto allowed me to make 3–4 portions from each lobster, using every part and bringing the cost down to an acceptable level. It's a special dish to me and always will be. It comes complete with an early Noughties foam sauce. Check me out!

1. For the basil oil, put the basil into a blender with the oil and blitz for 2 minutes. Pour the oil mixture into a jug and leave to infuse and settle for 24 hours. Strain the oil through a fine sieve into a sterilized bottle, keep in the refrigerator and use within 1 month.

2. To make the foam, in a medium saucepan, bring the lobster stock to a simmer and reduce to about 2 tablespoons. At this point, add the cream, bring to a simmer, then add the milk and season to taste. Set aside while you make the risotto.

3. Bring a pan of salted water to the boil over a high heat. Once the water is boiling, quickly take the lobsters from the freezer, place on a board and firmly insert the tip of your knife into the cross on the head to kill each one instantly. Plunge the lobsters straight into the boiling water and cook for 8 minutes. Remove from the water and place on a tray to cool. When cool enough to handle, carefully extract the meat (see page 194). Cover and refrigerate if not using straight away.

4. Before you start the risotto, chop the lobster meat into equal bite-sized pieces, not too big. Bring the lobster stock to the boil in a pan and keep it at a gentle simmer.

5. Place a large saucepan over a medium heat and add the olive oil and half the butter. When it is bubbling, add the shallots and garlic and cook for 1 minute without colouring, then add the rice and cook for 1 minute, stirring constantly. Add the hot stock to the rice a ladleful at a time, stirring and allowing each addition to be absorbed before adding the next. Continue in this way for 14 minutes, or until the rice is al dente and you have a creamy-looking risotto.

6. Warm the foam sauce until you see the steam rising, then use a hand blender or whisk to mix vigorously to create foam. Keep warm.

7. Turn the heat under the risotto down to its lowest setting. Add the chopped lobster and spring onions to the rice and cook for 1 minute, then add the Parmesan and the remaining butter in pieces. Warm gently for 2 minutes, stirring all the time. Finally, add the chopped orange and season with salt and pepper to taste. Serve immediately in 4 bowls, with the lobster foam spooned around and a good drizzle of the basil oil.

Whole Lobster & its Bisque

Serves 4

4 x live lobsters, roughly 500g (1lb 2oz) each, placed in the freezer 30 minutes before cooking
4 tablespoons extra virgin olive oil
1 sprig of rosemary, picked and finely chopped
1 garlic clove, finely chopped
2 large potatoes, peeled and halved
2-finger pinch of saffron threads
4 ripe tomatoes
sea salt and freshly ground black pepper

For the bisque

6 very ripe vine-ripened tomatoes
olive oil, for drizzling
100ml (3½fl oz) water
75g (2½oz) unsalted butter
1 onion, chopped
2 garlic cloves, chopped
2 carrots, peeled and chopped
2 sprigs of rosemary
zest and juice of 1 orange
100ml (3½fl oz) brandy
600ml (20fl oz) Roasted Fish Stock (see page 250)
100ml (3½fl oz) double cream

To serve

selection of herbs (fennel, chervil, dill), washed and picked

This dish is obviously for a special occasion, and I wouldn't expect anyone to be eating it as an everyday dinner, but never say never! Lobster needs celebrating, but I believe it should be kept simple. It's too beautiful to mess with and it would be a terrible shame to overcook or lose the flavour of lobster. This dish is actually relatively simple if you follow the recipe, and the bisque method can be used for crab shells as well.

1. Bring a large pan of very salty water to a simmer. Take your lobsters from the freezer and place them on a board. Insert the tip of a strong, sharp knife firmly into the cross on the back of each lobster's head. (This will kill it instantly, although it may still move a little.) Carefully pull the lobster tail away from the head, keeping the head for the bisque, and remove the claws, too. Add the claws and tail to the simmering water and cook for 2 minutes, then immediately remove from the pan and leave until cool enough to handle.

2. Crack open the claws and knuckles and extract the meat (see page 194). Keep all the shells. Hold the tail firmly with both hands and crack it. Placing your hands either side of the lobster and pull it apart. Cut through the centre of the tail at an angle to remove the dark intestinal tract. Set the lobster meat aside until ready to serve or put it in the refrigerator if not serving immediately.

3. For the bisque, preheat the grill. Cut the 6 tomatoes in half and place them on a grill tray. Grill for 20 minutes until coloured, blistered and soft but not collapsing, then remove and set aside.

4. Preheat the oven to 180°C Fan (400°F), Gas Mark 6.

5. Put the lobster heads and shells in a large roasting tray and drizzle them with olive oil. Roast for 20 minutes, then turn the shells over and return to the oven for a further 10 minutes. Take the tray from the oven and deglaze with the measured water, scraping up the sediment from the bottom. Reduce the oven temperature to 150°C Fan (340°F), Gas Mark 3½.

6. Place a large saucepan over a medium heat. When hot, add a good drizzle of olive oil and the butter. When bubbling, add the onion, garlic, carrots and rosemary and cook, stirring occasionally, for 3 minutes. Add the roasted tomatoes and orange zest and cook for another 5 minutes. Now add the roasted shells and pan juices along with the brandy. Flame the brandy carefully (watch out for your eyebrows!) Add the stock and bring to a simmer and cook gently, uncovered, for 30 minutes, skimming off any impurities that rise to the surface from time to time.

Recipe continued overleaf

Recipe continued

7. While the bisque is cooking, blanch the 4 whole tomatoes in boiling water for 10 seconds, then drain. When cool enough to handle, skin and quarter them. Spread them out on a baking tray, drizzle with olive oil and season with the rosemary, chopped garlic and some salt and pepper, then roast for 1 hour until semi-dried. Set aside.

8. Meanwhile, cook the potatoes in boiling, salted water with the saffron until tender, then drain and keep warm.

9. Once the bisque is cooked, strain through a fine sieve into a clean pan – discard the shells and vegetables. Add the cream and bring the bisque to a gentle simmer. Taste and correct the seasoning with salt, pepper and a few drops of the orange juice.

10. To serve, warm 4 bowls. Add the lobster to the bisque and gently heat through for 3 minutes. Share the potatoes and semi-dried tomato quarters among the bowls, and add the meat from 1 lobster to each bowl. Ladle the bisque equally between the bowls and scatter over the herbs. Serve immediately, I suggest with lots of bread and butter on the side for mopping up the wonderful bisque!

Braised Cuttlefish & Pea Pie
with Green Sauce Gravy

Serves 4

For the pie filling
sunflower oil
1kg (2lb 4oz) cleaned cuttlefish
1 onion, quartered
1 large carrot, peeled and left whole
2 garlic cloves, crushed
1 sprig of rosemary
2 bay leaves
200ml (7fl oz) red wine
600ml (20fl oz) Roasted Fish Stock (see page 250) or chicken stock
sea salt and freshly ground black pepper

For the pie sauce
50g (1¾oz) unsalted butter
1 onion, finely chopped
1 leek, washed and finely sliced
60g (2¼oz) plain flour
100ml (3½fl oz) red wine vinegar
200g (7oz) fresh peas, podded
2 tablespoons chopped mint leaves
2 tablespoons chopped flat-leaf parsley leaves

For the pastry
260g (9¼oz) plain flour, plus extra for dusting
1 teaspoon fine sea salt
2 teaspoons finely chopped rosemary leaves
75g (2½oz) unsalted butter, chopped
75g (2½oz) lard, chopped
1 tablespoon milk
1 egg yolk beaten with 1 tablespoon of milk, for the egg wash

Cuttlefish is as meaty as most animal meats, so in a lot of my recipes where I think meat would be nice, I use cuttlefish as an alternative. This pie is absolutely delicious and a great use of such an underrated and underused species. You can make a big pie, like I have here, or do individual ones. The pie mix will also freeze well and if you have any left over, you could turn it into a stew and add a few dumplings. Cuttlefish is a species with endless possibilities. It should go without saying that this dinner needs mashed potatoes and more peas!

1. Heat a frying pan over a medium heat and add a drizzle of oil. Once hot, add the cuttlefish and fry for 2 minutes until it starts to colour (you may need to do this in 2 batches if your frying pan is small). Season with salt and pepper and tip the cuttlefish into a large saucepan.

2. Wipe the frying pan clean and put it back over the same heat. Add another drizzle of oil and sweat off the onion, carrot and garlic for 2 minutes. Add the rosemary, bay, red wine and stock. Pour over the cuttlefish and bring to a gentle simmer. Cook for 1 hour. Once cooked, strain the stock into another pan and keep warm. Chop the cuttlefish into large pieces and set aside. Discard the vegetables and herbs.

3. For the pie sauce, melt the butter in a large pan and soften the onion and leek for 2 minutes, stirring occasionally. Season with salt and pepper, then stir in the flour. Cook for 2 minutes. Pour in the vinegar and gradually add the warm cuttlefish stock, ladle by ladle, stirring all the time until the liquid thickens. You want it quite thick, so you may not use all the stock. When the sauce is smooth, remove from the heat and add the cooked cuttlefish, peas and herbs. Taste and season with salt and pepper. Leave to cool in the refrigerator with a layer of clingfilm or greaseproof paper on the surface to stop a skin forming.

4. To make the pastry, put the flour, salt, rosemary, butter and lard into a bowl and rub in, using your fingertips, until the mixture resembles fine breadcrumbs. Add the milk and mix carefully until everything comes together as a dough; don't overwork it. Flatten the dough into a disc shape and wrap in clingfilm. Leave to rest in the refrigerator for at least 30 minutes.

Ingredients & recipe continued overleaf

Recipe continued

For the gravy
75g (2½oz) caster sugar
1 red onion, finely chopped
2 garlic cloves, finely chopped
2 teaspoons finely chopped rosemary leaves
1 tablespoon plain flour
100ml (3½fl oz) red wine vinegar
4 anchovy fillets, finely chopped
300ml (10fl oz) red wine
500ml (18fl oz) chicken stock
1 tablespoon capers
1 gherkin, finely chopped
1 teaspoon English mustard
2 tablespoons chopped flat-leaf parsley leaves
1 tablespoon chopped mint leaves

5. To make the gravy, heat a saucepan over a medium heat and add the sugar to the pan, leaving it to melt and caramelize. Toss in the onion, garlic and rosemary and cook, stirring, for 2 minutes until the onion has softened. Add the flour and cook, stirring constantly, for 1 minute, then add the wine vinegar and anchovies, stirring as you do so. Simmer for 1 minute. Pour in the wine and cook for another 5 minutes, stirring all the time. Now add the stock and simmer until the gravy is reduced and thickened to the consistency you like. When you hit your desired consistency, stir in the capers, gherkin and mustard. Keep warm while you bake the pie.

6. Preheat the oven to 180°C Fan (400°F), Gas Mark 6 and take the pie filling from the refrigerator. Roll out the pastry to the thickness of a £1 coin and line the pie dish (about 2 litre/3½ pint capacity) with two-thirds of the pastry, leaving the excess overhanging the edges. Brush the pastry around the rim of the dish with egg wash. Spoon in the cuttlefish mixture to about three-quarters full. Place the rest of the pastry over the mixture to make a lid, press the edges together to seal it and crimp, then trim off the excess. Brush the top of the pie with egg wash and cut a small cross in the centre to allow steam to escape.

7. Place the pie dish on a baking tray and bake for 45 minutes until the pastry is golden and the filling is piping hot.

8. When the pie is ready, heat your gravy and add the herbs. Divide the pie between 4 plates and serve with the gravy on the side.

Marinated Squid Salad
with Peas, Salami & a Sherry Dressing

Serves 4 as a starter or light lunch

2 handfuls of fresh peas
2 garlic cloves, chopped
600g (1lb 5oz) medium squid, cleaned, body cut into rings, fins scored (see page 198)
1 fennel bulb, finely sliced (ideally on a mandoline)
1 Baby Gem lettuce, leaves separated and washed
150g (5½oz) spicy salami, sliced and cut into strips
1 tablespoon chopped flat-leaf parsley leaves
1 tablespoon chopped mint leaves
1 punnet of pea shoots, cut and washed
sea salt and freshly ground black pepper

For the dressing
150ml (5fl oz) extra virgin olive oil
50ml (2fl oz) sherry vinegar
50ml (2fl oz) Fino sherry
1 shallot, finely chopped

Marinated and cooked this way isn't something you would probably think to do with squid. Most of the time it's coated and deep-fried or cooked whole on a plancha or in a hot pan, both of which are fantastic as well and I wouldn't turn my nose up at either of them. Marinating, though, is a lovely way to introduce extra flavour and improve the texture. You can serve this straight away, but it's better if you leave it for a few hours in the marinade. A salad is a wonderful thing when the textures and ingredients are a bit different – this one is certainly that!

1. For the dressing, whisk the olive oil, sherry vinegar and sherry together in a large bowl, then add the shallot and some salt and pepper. Set aside.

2. In a saucepan, bring around 2 litres (3½ pints) of water to the boil and season generously with salt. Blanch the peas for 2 minutes, then drain and refresh them in iced water. Add the garlic to the boiling water and simmer for 2 minutes, then add the squid to the boiling water and blanch for 30 seconds. Remove and drain well. Drop the squid straight into the dressing and mix. Leave to cool and marinate for 2 hours.

3. Drain the peas from the iced water and place in a big bowl with the fennel, lettuce and salami. Season with salt and pepper and mix well.

4. When ready to serve, add the chopped herbs to the squid and mix well, then tip the squid and dressing into the salad. Mix well and share among 4 plates. Scatter over the pea shoots and finish with a drizzle of any extra dressing. This dish requires a bread-mopping exercise, so make sure you have some!

Serves 4

75g/2½oz spelt
sunflower oil
30g (1oz) shallot, chopped
100g (3½oz) smoked streaky bacon
1 teaspoon smoked paprika
15g (½oz) sea salt
200ml (7fl oz) apple juice
175ml (6fl oz) double cream
300ml (10fl oz) pig's blood (pre-order from a good butcher)
50g (1¾oz) jumbo porridge oats
300g (10½oz) raw cuttlefish, finely chopped

For the apple relish

500g (1lb 2oz) cooking apples, peeled and chopped
2 shallots, chopped
250ml (9fl oz) dry cider
125ml (4fl oz) cider vinegar
75g (2½oz) caster sugar
1 red chilli, deseeded and chopped
1 star anise
2 cloves

For the watercress salad

1 bunch of watercress, picked and washed
1 green apple, peeled and chopped into small cubes
1 tablespoon cider vinegar
2 tablespoons extra virgin olive oil
1 tablespoon chopped chives
1 tablespoon chopped tarragon leaves
sea salt and freshly ground black pepper

Cuttlefish Black Pudding
with Apple Relish & Watercress Salad

Earlier in my career, I made a lot of black pudding. It's something I always enjoyed making, because the results were so much more impressive than the store-bought stuff. This recipe came about when we were writing a menu for a new restaurant. We wanted a seafood starter, but not one you'd expect. My chefs thought I was mad when I suggested it, but we set about creating a recipe with cuttlefish instead of the usual white fat that's found in most recipes. I'd always thought cuttlefish, when chopped, looked like that fat, so we had a go. It took several weeks to get it right, but when we did it came out so well. This recipe makes more than you need, but freezes well. The apple relish is the perfect condiment to go alongside. Surf and turf with a difference!

1. Cook the spelt for 30 minutes in lightly salted simmering water, then drain.

2. Preheat the oven to 140°C Fan (325°F), Gas Mark 3. Line a terrine mould with a double layer of clingfilm, with plenty of overhang.

3. Heat a sauté pan over a medium heat and add a drizzle of oil. Sweat the shallot and bacon for 2 minutes, then add the paprika and salt and stir in. Add the apple juice, cream and blood and heat gently until thick and darker in colour. Stir in the oats, cooked spelt and cuttlefish.

4. Transfer the mixture to the lined terrine and bring the overhanging clingfilm up over the top to seal it, then cover with foil. Place the terrine in a high-sided oven tray. Boil the kettle and pour in enough water to come halfway up the terrine mould. Carefully slide it into the oven and cook for 1 hour 10 minutes.

5. To check that it's cooked, the internal temperature should be 90°C (195°F). Once it is, leave it to cool and then place in the refrigerator for at least 6 hours. Ideally, make the day before and leave overnight.

6. To make the apple relish, place all the ingredients into a pan and cook at a simmer for 1 hour, stirring occasionally. When the mixture starts to catch on the bottom of the pan, reduce the heat and cook for 20 more minutes, stirring occasionally. Leave to cool, then place in the refrigerator.

7. For the salad, mix everything together and season with salt and pepper.

8. When you are ready to serve, unwrap the black pudding and slice it into 2cm (¾ inch) thick slices. Drizzle with oil, then cook the slices under a medium-high grill for 8 minutes until crisp and hot. Serve with the salad and apple relish on the side.

Barbecued Peppered Squid
with Ginger Yogurt & Charred Aubergine & Courgette Salad

Serves 4

8 squid, about 100g (3½oz) each, prepared (see page 198), tubes and tentacles whole, wings scored

For the rub
1 tablespoon fennel seeds
1 tablespoon black peppercorns
1 tablespoon coriander seeds
1 tablespoon sea salt

For the ginger yogurt
100g (3½oz) peeled weight of fresh root ginger
2 tablespoons water
200ml (7fl oz) Greek yogurt
2 teaspoons chopped coriander (optional, but preferable)

For the charred aubergine & courgette salad
1 aubergine, cut in half lengthways
2 courgettes, cut in half lengthways
olive oil
1 teaspoon ground coriander
1 teaspoon ground cumin
1 red onion, cut into 4 thick rings
1 tablespoon white wine vinegar
2 teaspoons chopped thyme leaves
2 tablespoons chopped fresh coriander, plus extra to serve

When you get very good, medium-sized, jigged-caught squid, cooking it on the barbecue is a delight. The pepper rub brings out a special characteristic from the squid alongside the smoke from the barbecue. The salad is a good way of utilizing the barbecue as it is starting to rise in temperature to get to a perfect heat for grilling the squid. I find a barbecue, when set up correctly, works best once it's been lit for over an hour. It goes without saying, I suppose, but a good prawn or lobster cooked with the pepper rub is great too.

1. To make the rub, dry-fry all the ingredients in a hot frying pan over a medium heat for 5 minutes until aromatic. Cool slightly, then blitz in a spice grinder or mortar and pestle.

2. Place the squid in a bowl with the rub, turning it a few times to make sure it's generously coated. Leave to marinate in a cool place for at least 1 hour.

3. Light the barbecue 1 hour before planning to cook.

4. Meanwhile, make the ginger yogurt. Put the ginger and water in a blender and blitz to a pulp. Tip the pulp into a piece of muslin, gather up the edges and squeeze tightly over a bowl to extract the juice. You'll need 3 tablespoons of ginger juice. Mix this into the yogurt with the coriander (if using) and season with a pinch of salt. Set aside.

5. Score the cut side of the aubergine and courgette halves and drizzle with 3 tablespoons of olive oil, then season with salt, the ground coriander and cumin. Season the red onion slices likewise.

6. When the barbecue coals are ready, place the aubergine and courgette halves skin-side down on the rack with the onions and cook, turning occasionally. The aubergine will need about 20 minutes, the onion about 20 minutes to soften and the courgettes just 10 minutes.

7. Chop the charred vegetables into bite-sized pieces, place into a bowl and mix. Season with salt, the white wine vinegar, the olive oil, thyme and chopped coriander. Arrange on a warm platter.

8. To cook the squid, place it on the barbecue and cook for 2 minutes on each side. Transfer to the platter and serve immediately, with a scattering of coriander and the yogurt on the side.

Pan-Fried Octopus in Red Pepper & Potato Broth
with Paprika Oil

Serves 4

8 litres (2 gallons) water
1 onion, roughly chopped
2 carrots, roughly chopped
1 red pepper, roughly chopped
1 fennel bulb, roughly chopped
2 teaspoons smoked paprika
1 teaspoon fennel seeds
1 teaspoon peppercorns
1 x 1kg (2lb 4oz) frozen double-sucker octopus, thawed overnight in the refrigerator
Paprika Oil (see page 251), to serve

For the red pepper & potato broth
finely pared zest and juice of 1 orange
2 teaspoons fennel seeds
100ml (3½fl oz) dry sherry
olive oil
1 banana shallot, finely chopped
2 garlic cloves, finely chopped
1 fennel bulb, trimmed and finely chopped
300g (10½oz) potatoes, peeled and finely chopped
100ml (3½fl oz) double cream
3 flame-grilled red peppers from a jar, finely chopped
4 small spring onions, trimmed and sliced
2 teaspoons chopped mint leaves
4 teaspoons fennel herb
sea salt and freshly ground black pepper

This dish has its roots from over 20 years ago when I started my first restaurant, The Black Pig in Rock, Cornwall. Back then I was in the kitchen with just one other chef, so I always had to have one-pot wonders in my pocket; this was one of those. I had to do it that way so I could make sure I looked after the main element, in this case the octopus, not an ingredient you want to ruin. I'm happy that I've been able to include this dish, it brings back good memories.

1. Bring the water to the boil in a large pan with the onion, carrots, fennel, red pepper, smoked paprika, fennel seeds and peppercorns.

2. Holding the head of the octopus between 2 forks, dunk it into the hot water, leave it for a few seconds then lift it out and bring the water back to the boil. Dunk it once more, then remove and return the water to the boil. Put the octopus into the pan, making sure it's fully submerged. Cover and leave to simmer for 50 minutes–1 hour, or until tender. If a skewer inserted into the thickest part of the tentacle goes in easily, it's done. Lift out the octopus and leave until cool enough to handle. Keep the cooking water, which is now your stock.

3. Cut the tentacles away from the head of the octopus, separate them and then cut the head in half. Remove the inedible part from inside and cut the head into bite-sized pieces. At this stage, you should have 8 tentacles and the head meat. Freeze 4 of the tentacles for another day and slice the remaining 4 into bite-sized pieces. Set aside.

4. For the broth, heat a saucepan over a medium-low heat, then add the orange zest and fennel seeds. Heat for a minute to allow the orange zest and fennel seeds to release their natural oils, then pour in 400ml (14fl oz) of the reserved octopus stock. Bring to the boil, then reduce the heat and simmer for 5 minutes. Set aside to cool, then pass through a sieve. Once cooled, add the orange juice and sherry.

5. Heat a drizzle of oil in a saucepan, add the shallot and garlic and sweat for 1 minute, without colouring. Add the fennel and continue to sweat for another 2 minutes, then add the potatoes and the cooled octopus stock. Simmer until the potatoes are tender. Now add the cream and red peppers and simmer for a couple of minutes. Season with salt and pepper to taste.

6. Heat a frying pan over a medium heat and add a drizzle of oil. When hot, add the octopus tentacles and chopped head meat. Colour for 2 minutes, then turn the tentacles over and stir the head meat. Cook for another 2 minutes. The aim is to crisp up and almost char the octopus fat.

7. To finish the broth, add the spring onions and herbs and simmer for 1 minute. Ladle the vegetables and broth into 4 warmed soup plates, top with the octopus and drizzle the paprika oil around. Serve at once.

Octopus & Fennel Gratin

Serves 4

8 litres (2 gallons) water
1 onion, roughly chopped
2 carrots, peeled and roughly chopped
1 fennel bulb, roughly chopped
1 teaspoon fennel seeds
1 teaspoon peppercorns
1 x 1kg (2lb 4oz) frozen double-sucker octopus, thawed overnight in the refrigerator

For the gratin
2 tablespoons olive oil
2 shallots, finely sliced
2 fennel bulbs, trimmed and finely sliced on a mandoline
1 green chilli, deseeded and finely sliced lengthways into strips
2 garlic cloves, finely chopped
2 teaspoons chopped thyme leaves
zest and juice of 1 orange
300g (10½oz) crème fraîche
100g (3½oz) Parmesan, grated
2 tablespoons fennel herb or fennel fronds, to serve
sea salt and freshly ground black pepper

For the crumbs
75g (2½oz) fine breadcrumbs
2 tablespoons wild fennel herb (if unavailable, use dill or fennel tops)
finely pared zest of 1 lemon, finely chopped
50g (1¾oz) Parmesan, grated
50ml (2fl oz) olive oil

Unlike our native curled octopus, the double-suckered Mediterranean octopus is very good to eat, and seeing a huge increase of the species here means we can enjoy them for dinner. When cooked gently they are unlike any other species, in my opinion. The dish below is all about the preparation, but to bring it together it's just a visit to the oven. The fennel flavours work so well with octopus. Serve this alongside a green salad dressed with extra virgin olive oil and a nice vinegar.

1. Bring the measured water to the boil in a large pan with the onion, carrots, fennel, fennel seeds and peppercorns.
2. Cook and prepare the octopus according to the method on page 244, finely chopping the tentacles. Once cooked, discard the stock.
3. Preheat the oven to 180°C Fan (400°F), Gas Mark 6.
4. To make the gratin, warm a frying pan over a medium heat and add the olive oil. When hot, add the shallots and fennel and fry for 3 minutes, stirring occasionally. Now add the chilli and garlic and cook for a further 2 minutes. Transfer to a bowl.
5. Mix the cooked mixture with the octopus head meat, thyme, orange zest and juice and crème fraîche. Season with salt and pepper. Mix well, then transfer to a baking dish. Lay the chopped tentacles on top and sprinkle over the Parmasan. Bake in the oven for 25 minutes until golden and bubbling.
6. Preheat the grill to the highest setting.
7. Mix together the crumb ingredients and sprinkle evenly over the top of the gratin. Grill until golden.
8. Serve in the oven dish, sprinkled with fennel herb or fronds.

Serves 4

8 litres (2 gallons) water
1 onion, roughly chopped
2 carrots, peeled and roughly chopped
1 red pepper, roughly chopped
1 fennel bulb, roughly chopped
1 teaspoon fennel seeds
1 teaspoon peppercorns
1 x 1kg (2lb 4oz) frozen double-sucker octopus, thawed overnight in the refrigerator
2 tablespoons olive oil
2 banana shallots, cut into pieces the size of the octopus
2 green peppers, deseeded and cut into pieces the same size as the octopus
2 teaspoons Szechuan peppercorns, toasted and blitzed
3 teaspoons sea salt

For the grilling liquid
200ml (7fl oz) white wine
200ml (7fl oz) soy sauce
100ml (3½fl oz) white wine vinegar
100g (3½oz) soft light brown sugar

For the radish & cucumber salad
1 white radish (mooli), peeled and cut into matchsticks
1 cucumber, peeled and cut into matchsticks
1 green chilli, deseeded and finely chopped
1 tablespoon chopped chives
1 tablespoon extra virgin olive oil
juice of 1 lime

Grilled Octopus Skewers
with a Radish & Cucumber Salad

Who doesn't like food cooked on a skewer? Well, I do! These octopus skewers are really something and are a great start to a meal. The grilling liquid is well worth making, because as the skewers cook it starts to glaze and caramelize, giving the octopus a tasty coating. If your lips go numb, don't worry, it's the Szechuan peppercorns!

1. Bring the water to the boil in a large pan with the onion, carrots, pepper, fennel, fennel seeds and peppercorns.

2. Cook and prepare the octopus according to the method on page 244, chopping the tentacles into chunky sections. Once cooked, discard the stock.

3. To make the grilling liquid, place all the ingredients into a pan and simmer to reduce until you have 400ml (14fl oz). Transfer to a container and leave to cool.

4. In a frying pan, heat the olive oil over a medium heat and add the shallots and green peppers. Slowly cook the vegetables, stirring occasionally, then season with the Szechuan peppercorns and the salt. When the vegetables are collapsed and soft, transfer to a tray to cool.

5. Take some metal skewers and push on a piece of green pepper, followed by a piece of shallot, then a piece of octopus. Continue with the same pattern until you have 4–5 octopus pieces on each skewer.

6. To make the salad, mix all the ingredients together with 1 tablespoon of the grilling liquid. Set aside.

7. Preheat the grill to the highest setting.

8. Use a brush to paint the grilling liquid all over the skewers. Place them under the grill and cook for 30 seconds, then repeat the brushing with the grilling liquid. Continue this process for 3 minutes, then turn the skewers over. Do the same on the other side, cooking for another 3 minutes.

9. To serve, place the skewers onto 4 warm plates with a pile of the salad on the side.

Roasted Fish Stock

Makes about 500ml (18fl oz)

1kg (2lb 4 oz) turbot, brill or sole bones, washed and all blood removed

1. Preheat the oven to 180°C Fan (400°F), Gas Mark 6.
2. Line a large roasting tray with baking paper and lay the fish bones on it. Roast for 30 minutes, then turn the bones over and roast for a further 10 minutes.
3. Transfer the roasted bones to a large saucepan and pour over enough water to cover. Bring to a simmer over a medium heat and skim off any impurities from the surface. Simmer for 30 minutes, then remove from the heat and strain the liquid into another pan, discarding the contents of the sieve. Bring the stock back to a simmer and reduce by half. Remove from the heat and allow to cool. The stock is now ready to use. Store in the refrigerator for up to 3 days or freeze for up to 2 months.

Roasted Garlic

Makes 2–3 tablespoons

1 teaspoon sea salt
1 large whole garlic bulb
olive oil to drizzle

1. Preheat the oven to 200°C Fan (425°F), Gas Mark 7.
2. Take a piece of foil large enough to enclose the garlic and sprinkle it with the salt. Place the garlic bulb in the middle of the foil and drizzle with the olive oil. Wrap the garlic in the foil and place it on a baking tray. Bake for 20 minutes until the cloves are soft.
3. When cool enough to handle, snip the tips off the top of the cloves, squeeze out the flesh, then use in dishes as required.

Lobster Stock

Makes about 500ml (18fl oz)

1kg (2lb 4 oz) lobster shells
olive oil, for cooking
2 onions, peeled and chopped
6 ripe tomatoes, chopped
3 carrots, peeled and chopped
6 garlic cloves, peeled and chopped
finely pared zest and juice of 1 orange

1. Preheat the oven to 200°C (425°F), Gas Mark 7.
2. Line a large roasting tray with baking paper and lay the lobster shells on it. Roast for 30 minutes.
3. Meanwhile, heat a large saucepan over a medium heat, add a drizzle of olive oil and sweat the onions, tomatoes, carrots, garlic and orange zest for 5 minutes until lightly coloured.
4. Once the shells are roasted, chop them roughly and add them to the pan. Pour over enough water to cover, then add the orange juice. Bring to a simmer and cook for 1 hour.
5. Remove from the heat and strain the liquid into another pan, discarding the contents of the sieve. Bring the stock back to a simmer and reduce by half. Remove from the heat and allow to cool. The stock is now ready to use. Store in the refrigerator for up to 2 days or freeze for up to a month.

For Roasted Garlic Cloves: Follow the recipe for Roasted Garlic but omit the foil and reduce the cooking time to 15 minutes. Once cooked, separate the individual cloves and use them as a garnish.

For Roasted Garlic Purée: Follow the recipe for Roasted Garlic, then blitz the pulp in a small blender. To store, place in a small jar and cover with a thin layer of olive oil. Store in the refrigerator for up to a month.

Mint Oil

Makes about 300ml (½ pint)

30g (1oz) mint leaves
30g (1oz) flat-leaf parsley leaves
300ml (10½oz) light olive oil
sea salt

1. Bring a saucepan of salted water to a simmer and have a bowl of iced water ready. Add the herbs to the simmering water and blanch for 30 seconds, then immediately scoop them out with a slotted spoon and plunge them straight into the iced water to cool quickly. Drain, then squeeze out all excess water from the herbs.

2. Put the blanched herbs into a blender with the olive oil and blitz for 2 minutes. Transfer the mixture to a container and refrigerate for at least 3–4 hours, preferably overnight.

3. Transfer the oil to a saucepan and heat slightly, then strain it through a fine sieve into a clean container. The oil is now ready to use. Store in the refrigerator for up to 1 week.

Lemon Oil

Makes about 400ml (14fl oz)

finely pared zest of 4 unwaxed lemons
300ml (½ pint) light rapeseed oil
100ml (3½fl oz) light olive oil

1. Put all the ingredients into a blender and blitz for 2 minutes. Pour the mixture into a jug and leave to infuse and settle for 24 hours.

2. Next day, decant the oil into a clean container straining it through muslin. Store in the refrigerator for up to 1 month.

Curry Oil

Makes about 400ml (14fl oz)

4 teaspoons mild curry powder
400ml (14fl oz) light rapeseed oil

1. Sprinkle the curry powder into a dry frying pan and toast over a medium heat for 1–2 minutes until it releases its aroma – don't let it burn. Remove the pan from the heat, then stir in the oil. Pour the mixture into a jug and leave to infuse and settle for 24 hours.

2. Next day, decant the oil into a clean container, straining it through muslin. Store in in a dark cupboard for up to 3 months.

Paprika Oil

Makes about 250ml (9fl oz)

2 teaspoons smoked paprika
250ml (9fl oz) rapeseed oil

1. Sprinkle the smoked paprika into a dry frying pan and toast over a medium heat for 1–2 minutes until it releases its aroma – don't let it burn. Remove the pan from the heat, then stir in the oil. Pour the mixture into a jug and leave to infuse and settle for 24 hours.

2. Next day, decant into a clean glass jar, straining it through muslin. Store in the refrigerator for up to 3 months.

Index

Aïoli
  cauliflower 130
  lemon 113
anchovies 11, 16, 146
  anchoïade sauce 99
  anchovies with crispy potato wedges 152
  anchovy, saffron & lemon mayonnaise sauce 168
  braised cuttlefish & pea pie 235
  tomato, anchovy & basil salad 133
  tuna fish balls in tomato sauce 159
apples 90, 130, 163, 204
  apple relish 240
  champagne-pickled oysters with apple & grape relish 212
  crab with apple & carrot salad 224
  pan-fried ling with braised white cabbage & apple 117
  raw scallops with cicely, apple, lemon and a roe mayonnaise 215
  steamed ray with cauliflower & apple salad & cauliflower aïoli 130
  white apple & cabbage salad 200–1
asparagus
  barbecued whole mackerel 171
  pan-fried black bream 86
aubergines
  charred aubergine & courgette salad 243
  griddled tuna belly 156
  pan-fried trout on baked aubergine 142
  plaice, aubergine & mushroom curry with a lime oil 51
avocados
  scallop ceviche with watermelon, cucumber & avocado 219

Baked fish 20, 25, 27, 36, 47, 67
  en croute 20
  en papillote 20
barbecue sauce 211
barbecued fish 20, 64, 67, 69
  barbecued whole mackerel 171
basil
  lobster cocktail flatbreads with orange & basil 227
  tomato, anchovy & basil salad 133
bass 11, 17, 20
  baked in puff pastry 82
  cured bass with tomato & horseradish 80
  raw 16
  rosemary & garlic pan-fried bass 85
beans
  green 160
  roast turbot steak with mustard sauce & butter beans 55–7
  white bean & apple soup 207
  whole baked peppered John Dory 113
beetroot 126
  beetroot ketchup 138
  mackerel tartare with beetroot & apple 163
  sweet & sour beetroot 39
black bream (porgy) 61
  pan-fried black bream 86
black pudding, cuttlefish 240
black spot sea bream 61
bleeding raw fish 16
boiled seafood 18–19
bouquerones 152
braised fish 18–19, 67
bread
  flatbreads 227
  soda bread 204
bream 16, 17, 19, 20, 61–2
  black bream 61, 86
  gilt-headed bream 20, 62, 89–90
  raw 16
brill 16, 18, 19, 24
  cured in white wine 32
  steamed brill with pea, shallot & cider stew 35
butterflied fish 77, 133
butternut squash
  baked scallops on a squash purée 216

Cabbage 200–1
  pan-fried ling and pancetta with braised white cabbage & apple 117
carrots 103, 125, 138, 224
  carrot & fennel seed vinaigrette 137
  salt hake fishcakes with pickled carrots & Béarnaise mayonnaise 103
cauliflower
  baked hake and cauliflower purée with a pine nut, smoked chilli & rosemary butter 108
  steamed ray with cauliflower & apple salad & cauliflower aïoli 130
celeriac salad 129
celery 110
cephalopods 12, 19, 189–90, 198–9
champagne-pickled oysters with apple & grape relish 212
cheese 100, 159, 176
chicory
  grilled plaice on the bone in a star anise & lemon rub with braised onion & chicory 48
  hot-smoked mackerel salad with sweet potatoes & raspberries 172
cider 216, 240
  cider-pickled cockles 200–1
  mussel pâté & cider jelly 204
  steamed brill with pea, shallot & cider stew 35
  steamed mussels in a white bean & apple soup 207
clams 12, 18, 181
  poached clam wontons in a mushroom broth 203
cockles 12, 18, 180
  cider-pickled cockles 200–1
cod 10, 63
cold-smoked fish 151
Cornish sole see megrim sole
Couch's bream 61
courgettes 243
court bouillon 18
crab 6, 184–5
  boiling 18–19
  crab with apple and carrot salad 224
  curried brown crab dressing 224
  freezing 13
  potting 10, 185
  shore crab soup with steamed crab dumplings 220
  spider crabs 10, 223
  varieties 184–5
crawfish 10
croaker see gurnard
crustaceans
  barbecuing 20
  boiling 18–19
cucumber 118, 141, 167, 208
  cucumber & ginger mayonnaise 43
  cucumber, carrot & sesame salad 125
  cucumber, mint & pea soup 155
  radish & cucumber salad 248
  scallop ceviche with watermelon, cucumber & avocado 219
cured fish 16, 24, 72
  freezing 32
  gin-cured trout 141
curry oil 207, 224, 251

cuttlefish 12, 19, 189
    braised cuttlefish & pea pie 235
    cuttlefish black pudding 240
    ink 189

Deep-fried fish 21, 43, 44
defrosting 13
Dover sole 17, 25
    soused Dover sole with sweet &
        sour beetroot & shallots 39
    whole baked Dover sole with
        blistered olives & tomatoes 36
Dublin Bay prawns 188

Eggs
    lobster kedgeree with turmeric
        poached eggs 228
equipment 14

Fennel
    baked megrim sole on fennel with
        orange and gochujang butter 47
    breaded butterflied mackerel 168
    cider-pickled cockles 200–1
    lobster kedgeree with turmeric
        poached eggs 228
    octopus & fennel gratin 247
    spider crab croquettes 223
fish and chips 21
fish pies 20
fish stock, roasted 232, 250
fishcakes
    salt hake fishcakes with pickled
        carrots & Béarnaise mayonnaise
        103
fishing methods 10–11
    flat fish 10, 11, 25, 27, 28, 29
    oily fish 146, 147, 148, 149, 150
    round fish 60, 61, 62, 64, 65, 67, 68
    shellfish 180, 183, 185, 186–7
flat fish 12, 23–57
    filleting and pinboning 30–1
    fishing methods 10, 11, 25, 27, 28, 29
flatbreads 227
freezing fish 12–13, 32

Garlic 52–4, 250
gilt-headed bream 20, 62
    raw gilt-headed bream with
        pickled fennel & horseradish
        crème fraîche 89
    salt-baked bream with cider &
        brown butter dressing 90
gin salad cream 142
gin-cured trout 141

ginger beurre blanc 208
grapes 32, 212
grey mullet 11, 17, 21, 72
    hot-smoked grey mullet pâté 138
    orange & fennel pan-fried grey
        mullet 137
grilled fish 19, 65, 69, 72
gurnard 21, 64
gurnard curry & fried rice noodles
    with a pineapple chutney 95–6
gurnard soup with gurnard fritters
    and green olive tapenade 93–4

Haddock 21, 54, 65
    grilled haddock 99
    roasted haddock and roasted
        Portobello mushroom rarebit
        100
    smoked haddock fritters with
        cheese sauce 176
hake 10, 20, 66
    baked hake and cauliflower purée
        with a pine nut, smoked chilli &
        rosemary butter 108
    hake and mussels in a bag 104
    salt hake fishcake 103
    smoky hake steak with 107
harissa-roasted monkfish 121
hazelnuts 216
health benefits of fish 6
herring 11, 16
hollandaise, olive 121
horseradish
    cured bass with tomato &
        horseradish 80
    raw gilt-headed bream with
        pickled fennel & horseradish
        crème fraîche 89
hot-smoked fish 151
    grey mullet pâté 138

John Dory 67
    braised fillets of John Dory 110
    whole baked peppered John Dory
        113
juniper-pickled cucumber 141

Kale
    crispy 121
knives 14

Langoustines 18–19, 188
leeks 99, 104
lemon sole 26
    crispy breaded lemon sole with
        cucumber & ginger mayonnaise
        & herb oil 43

lemon sole in sherry sauce with
    braised lettuce & green peppers
    40
lemons
lemon & garlic crème fraîche 152
    lemon oil 251
    raw scallops with cicely, apple,
        lemon and a roe mayonnaise
        215
    white baked peppered John Dory
        with white bean & lemon aïoli
        113
lettuce
    lemon sole in sherry sauce with
        braised lettuce & green peppers
        40
limes
    plaice, aubergine & mushroom
        curry with a lime oil 51
    scallop ceviche with watermelon,
        cucumber & avocado 219
    spiced pan-fried red mullet with
        mushroom soup & lime cream
        134
ling 10, 68
    crispy ling with smoked chilli jam
        114
    pan-fried ling and pancetta with
        braised white cabbage & apple
        117
lobster 16, 20, 186–7
    boiling 18–19
    buying 12
    fishing 10, 186–7
    freezing 13
    lobster cocktail flatbreads with
        orange & basil 227
    lobster kedgeree with turmeric
        poached eggs 228
    lobster risotto with spring onions,
        orange & basil 231
    lobster stock 228, 231, 250
    preparing cooked lobster 194–5
    whole lobster & its bisque 232–4

Mackerel 16, 19, 20, 21, 149
    barbecued whole mackerel 171
    breaded butterflied mackerel 168
    butterflying 77
    hot-smoked mackerel salad with
        sweet potatoes & raspberries
        172
    mackerel tartare with beetroot &
        apple 163
    pickled in pastis 164
    salt & vinegar-cured mackerel 167
    smoked 17, 151, 175

mayonnaise
  anchovy, saffron & lemon
    mayonnaise sauce 168
  Béarnaise 103
  black olive 160
  cucumber & ginger 43
  lemon mayonnaise sauce 142
  mustard 118
  mustard & herb 129
  scallop roe 215
megrim sole 27
  baked megrim sole on fennel with
    orange & gochujang butter 47
  deep-fried megrim sole with a
    chilli & seed dressing 43
mint
  cucumber, mint & pea soup 155
  grilled butterflied red mullet with
    a tomato, anchovy, mint & basil
    sauce 133
  mint oil 155, 251
  mint, tarragon & caper crème
    fraîche 175
monkfish 10, 69
  filleting 78–9
  harissa-roasted monkfish 121
  livers 69
  monkfish karaage 122
  sticky sweet & sour monkfish 125
  Szechuan cured monkfish with
    mustard mayonnaise &
    cucumber salad 118
mushrooms
  plaice, aubergine & mushroom
    curry with a lime oil 51
  poached clam wontons in
    mushroom broth 202–3
  roasted haddock and roasted
    Portobello mushroom rarebit 100
  spiced pan-fried red mullet with
    mushroom soup & lime cream
    134
mussels 6, 12, 18
  farmed and wild 181
  hake and mussels in a bag 104
  mussel pâté & cider jelly 204
  steamed mussels in white bean
    & apple soup 207

Noodles, gurnard curry & fried rice
  noodles 95–6

Octopus 12, 190
  grilled octopus skewers with a
    radish & cucumber salad 248
  octopus & fennel gratin 247
  pan-fried octopus in red pepper &
    potato broth 244
oils, flavoured 251

oily fish 6, 11, 12, 145–77
  fishing methods 146, 147, 148,
    149, 150
olives 36, 160
  olive hollandaise 121
  tapenade 93–4, 142
onions
  grilled plaice on the bone in a star
    anise & lemon rub with braised
    onion & chicory 48
  onion confit 82
  smoked mackerel & baked red
    onions 175
oranges
  baked megrim sole on fennel with
    orange and gochujang butter 47
  lobster cocktail flatbreads with
    orange & basil 227
  lobster stock 250
  orange & fennel pan-fried grey
    mullet 137
  shore crab soup with steamed
    crab dumplings 220
  soused ray with beetroot, orange
    & ginger salad 126
  whole baked peppered John Dory
    with white bean & lemon aïoli
    113
oysters 6, 10, 12, 16, 20, 191–2
  champagne-pickled oysters with
    apple & grape relish 212
  deep-fried oysters in a seeded
    crumb 211
  preparing 193
  steamed oysters with a ginger
    beurre blanc 208

Pan-fried fish 20–1, 61, 62
pans 15, 20
paprika oil 244, 251
peas
  braised cuttlefish & pea pie 235
  cucumber, mint & pea soup 155
  marinated squid salad 239
  steamed brill with pea, shallot &
    cider stew 35
peppers
  crispy ling with smoked chilli jam
    114
  lemon sole in sherry sauce with
    braised lettuce & green peppers
    40
  pan-fried octopus in red pepper &
    potato broth 244
  rosemary & garlic pan-fried bass
    85
  sherry-roasted pepper potatoes
    107
pesto 159

pickled fish 16–17, 160, 164
pies, braised cuttlefish & pea pie 235
pilchards 17, 150
pine nuts
  baked hake and cauliflower purée
    with a pine nut, smoked chilli &
    rosemary butter 108
pineapple
  gurnard curry & fried rice noodles
    with a pineapple chutney 95–6
plaice 18, 19, 28
  grilled plaice on the bone in a star
    anise & lemon rub with braised
    onion & chicory 48
  plaice, aubergine & mushroom
    curry with a lime oil 51
poached fish 18, 65
pollack 10
potatoes
  anchovies with crispy potato
    wedges 152
  pan-fried octopus in red pepper &
    potato broth 244
  sherry-roasted pepper potatoes
    107
  steamed turbot fillet & parsley
    sauce with roast garlic potato
    dumplings 52–4
  whole lobster & its bisque 232–4
puff pastry, bass baked in 82

Radishes 167, 168
  mussel pâté & cider jelly 204
  radish & cucumber salad 248
raspberries
  hot-smoked mackerel salad with
    sweet potatoes and raspberries
    172
raw fish 16, 62, 72
raw gilt-headed bream with pickled
  fennel & horseradish crème
  fraîche 69
ray 17, 70
  ray scumpets & celeriac salad 129
  soused ray 126
  steamed ray 129
razor clams 181
red mullet 10, 21, 71
  grilled butterflied red mullet 133
  livers 71
  spiced pan-fried red mullet with
    mushroom soup & lime cream
    134
red sea bream 61
rhubarb, pickled 164
rice
  lobster kedgeree with turmeric
    poached eggs 228

lobster risotto with spring onions,
    orange & basil 231
roasted fish stock 232, 250
rosemary
    baked hake and cauliflower purée
        with a pine nut, smoked chilli &
        rosemary butter 108
    rosemary & garlic pan-fried bass
        85
    rosemary crackers 138
round fish 59–143
    fishing methods 60, 61, 62, 64,
        65, 66, 67, 68
    preparation 74–9

Salami
marinated squid salad 239
salt cod 16
salt hake fishcakes with pickled
    carrots & Béarnaise mayonnaise
    103
salt-baking fish 20, 62
    salt-baked bream with cider &
        brown butter dressing 90
sardines 11, 17, 150
scallops 10, 12, 16, 20, 21
    baked scallops on a squash purée
        216
    fishing 183
    raw scallops with cicely, apple,
        lemon and a roe mayonnaise 215
    scallop ceviche with watermelon,
        cucumber & avocado 219
scampi 188
sea bass 19
sea robin see gurnard
sea trout 20
seaweed tartare sauce 122
sesame sauce 167
shallots
    soused Dover sole with sweet &
        sour beetroot & shallots 39
    steamed brill with pea, shallot &
        cider stew 35
shopping for fish 12
shore crab 184, 185
skate 70

slip soles 25
smoked fish 151
    smoked haddock fritters with
        cheese sauce 176
smoked mackerel 17, 151
smoked mackerel & baked red
    onions 175
smoked salmon 17
smoking fish 17, 72
    hot-smoked grey mullet pâté 138
soda bread 204
soups
    cucumber, mint & pea soup 155
    gurnard soup 93–4
    mushroom broth 203
    shore crab soup with steamed
        crab dumplings 220
    spiced pan-fried red mullet with
        mushroom soup & lime cream
        134
    white bean & apple soup 207
soused fish 16–17, 25
    ray 126
    soused Dover sole with sweet &
        sour beetroot & shallots 39
spider crab 10, 184, 185
sprats 11
squid 12, 19, 21
    barbecued peppered squid 243
    marinated squid salad 239
    preparing 198–9
steamed fish 17–18
    ray 129
stock
    lobster stock 228, 231, 250
    roasted fish stock 232, 235
storing fish 12–13
sweet potatoes
    hot-smoked mackerel salad with
        sweet potatoes and raspberries
        172
sweetcorn
    spider crab croquettes with
        sweetcorn sauce 223
    Szechuan cured monkfish with
        mustard mayonnaise &
        cucumber salad 118

Tapenade 93–4, 142
tarragon 175
tartare sauce
    seaweed 122
tomatoes
    cured bass with tomato &
        horseradish 80
    grilled butterflied red mullet 133
    rosemary & garlic pan-fried bass
        85
    shore crab soup with steamed
        crab dumplings 220
    tomato, olive & cumin dressing
        156
    whole baked Dover sole with
        blistered olives & tomatoes 36
    whole lobster & its bisque 232–4
trout
    ceviche 73
    farmed 73
    gin-cured trout 141
    pan-fried trout on baked
        aubergine 142
tuna, blue-fin 155–60
    griddled tuna belly 156
    pickled tuna & pickled shallots on
        toast 160
    raw 16, 155
    tuna fish balls in tomato sauce 159
turbot 10, 19, 20, 24
    roast turbot steak with mustard
        sauce & butter beans 55–7
    steamed turbot fillet & parsley
        sauce with roast garlic potato
        dumplings 52–4

Velvet crab 184, 185
vinaigrette, carrot & fennel seed 137

Watercress salad 240
watermelon, with scallop ceviche 219
whole fish 20
wontons 203

Yoghurt, ginger 243

Picture Credits

Biodiversity Heritage Library: A history of the fishes of the British Islands v.3 (1877)/MBLWHOI Library 27, The fishes of Great Britain and Ireland, 1880-1884/Smithsonian Libraries and Archives 26; iStock: channarongsds 189a, Christine_Kohler 24, 62, 64, duncan1890 66, 70, 149, 190, Evgeniy Zotov 147, Hein Nouwens 184, Ievgeniia Lytvynovych 181, ilbusca 29, 60, 68, 69, 71, 148, 150, 180, 183, 186, 188, Nastasic 189b, NSA Digital Archive 67, 182, pleshko74 191, powerofforever 72, THEPALMER 65, 73, TonyBaggett 28, 63, Vladayoung 146.

Acknowledgements

Rachel, my love and best friend, thank you for all your support and patience.

Jessica, thanks for all your help and contributions to the book, love you.

Jacob, thanks for being you, love you.

Mum, thanks again for all your support, help, love and nagging. You know this book doesn't happen without your help, so I am eternally grateful.

Dad, I hope you enjoy this shoal of recipes. You inspire me still to this day. Proud of you.

Pete, thanks for your support and friendship over the last 24 years. Your help on this book was amazing and I could not have done it without you.

Tim, thanks again for your help with this book and continued support over the last 15 years, it means a lot.

The class of 2025 at Outlaw's New Road, Outlaw's Fish Kitchen and Outlaw's Guest House. Thanks for keeping the ship sailing while I wrote this book. Proud of everyone.

Mitra, thank you for helping with the publishers and looking out for me in the wider world. Your support means a lot.

The team at Kyle Books – publisher Joanna Copestick; senior managing editor Sybella Stephens; creative director Jonathan Christie; designer/illustrator Paul Palmer-Edwards, and senior production manager Katherine Hockley. Thank you so much for making my mind and ideas look amazing in a book. The real stars behind the authors.

Kate Whitaker. Another book together, thank you for letting me take over your studio with lots of fish. You are one of the most talented and amazing people I've ever met. I'm gobsmacked at how you can make my food look so great. Thank goodness!

Thanks to all our customers for their continued support at our restaurants and at the guesthouse.

Thanks to all the readers out there, please share your recipe creations with me on my Instagram page: @nathanoutlaw – I love to see the results.

To all the fisherman, growers and producers who supply us with amazing ingredients, thank you. We couldn't do it without you – either this book or the restaurants.

UK–US Glossary

UK	US
aubergine	eggplant
bicarbonate of soda	baking soda
broad beans	fava beans
butter beans	lima beans
caster sugar	superfine sugar
celeriac	celery root
chicory	endive
chickpeas	garbanzos
cicely	sweet cicely
cider (dry)	hard cider
clingfilm	plastic wrap
coriander	cilantro
cornflour	cornstarch
courgette	zucchini
cream (double)	heavy cream
grill	broiler
mushooms, chestnut	crimini mushrooms
muslin	cheesecloth
peppers (red, yellow)	bell peppers
plain flour	all-purpose flour
prawn	shrimp
rapeseed oil	canola oil
sieve	strainer
spring onions	scallions
yogurt (natural)	plain yogurt

Nathan Outlaw is a Michelin-starred British seafood chef. Having trained with Rick Stein he went on to open two restaurants and a guest house in Port Isaac, Cornwall. He is passionate about using local, seasonal and sustainable produce, and the importance of ethical fishing and seafood consumption. He is the author of *Fish for Dinner*, also published by Kyle Books.